Shared Visions

Shared Visions

TWO FRIENDS EXPLORE THE
PLEASURES OF GARDENS & FOOD

Maggie Barry
Mary Greene

We would like to thank

Mrs Bev McConnell
Mrs Anne Coney
Mrs Barbara Myers
Ms Diana Firth
Mrs Christine Horton
Mrs Kathy Boardman
Mr John Heard
Mrs Nan Raymond
and
Mrs Sharon Carew

for sharing their own visions of paradise with us.

All the photographs are by Alan Hough except the jacket photographs, which are by Cindy Wilson, and the photographs on the following pages from the collection of Maggie Barry: 10 (bottom), 11, 14, 16, 18, 22, 24, 38, 40, 44, 48–49, 76, 80, 88, 92, 110, 120, 134, 135, 144–145

A RANDOM HOUSE BOOK
Published by
Random House New Zealand
18 Poland Road, Glenfield, Auckland, New Zealand

First published 1998

© 1998 (text) Maggie Barry and Mary Greene; (photographs other than those listed above) Alan Hough

The moral rights of the authors have been asserted

ISBN 1 86941 352 0

Design: Christine Cathie
Cover photograph: Cindy Wilson
Cover design: Juliet Hughes
Printed in Hong Kong

Contents

Foreword   6

BREAKING NEW GROUND   9
   Alternatives to lawn   10
   Breaking the monotony   12
   Soft touches   15
   Tied up in knots   18
   Boxing on   25
   Planting a knot garden   26

MEDITERRANEAN ASSOCIATIONS   29
   The olive grove   32
   Go gravel   35
   The importance of the vessel   45
   Pelargoniums Mediterranean style   48
   Indestructible succulents   50

TROPICANNA   55
   Hot high fashion   56
   Flowering subtropicals   61
   The non-subtropical tropicanna look   65
   Tropicanna accessories   70

FRUIT OF THE GODS   73
   The stuff of legends   74
   Winter assets   78
   Hardy lemons   82
   Grapes   83

THE KITCHEN GARDEN'S COMEBACK   87
   Le potager   88
   The herb garden   106
   Salad herbs   120
   Blooms to consume   125

ROMANCING THE ROSE   129
   The edible rose   131
   War of the roses   134
   Roses in winter   136

PLEASURE GROUNDS   141
   Moonlighting   142
   Barbecues   152

THE RECIPES   160

INDEX   167

Foreword

It's fair to say I've been in the grip of gardening most of my life. My mother had a florist shop in Molesworth Street in Wellington, so there were always flowers in the house when I was growing up and weekends at the beach house at Paraparaumu working up a head of steam in the garden. As a child my job was to chase the frogs away from Dad's motor-mower blades, and when Mum visited her friends I tagged along as the little carrier of garden cuttings.

I was promoted to pouring water into vases as my contribution to arranging the church flowers for big events like weddings and Christmas, when everything had to look perfect. After the gardens of the parish had been stripped of anything usable, there was the last-minute, early-morning trip to the market to buy the freshest flowers and fragrant lilies for the nuptial or midnight mass.

Despite Mum's fondness for flowers, my parents were none too pleased when their only child left university to work as a gardener for the local council. Most of my friends regarded the move as the career equivalent of a suicidal catapult into certain oblivion. It was a comfort to meet Mary in the enrolment queue at Lincoln University, and our friendship was consolidated over welding our first vice together in metalwork class and eating bacon-and-egg toasted sandwiches in the cafeteria.

We didn't have to eat there often. Thanks to Mary, the trained chef, we dined like royalty on the student bursary, feasting on rabbit, unbeatable chicken livers and whatever could be scavenged from the garden.

Greene family legend has it that Mary's been on more courses than Lester Piggot: journalism, graphic art and cooking, of course. She swore the diploma of horticulture would be her last, but even without the formal instruction, Mary was bred to be a food stylist. Hospitality is always outstanding at the Greenes', with Kevin, ever the convivial host, alongside Elizabeth, paramount queen of the kitchen. Brought up on the complexities and subtleties of the finest cooking, Mary became acquainted early on with the path from the garden to the kitchen. Later, as an innovative restaurateur, she was not deterred when what she needed was not available in the shops. Mary did what any determined cook would do and went out and grew her own.

Meanwhile, after working as a self-employed gardener for a couple of years,

I'd retired indoors to the relative heat of a career as a broadcaster. I took a few months leave from my job at National Radio, and that's when my second garden vice kicked in. What began as a solitary habit looking at other people's gardens in Europe led to years of filming them, taking tours to them and writing about them.

Mary has been there since day one of the garden show and proved herself equal to every challenge. When her fruits from the garden were given an extra grilling under the harsh studio lights, she learned the indispensable craft of the resuscitator. In the past seven years, we've filmed in some unaccommodating environments, and behind the scenes is the skilled hand of Mary turning out great-looking food anywhere in any weather.

I'm often asked if the food tastes as good as it looks and, hand on heart, it does. We have to fight to keep the ever-appreciative Bill and Jack off the seasonal fare long enough for us to film it. Afterwards Mary hands out recipe sheets to the crew and is always the first port of call for advice when someone has a crowd coming round for a barbeque.

Unlike many chefs, Mary wants a garden not only to service the kitchen but to be the perfect setting for a great meal. That's our common meeting ground and a very pleasant one it is, too. Having little of value to contribute on the subject of cooking, I've focused on what I know best: gardens. The more I see, the more I'm inclined to believe style is an individual, singular and deeply personal matter. Me, I'm partial to big and grand, hence my high regard for Vaux-le- Vicomte, but I couldn't live with it every day. Gamberaia's my pick for a summer bolthole in Florence, outstanding by day and by moonlight. Both gardens have spadefuls of what I tend to think of as presence and personality.

The gardens speak eloquently enough for themselves, but talking to the people who made or maintain them is when it all starts to make sense. So we've included practical tips from the people who know what to do. Gravel and hot 'Tropicanna' gardens are a worldwide trend, but how do you turn the front lawn into a Xerilandscape or get that subtropical look in Invercargill?

This book is an eclectic collection of what we think works well. It is not a definitive guide to gardening nor a comprehensive cooking tome.

For the two of us, gardening and food are inextricably linked . . . and this book reflects our shared vision of the pleasures we have found in both.

Maggie Barry

Breaking New Ground

Maggie: There's more to gardening than plants alone. Sometimes, though, gardeners can focus their entire attention on cultivating plants at the expense of layout and co-ordinating the big picture. 'Landscape design' is sometimes regarded as being synonymous with soulless and expensive.

So for those and others who want to take a do-it-yourself approach, we've presented a selection of alternative ways of arranging plants, including a recipe à la Mary for making your own unique pavers.

ALTERNATIVES TO LAWN

The extraordinary hummocks of Scleranthus biflorus make a surprisingly natural groundcover between pavers.

The notion of a well-manicured lawn is deeply impressed in our minds as one of the most important elements in the garden, but these days many people have neither the time nor the space to accommodate such verdant luxury and are seeking alternatives. This is not a new fad, for surprising though it may seem, grass lawns as we know them were not grown until the eighteenth century. In Tudor England aromatic herbs were planted underfoot. According to Sir Francis Bacon, Chancellor and budding gardener, 'Those which perfume the air most delightfully, not passed by as the rest, but being trodden apon and crushed … have the pleasure when you walk or tread.' Lawns were planted with chamomile and wild thyme. Sir Francis Drake was probably bowling on a chamomile lawn when he spotted the Spanish Armada.

Scented lawns are established in much the same way as ordinary grass. They are best sown in spring or early summer to give the plants a good chance to take hold before the onslaught of winter. The ground should be cleared of grass and weeds, then raked over. A covering of clear plastic will encourage any remaining weeds to germinate quickly — three weeks at the most. Rake the soil once more. It isn't necessary to go too deep. To achieve a relatively even spread of plants, it's a good idea to mix the grass seed with dry sand. Once scattered, sprinkle over some more sand or dry soil. Water gently and keep the soil moist until the plants are up and running. Any clumps of seedlings can be thinned out to about 10 cm apart and the excess transplanted to any bald patches.

Once planted, a sweet-smelling lawn makes few demands on our time. In fact, most problems with cultivating thyme arise from over watering and over feeding. The plants thrive in an open, dry situation. Chamomile needs watering over hot summers to prevent drying out and leaving embarrassing gaps but if these occur they can be filled with divisions from mature plants. If a thyme lawn shows signs of losing its vitality, a weekly topdressing of potting mix for three consecutive weeks will bring it back to life. The plants will layer themselves by growing new roots from the stems, and fresh new leaves. The herb can be propagated in much the same way by filling a tray with potting mix and laying the cut stems on top. Sprinkle over a little more potting mix, allowing the leafy parts to still show. Water and place the tray in a warm, sheltered spot. The plants should have rooted and be ready for use within a month in spring and summer, longer in the colder months.

Three different types of lawn chamomile (*Chamaemelum nobile*) are available. There are single and double-flowered varieties. The flowers should be clipped back — either with the mower on its highest setting, or harvested by hand to make relaxing chamomile teas. Mowing every few months in the first two years will encourage the plants to thicken. There is also a non-flowering type, 'Treneague', which doesn't send up long flowering shoots, so there's no need to mow. All types will release a refreshing apple fragrance when trodden on. In Spain chamomile is known as *manzinella*, which means 'little apple'. Chamomile is known as the 'physician plant' since it reputedly improves the health of ailing plants nearby and will attract battalions of bees when located near fruit trees.

Matting or creeping thymes are the types to use as a substitute for grass. These are the smaller-leaved varieties that will spread rapidly rather than form clumps. Some will give off strong lemon scents, others smell of nutmeg and caraway. Some leaves are dark and glossy, others golden, grey and woolly or variegated. Some have tiny white flowers, others range from pink to purple, and *Thymus coccineus* produces a magnificent carpet of scarlet flowers.

A patchwork of various coloured thymes is a lovely notion but can look, well, patchy, as you can never rely on uniform or sequential flowering. For a glorious show it would be safer to stick to one colour. Besides, these alternative lawns work better in small spaces, not on a grand scale. They'll stand up to the pitter patter of tiny and not-so-tiny feet, but not heavy-duty traffic. They can be planted in alternate squares with pavers to chequer a courtyard — you could have your own 'thymes square'. Planted between pavers, the herbs' heady perfumes are naturally released by the concentrated heat.

Another alternative to everyday grass is our own native *Pratia angulata*, a hardy ground creeper with dense masses of the tiniest soft leaves. It will not fill the air with striking fragrance but the generous white starry flowers over the summer months, followed by displays of red berries, compensate for the absence of scent. It will need more watering than other lawn alternatives and appreciates a little respite from direct sun, although I have seen a flat garage roof totally covered with pratia. The roof was quite visible from the front of the house and the planting struck me as an ingenious way to conceal the corrugated iron.

Bees also find the bright flowers of the wild thyme Thymus coccineus *particularly appealing, so be wary of walking on such lawns in bare feet.*

A groundcover that I can't walk past without stooping to pat is *Scleranthus biflorus*, found both here and in Australia. It grows into a spongy mound with a distinctive mossy look to it. But unlike a moss, scleranthus is best planted in full sun. Like some scientific experiment gone weirdly wrong, it will slowly spread, doubling its size every two years. It doesn't take kindly to frequent frosts nor constant rain. This bright green cushion is studded with tiny flowers over summer. These cushions are striking if set between paving or rocks in what's often referred to as an architectural garden. They also look great sitting just above the rim of a clay pot. That way there is less stooping and more stroking.

BREAKING THE MONOTONY

Not long ago, Mary finally summoned up the courage to tackle a niggly area in her parents' garden. This particular spot was too narrow to be a courtyard yet too wide to be called a path, although it put up with a lot of foot and paw traffic — there were two dogs. Both the bricks and the herbs that were once nurtured between the cracks had become blackened with the rigors of time.

Mary's recipe for hand-made pavers

Construct a simple wooden frame by nailing **four pieces of wood** together to form a square. (The old 2 by 1 (inch) is perfect. I chose to make small tiles and found the lengths found in boxes of kindling quite adequate. The resulting tiles were roughly 22 cm square. You will need stronger, thicker lengths of wood for larger tiles, to stand up to the weight of the concrete.) Lay the frame on a flat surface and, as a trial, arrange **a selection of smooth pebbles and shells** (think of your vulnerable bare feet and avoid jagged surfaces) within the frame to make a pattern. Any unusual shapes can make an interesting centrepiece. Lift the frame to another flat surface. This time lay it on a **plastic rubbish bag** to protect whatever's underneath. Mix **easy-mix cement** with a little water to a thick cake-batter in a **plastic bucket**. Pour this mix into the frame. Be generous — the thinner the tile, the more likely it is to crack. Ever so carefully, transfer the pebbles and shells into the frame, following your trial design. Push each stone gently into the cement.

Try not to be impatient and allow the cement to dry thoroughly without any nudging or prodding at your work of art. The drying process may take a couple of days. When the cement has set, the wooden frame is easily removed and you can use your new tile to good effect. The frame can be used again for the next one.

The gentle mauve flowers of nepeta blend beautifully with the various purples, pinks and crimsons in this cool border planting.

Mary thought about replacing the bricks with concrete pavers, but when she looked at what was available, it was 'Woah. Reach for the sunglasses.' They seemed way too brash, especially piled high, all gleaming and new at the supplier's yard. The starkness of the concrete would need some relief — for the spirit as much as the eye. I suggested she tinted the slabs. Touring other gardens, I'd seen some wonderful coloured concrete in subtle shades of ochre and others that looked like pink marble and black slate, but Mary was informed that the tinting worked best when the concrete was poured in situ, popping the powdered oxides or acrylics straight from the tube into the wet mix. And you have to add a lot more colour than you might think to achieve even the most subtle of hues. She concluded that this was probably all a bit beyond a novice, and decided instead to make her own pavers and decorate them with pebbles and seashells. This would result in a more natural effect and add a little warmth.

The procedure turned out to be very straightforward. This came as a very

Saying it with flowers

The garden surrounding the Château Villandry in the Loire Valley is most famous for its elaborate potager, but as anyone who has been there will tell you, its Jardins d'Amour, which I was lucky enough to visit, are equally fascinating.

It seems only fitting that the French, who consider themselves pre-eminent as arbiters of passion and romance, have created an intricate gardening tribute to love. The Jardins d'Amour depict in box hedge and flowers the symbolic meanings of four types of romance. For the amusement of the household, the ornamental gardens were laid out beneath the main salon of the château. From there, the four separate beds of the parterre, or 'embroidery on the ground', can be seen to great effect.

In 'l'Amour Tragique', the box hedges are pruned in the shape of swords and daggers, with red flowers used to represent the blood spilled in the name of love.

'L'Amour Adultère' (fickle love) incorporates horns, the symbol of the cuckold, and fans to recall the airiness of flirtations complete with a love letter in the centre pledging worthless constancy. Yellow flowers are predominant, for since time immemorial that colour has symbolised betrayal.

'L'Amour Tendre' features heart shapes, separated by orange flames of love with masks in the centre, used to hide tender whisperings at a costume ball. In 'L'Amour Passionné' the hearts are shattered by passion, their dancing shapes enlivened by dramatic blue and purple flowers.

How can people ever think gardens are dull and boring? For the statisticians among you, the four gardens of love are replanted twice a year, requiring a total of 25,000 plants. The spring displays usually include tulips and forget-me-nots, with dahlias, petunias and salvias taking over in the summer.

pleasant surprise to one who considered anything vaguely associated with wood and nails, let alone concrete, to be a 'guy thing' and who recalled with horror the classes on concrete stress, complete with mathematical equations, that we both attended at Lincoln. Stress was definitely the operative word, then, though we wished we had listened a little more attentively as neither of us knew much about the stress capacity of hand-made tiles. So far, though, Mary's are standing up well to parents, dogs and even the occasional admirer. For a heavy-duty path, a row of your 'originals' could be alternated with a bright but perhaps more durable row of pavers from the supplier's yard. Even a single one or two decorated paver set in among the rest would give some variety to the overall look.

SOFT TOUCHES

Most hard surfaces — pavers, a yard, steps or the edges of a raised bed — will benefit from a little softening. There's a danger such areas will look raw, more like an afterthought than part of the garden itself. A good edging plant can help blend the paving into its new surroundings. The neglected nepeta, or catmint, is a natural softener. For years it has been banished to the wilderness because of cats' predisposition towards the humble plant and the resulting mangled mess in the garden. My tried and true tip for manipulating moggies is to put a wire hanging basket upside-down over the top of the catmint plant. Push it down firmly, and within a couple of months the catmint will be cascading through the supportive wire frame, which protects the crown of the plant from being crushed by any marauding moggies. The one the cats really go for is *Nepeta cataria*, the true catmint. There is a hybrid, *N. cataria liminoides*, which gives off a lemony smell that is far less to the feline's liking, but the best nepetas for the garden are *N. faassenii* and *N. racemosa* (syn. *N. mussini*), which do not attract the furry creatures to quite the same degree.

There is so little difference between these two garden perennials that they are often mistaken for each other. The former tends to grow higher — 45 cm as opposed to 30 cm. One cultivar, 'Six Hills Giant', grows up to 1 metre and its mass of lavender-blue flowers makes it a better subject for the border rather than edges. Both species are easy to grow. They're quite happy to be left alone in a reasonably

A generous planting of lavender and ivy helps soften the hard lines of the brick paving.

Breaking New Ground 15

Penstemon *'Purple Passion'* will form a strong bush about 90 cm tall.

sunny situation with well-drained soil. They have a long flowering season, mostly blooming in shades of lavender-blue, which over summer produce a lovely indeterminate haze in the garden. These clouds of colour will soon mellow the hardest of edges. In warm areas this haze can be cut back to soil level at the end of summer. This will promote fresh growth the following season. In areas prone to severe frosts it will pay to wait until spring. Nepetas are quickly established and fairly long lived. They will grow readily from cuttings, so even the longest path can benefit from their gentle touch.

No sooner had Mary exercised her abilities with concrete than she shifted to a property that happened to have a really striking rose garden. I mean striking. It was full of all the bright colours — you might say gaudy. Bright colours may be the height of fashion, but she wanted to tone things down while keeping the roses in place. She cleverly did this with some subtle underplanting. Nepeta is the perfect mixer, gliding from one blousy partygoer to the other with confidence and making each feel at ease as it passes by. Its soft lavender-blue flowers and grey-green foliage make a good foil for the bright sparks, while discreetly binding the magentas with the pinks and apricots.

There are several other plants that would have been just as good at working a 'garden room' in this way. *Campanula persicifolia* is an old hand at it. Having started off in Eastern Europe, it had colonised most of Europe by the 1500s, before taking on the world. Needing but a casual invitation into the garden, it grows easily from seed and will thrive in most garden soils under the full glare of sun or in light shade. It is one of those guests that, once it's got its foot through the door, will never want to leave. It's known as the 'peach-leaved bellflower', which more or less describes the plant. Its bright green leaves form a good-looking rosette and the purple nodding flowers grow up to about a metre. Some of the flowers have less violet and more of a lavender tinge. There are single and double-flowered varieties as well as a white cultivar, which is not so useful a mixer as the purplish ones. The mauve colouring has a tempering influence on yellows, oranges and even the angrier magentas and crimsons. It also blends beautifully with greys and silvers. Regular deadheading will ensure blooms all summer long. Clumps can be lifted and divided every three to four years.

Penstemons will also prove an able match for the tough colours. Again, they love the sun and will tolerate a partially shaded position but they must be in a well-drained soil as they are very susceptible to root rot. By removing the spent blooms, you should see flowers right through the summer and on into autumn. This long flowering season can take its toll on the plants and they can soon exhaust themselves, so take a supply of cuttings by removing the non-flowering side shoots in autumn. Clumps can wait until spring to be divided. The rich reds of 'Garnet' and 'Firebird' look fantastic planted en masse, but they're not always compatible alongside other fiery hues, and the resulting colour scheme can end up more of a miss than a hit. Far safer are the various shadings of purple, some beautifully subtle, found in the hardy varieties 'Sour Grapes' and 'Stapleford Gem'. These will grow to 50 cm.

If you're looking for a mixer that would stand taller in the bed, it's hard to ignore the reliable lavateras. Blending well into most garden styles they can be relied upon to flower all summer long. They prefer full sun and a well-drained but only moderately rich soil, as too much of a good thing will result in a surfeit of leaves at the expense of the attractive mallow flowers. *Lavatera* 'Barnsley' will clothe itself in flowers of the palest pink that deepens as they age. They usually appear on the tips of new wood, which gives an airy-fairy look to the plant. Its stems carry shades of purple and brown, which allow the plant to blend well into the background, and its dull sage-green leaves fit easily into silver planting schemes. It will grow to around 2 metres high and wide and requires only the lightest of trims with the secateurs. Taller again is *L.* 'Bredon Springs', which produces blooms in a dusky pink-mauve colour. It can be kept in line with a reasonably hard prune — cut back by about two-thirds — before new growth commences in early spring.

If it's contrast you're after, cushions of lime-green *Alchemilla mollis* are a striking sight beneath the roses. Lady's mantle, as it is also known, is an easy plant that does well in sun or light shade, although it requires plenty of water over the hotter months. A mulch would help retain the moisture. At first glance the 'greenery-yallery', as Gilbert and Sullivan coined it, that is so predominant in the plant when it is in flower over the summer months may seem at odds with the bright reds of the roses. But the gentle, slightly downy leaves and the soft shape of the plant itself help it to blend smoothly with its neighbours, and its lush growth more than compensates for the stark bases of the rose bushes.

When placing *Alchemilla mollis* against the really bright reds it helps to include some blue-green in the planting to ease the eye and bring the whole picture together. The giant European spurge, *Euphorbia characias* subsp. *wulfenii*, is a good 'anchoring' plant. It is quite densely clothed with healthy blue-green foliage and produces a spectacular show of large domes of long-lasting chartreuse flowers over winter and early in spring, just when they are most needed. The plant can be persuaded to form a rounded bush 1.5 metres high but seems happier sprawling at a slightly lower level and stretching out into the shapes that would make an acrobat envious. It's dependable, hardy and thrives in a well-drained soil in sun or shade, and the plants seed freely once established. You can also propagate by dividing when the flowering eventually comes to an end.

This euphorbia is one of the best 'mixers' of all. Its colouring should assure it a place among a spring planting of blue and yellow bulbs because it actually seems to combine well with most plants — in mixed borders, seaside gardens and in a light woodland setting with perhaps hostas, hellebores and aquilegias. Being reasonably drought tolerant, it's also good in containers.

Vita Sackville-West appreciated the impact of euphorbias, and her extensive collection is shown to great advantage at Sissinghurst, justifiably regarded as one of England's finest gardens. She boldly planted *E. c.* subsp. *wulfenii* in a pair of large terracotta urns placed at each end of the pleached lime walkway, designed by her husband Harold Nicholson. The stately plants are a dramatic focal point and a mesmerising drawcard to stroll the length of the path.

Euphorbia characias *subsp.* wulfenii *at Sissinghurst.*

TIED UP IN KNOTS

Parterres these days refer to almost any horizontal patterned bed or border, and this flexible approach has ensured they have a place in the thoroughly modern garden. The clean, straight lines of hedging sit neatly alongside modern buildings and for the impatient gardener, it's remarkable how quickly a heap of builder's rubble can be transformed into an elegant show of pattern and plants. Parterres look good almost as soon as they're planted. They fit into small spaces with ease and are often the ideal solution to those mysterious poky little areas that seem to be the legacy of new townhouses — especially if there's an upstairs balcony from which to better view the masterpiece. Parterres can also look

The flimsy lime-green sprays of Alchemilla mollis *contrast well with the bold leaves of the hosta in the background.*

appropriate in the gardens of some of our older villas and bungalows, where the clipped low hedges guide visitors effortlessly to the front door while giving the entrance a becoming air of formality.

History has shown us how utterly grand parterre gardens can be — the quintessence of formality. These elaborate manifestations can be scaled down to a couple of square metres and still convey the same sense of formal style as those august precedents. The highly structured, geometric pattern is not to everyone's taste and to some the orderly lines of cropped hedge appear neither plant nor people friendly. The horror of human footprints in the freshly raked gravel. Perhaps it's better not to take it all quite so seriously, just adopt certain aspects of the parterre and use it to your advantage.

Lines of low hedges make wonderful living frames in a smaller area where they somehow manage to bring the garden together while making divisions within it at the same time. Using the same hedging plant clipped to the same height will give continuity throughout the garden, and a sense of simplicity that can be difficult to achieve by other means. This can be a lifesaver to those new to gardening during those first few years of hit and miss when, even though a lot of hard work and money might be put into landscaping, the result is often a mish-mash of ideas and plants. The hedging frames will unite it all together while the experiments can continue, thankfully partially obscured, within the spaces.

Inside the hedges a layer of seashells would make a more playful alternative to gravel, and seems more appropriate in a country where the ocean is never that far away. Another option might be a vigorous groundcover that would quickly colonise its territory and provide a carpet of foliage and flower without much encouragement on the gardener's part. Covers that may prove outright invasive in a natural-look garden will know their limitations within the hedge boundaries. A great cover, if there's some shade, is ajuga. Though it will take over whatever ground it's given, varieties of *Ajuga repens* will not steal the show, but gently beguile with their year-round beauty. Ajuga grows as a neat rosette of fleshy leaves, the colour depending on the variety. 'Atropurpurea' has deep purple-bronze leaves; 'Burgundy Lace' and 'Multicolour' are mottled rose pink and magenta with cream edges; 'Variegata' has grey-green leaves edged in cream and likes deep shade. For added drama, the foliage of 'Braunherz' is purple-black. Ajugas will flower in spring, or early summer in cooler areas. Flowers are usually blue but there is a

In Tudor England 'royal knots, alleyed and herbed' were laid beneath the upper rooms of the queen's quarters so that the pattern was better unravelled from the height and comfort of her lodgings. This more recent parterre, based on an Islamic design, is planted beneath a first-floor veranda. Seashells replace the traditional gravel inset to give it a New Zealand flavour.

Het Loo

For a 'living history lesson' on seventeenth century gardening style, you could join the queues to see one of England's most visited tourist sites at Hampton Court, or save yourself for Het Loo, located in Apeldoorn, about 80 km from Amsterdam.

Even if strong formality and a well-manicured look are not your chosen style, Het Loo Palace is worth seeing as the very embodiment of the aesthetic ideals of its age. From the mathematical precision of the filigree-patterned parterre to the elaborate topiary and ornamentation, the gardens are authentic seventeenth century Baroque in every detail. This was an era when Dutch mercantile activities were at their height, and new plants and flowers were collected with fervour from all around the world. In those days, expensive and often rare specimens stood alone in garden beds, where the soil was deliberately mounded up in the middle to give the star performers greater height and prominence. To the twentieth century eye, this style of planting can seem austere or even stingy, but such criticisms are quickly cast aside after a stroll through the lavish series of green corridors known as the Queens' Bowery.

Replanted in 1970, the hornbeam (*Carpinus betulus*) has been trained and interwoven on a network of vaulted wooden archways to dazzling effect. In every sense over the top, the Bowery was designed to protect the ladies of the Court from the sun that might blemish their fashionably pale complexions. Borrowed from an Italian tradition, it could be regarded as an affectation. Some have observed that Holland's milder climate scarcely required such elaborate protection, but as someone who has always welcomed a leafy retreat, I see the Bowery as a superb and welcome feature.

Maintenance of these elaborate estates has always been on an epic, and expensive, scale. Over the centuries, the original garden layout at Het Loo was simplified and altered, gradually falling into decline. The former hunting lodge that became the palace of Prince William of Orange (later King William III of England) was turned into a State museum following the death of Queen Wilhemina twenty years ago. After meticulous and costly restoration, the gardens were finally opened to the public in 1984. These days there's plenty to keep Het Loo's sixteen full-time gardeners working flat out. After the frosts, they have to transport the hundreds of container-grown bay and orange trees from their winter quarters into their summer positions. Then, of course, there's the 33 km of box hedging to be carefully clipped in spring . . . truly, a gardener's work is never done.

white-flowering variety, 'Alba'. 'Jungle Beauty' has an impressive show of flowers that stand considerably taller than other ajugas. It is very vigorous and its leaves are green tinged with bronze. You will need to weed ajuga beds for the first year until they get established. From then on they should suppress any unwelcome visitors themselves.

In the modern parterre the spaces can, in fact, hold anything from cabbages to roses. Many groups of plants tend to look very straggly at their bases at various times of the year and others just plain gloomy (like roses in winter). Any untidiness and cheerlessness can be concealed with a skirt of neatly clipped hedging. For visual accord, clusters of the same plant are best planted in each compartment — and it pays to be generous. Parterres can also be used to harbour those delicate specimens that require shelter from the wind, or those demanding plants whose every need you can cater for within the confines of the hedges.

The choice of the parterre hedging plant can be based around three things: what looks good all year round (an upright habit with dense evergreen or 'evergrey' foliage); what suits the site (sun or shade, dry or damp); and what will forgive you for the constant and often brutal haircuts. The tried and true plants for low silvery grey hedges are lavender, santolina, rosemary and germander. All these will give you sweet smells and pretty flowers (if you like) as well as good definition within the garden. They should all be clipped — little and often — to maintain dense growth and always trimmed immediately after flowering. The greys make a good foil for really bright flowers or would contrast well with green hedging when entwined in a pattern. They would all appreciate an open, sunny situation. So would the curry plant, *Helichrysum italicum*. Its grey spiky foliage likes to be clipped and if left unpruned will sport clusters of yellow button flowers in summer. This plant can look a bit bedraggled after a wet winter and benefits from being cut back hard to the old wood each spring. You could hardly call it sweet smelling but it will fill the air with an intriguing aroma of curry — especially after rain, when you'd swear you had just walked past an Indian restaurant. Mary tells me, the leaves are actually too bitter to use much in cooking, although very small amounts can be added to a soup or stew.

Hyssop was much used as a hedge in Elizabethan times but seems to have been forgotten, which is a shame as it makes a pretty hedge plant with narrow,

Top: Berberis thunbergii 'Atropurpurea Nana' is a compact plant with deep purple-wine foliage that will turn bronze then sometimes scarlet before baring itself to winter. This creates dramatic contrasts when interlaced with the dark-green box, but beware that most of the drama doesn't come from the barberry's vicious thorns.

Above: Finely clipped hedges at Hatfield's foot maze.

dark-green leaves and purple-blue flowers in late summer. There are also white and pink-flowering varieties, 'Albus' and 'Roseus'. Hyssop enjoys a sunny spot but doesn't cope well with humid weather. The aromatic leaves taste of a bitter combination of sage and mint and are best used sparingly. Hyssop is a useful herb that Mary uses with fruit sauces such as a cherry sauce, or with duck or a raspberry purée, when it cuts the sweetness and adds its own piquancy. It's one of the flavours in the liqueur Chartreuse.

Another good-looking plant for a hedge is the Australian native *Westringa fruticosa*. Its former name, *W. rosmariniformis*, better describes the small, deep-green aromatic foliage, although I wouldn't toss it in with the roast of lamb. It will grow in dry soils and doesn't mind salty winds, making it ideal for seaside gardens.

The very amenable *Choisya ternata*, or Mexican orange blossom, will feel as much at home in full sun or a shady corner. It is also one of the most frost-hardy evergreens, with glossy, deep-green leaves that are fragrant when crushed. In spring the shrub covers itself in masses of sweet-smelling white flowers. It will flower again in autumn in warmer areas. Trim after each flowering to keep the foliage dense at the base.

Some of our own hebes make very good low hedges and will add charm to the garden with their rather quiet blooms. *Hebe* 'Lavender Lace' will give you pale lavender flowers in spring and autumn, and *H. speciosa* 'Mauve Knight' will, strangely enough, produce mauve flowers over summer. Neither will mind clipping, but *H. speciosa* cultivars are not happy with really cold conditions.

Many of the small-leaved coprosmas and corokias will adapt to the formality of a parterre. They will also add rich hues to the threads of your embroidery — lending wonderful contrasts of woven hedges and subtle and not so subtle combinations of hedging and planting within them. *Coprosma* 'Beatson's Gold' has golden-yellow leaves edged with green. Those of *C.* 'Beatson's Brown' have a brown edge to the golden centre, while *C.* 'Coppershine' is aptly named, with dark, coppery green foliage. There are even more combinations with some corokias as they will give you small starry yellow flowers in spring and colourful berries in late summer. *Corokia* x *virgata* 'Cheesemanii' has dark-green leaves with a silvery underside and red berries. The foliage of 'Geentys Green' is bright green while that of 'Frosted Chocolate' is a glossy chocolate-brown, which becomes more intense over winter. 'Yellow Wonder' has yellow berries — no wonder there.

BOXING ON

By far the most popular plant for low hedging is box. There are many good reasons for its prevalence in our gardens. Box is slow growing so there is less clipping. It has dense, compact foliage, which makes it very malleable to the clipping shears, which, furthermore, it will forgive you for using. It's a courageous plant, enduring droughts, frosts, snow, indifferent soils — probably even plagues of locusts. It's easy with sun and shade — although it would appreciate a burst of heat sometime during the day and, like the best of us, ends up rather blistered and parched if it's in the full glare of the searing sun all summer long. The strong, erect form will bounce back into shape after the occasional altercation with Frisbees, footballs and even man's best friend. Perhaps the main reasons for box finding so much favour in parterres is that it is always neat and tidy and it knows how to behave itself. If it is planted in a straight line, it will keep to that straight line and this lack of deviation means that various planted patterns remain the same for years. It also knows its place, content with playing the reliable consort, walking so many paces behind so as not to outshine the radiant bride. Good old box will allow your showier blooms to hold centre stage.

Buxus sempervirens, the European or common box, is the most suitable for formal training. This will generally grow between 1 and 2 metres high. It's hard to believe that this plant that we think of as a shrub is really a tree that will naturally grow as high as 10 metres. And, yes, its wood was used for boxes. It was also used for mathematical instruments and in wood engraving, as the wood boasts an exceptionally even grain and great durability. Cloning has brought about even smaller varieties, the most useful and well known being *B. sempervirens* 'Suffruticosa', the dwarf box, which will grow up to 30 cm. There are variegated forms, 'Elegantissima' probably being the pick of them. Its olive-green leaves are splashed and margined with gold. Silver and blue-green varieties are in the pipeline. There are also pendulous, prostrate and mound-forming types of this very amenable plant.

Because of the actual numbers of plants required to form any sort of pattern, creating a parterre can be a costly exercise. Fortunately, for those of us who don't want to take out a bank loan to finance a knot garden, most hedge plants grow easily from cuttings.

Those flushes of new spring growth need several weeks to mature suffi-

Once box cuttings have taken root and their uncomely plastic protection removed, they can look decorative sitting in pots until they have attained the required height for planting out or clipping into simple geometric shapes.

Breaking New Ground 25

ciently before cuttings can be taken, so hold back on your trimming. Take cuttings of about 5 cm length, remove the bottom leaves and plant them in a pot of coarse sand.

Water and cover the pot with a plastic bag and keep in a cool location until the cuttings form roots. They can then be repotted in potting mix.

Larger cuttings can be taken in autumn and winter, stripped of their lower leaves and planted directly into the garden — some will take and some may not. Box plants are fibrous rooted and hold a good ball of soil and are consequently easily transported and transplanted at almost any size.

PLANTING A KNOT GARDEN

As this is going to be a relatively permanent planting, the ground should be thoroughly cultivated. It is best to plant in spring or early autumn, allowing the fledgling plants to become established before winter.

Draw up a pattern on paper remembering basic geometric shapes can be just as, if not more, effective than a complicated plan. Mark out your pattern on the ground with stakes, string and sand. Straight lines and right angles should be accurate as any errors will be gratingly visible. There is a little more leeway with curves. A bottle of sand tied to a fixed length of string will help you mark out sweeping circles and semi-circles.

Spacing between the plants depends on your patience, or perhaps more to the point, your impatience. Placed too close together, the plants run the risk of starving each other by the time they are mature. For those who just can't wait, the small varieties of box can be planted 10–15 cm apart. Larger plants can be spaced at 45 cm intervals. When in doubt, ask the experts at your local nursery. Keep some plants of the same size in reserve to compensate for any losses and that stray cricket ball. Allow the hedge plants to settle into their new surroundings before considering in-filling with other plants.

Once the plants have reached the desired height, they may require trimming up to four times a year. A cut after the first flush of growth in spring will give your hedge a tidy appearance for the summer months. Another clipping in autumn should be undertaken early enough to let the plants achieve a little

As well as containing the central swathe of mondo grass (Ophiopogon japonicus), box is cleverly partnered here with a pleached screen to conceal the garage in the background.

more growth before winter sets in. When trimming, try not to cut into the old wood. Unless you have a very keen eye, that good old piece of string may come in very handy again to help you maintain a straight line with the garden shears.

Each time you trim the hedges you are removing nutrients from the plants — and their potential capacity to take in food — so it's a good idea to replenish with a slow-release fertiliser. A mulch of well-rotted compost at the base of the plants will also give them food as well as help retain some moisture in the ground and keep the weeds at bay. A little patience is also required with a knot garden. It may take up to eighteen months to have a recognisable knot, but in the space of about three years it will look as if it's been there forever.

Mediterranean Associations

Maggie: While I wouldn't deny gardeners can be very stubborn, I'm often surprised when I'm filming round the country just how far some will go to grow completely unsuitable plants for their climate. I've done it myself: peonies in Auckland and tender agave in the Wairarapa: all doomed. In my saner moments I'm reminded that for best results for both the gardener and the plants it makes more sense to take note of the surrounding conditions.

In dry regions, why not abandon the thirsty perennials and go gravel? Look to the Mediterranean countries that share a similar climate; I'm drawn to their stylishly simple gardens and Mary revels in their exquisitely tasty cuisine.

Entertaining al fresco

Both the fruit and the oil of the olive tree lend themselves to very easy entertaining. They're also a good earthy reminder that life's pleasures should be kept simple. That way they remain timeless and are not swayed by changes of fashion. The charms that we can bring to our tables are the same uncomplicated delights enjoyed by people from all over the world for thousands of years. What could be more agreeable than some fresh crusty bread and a pristine saucer of good olive oil in which to dip it? For such a simple repast it would be as well to keep the table correspondingly uncluttered, maybe using plain white ramekins for the oil and wrapping both the bread and table in white cloths. No knives or sideplates. Part of the enchantment is in the communal breaking of the bread and crumbs scattered across the cloth for the birds later on.

Crusty bread, white cloth and if you add to the table a bowl of ripe peaches, flushed red and pink with the summer sun, you'd have your own tribute to Cézanne. Those shallow glazed terracotta saucers, along with a willow basket or wooden board for the bread, would fit right into a garden setting.

If you don't think your oil is quite up to such full-on scrutiny, you can add a sprig of thyme or rosemary to the bowl. If you're lucky enough to have a yield of bright red tomatoes ripened in the sun, go ahead and slice them, adding a leaf of basil and drizzling over a little oil to make it all glisten.

If you think you could go a step further and still maintain that nonchalant air so necessary with such plain fare, you could bake your own bread. There is no better welcome than the smell of bread just out of the oven. Making your own focaccia is an easy, straightforward procedure and it really tastes wonderful. (See recipe, page 160) And you wouldn't be overtaxing yourself by serving some tapenade with the bread. It's also a great topping for grilled or toasted breads.

Antipasto means 'before the meal' in Italian and referred to the tempting morsels that were served to stimulate the diner's appetite. More often than not they consisted of a few olives, some freshly dug radishes and maybe some slices of celery, tomato and salami — nothing fancy as the Italians have yet another phrase for more lavish displays, calling them *la morte del pranzo*, the death of the dinner. A generous selection was greeted with the frightening suspicion that the hostess may be planning to follow up with a meagre main course, giving rise to another term, *la malizia degli osti*, the host's trick. Those little plates have grown considerably over the past few years to large colourful platters containing all manner of delicious tidbits, and the appetizer has now become a meal in itself, a meal of tastes. This way of serving food suits our casual approach to entertaining. Friends can congregate in the charm of a terrace or courtyard and partake as they wish of various taste sensations without the reserve so often shown at 'real' meals and without the poor cook being confined to the kitchen. Although we've embraced the antipasto platter as our own, it still retains, quite literally, the flavour of its more humble origins. The olive and its wondrous oil have a good deal to do with this.

Once your simple meal is on the table, sit back with a chilled wine and enjoy your guests, the garden, the meal and all the good things the olive has contributed.

THE OLIVE GROVE

The darling of the nineties, the olive tree has found fresh surroundings in the antipodean home garden and there are several varieties perfectly suited to New Zealand conditions. Ideally, they should have quite a sharp winter followed by a long, warm summer. They're a great choice for planting by the sea as they seem quite resilient to salt wind and dry conditions. They have, after all, survived many thousands of years in some very inhospitable environments. Edward Gibbon, in his *Decline and Fall of the Roman Empire*, observed, 'The olive, in the western world, followed the progress of peace, of which it is considered the symbol.' Olives were also considered a staple food crop, along with wheat, for whole civilisations. It was the tree's magical oil that nourished the masses, soothed the ailing and anointed the princes of the many countries that bordered the Mediterranean Sea.

Coinciding with the love affair we are currently enjoying with all things Italian, there is the wonderful news that, along with red wine, olive oil is actually good for you. It is low in saturated and polyunsaturated fats and very high in monounsaturates, which lower the harmful kind of cholesterol while stimulating the beneficial kind. This apparently accounts for all those black-shawled women in Italy and Greece living to incredibly ripe old ages.

Olive oil is liquid gold. It is made from olives crushed to a pulp, from which is pressed the fruity, golden 'extra-virgin' oil. Cold water is added to the remaining pulp to make the second pressing, which is labelled 'fine' or 'extra-fine'. This is more bland in flavour but clearer in colour. The addition of hot water to the almost dry olive pulp makes the third pressing. Further pressings produce oil for soaps, fertilisers and the likes to ensure that not a drop is wasted.

The colour, nose and taste of olive oil are conditioned by many different factors — the climate, the soil, the varieties of olive and the ripeness of the fruit. Then there is the expertise in the production itself. Making a good olive oil is like making a good wine. In fact, there are even olive-oil tastings. The different oils are usually tasted on small pieces of plain white bread, although in the larger oil 'houses' of Europe, tasters will don their white coats, swirl the oil in a glass, hold it to the light to check the colour, take a big sniff and finish with a good mouthful. The oil's distinguishing qualities are described in the same way as wine — grassy,

fruity, peppery, flowery and the like. As in the wine industry, as well as houses, there are the smaller boutique or single estates where the olives are grown, harvested, pressed and then bottled in the same place. Most of us will be buying the oil, not pressing it. If you can, use the best. You'll need less of it and very good oil calls for minimum embellishment. Buy little and often, as this is where oil differs from wine — it does not improve with age.

Meantime we can enjoy the tree in our gardens. Good fruiting varieties of *Olea europaea* subsp. *europaea* make extremely elegant specimen trees, with dense willowy leaves of grey-green and silvery undersides. The trees may look a bit spindly and precious initially, but will slowly toughen up into fine examples of rugged good looks. Being evergreen and relatively undemanding in the soil and water departments, the olive makes a robust alternative to the ornamental pear (the darling of the eighties).

Olives are obliging trees and will adapt to life in a large container or even espaliered against a warm wall. Little pruning is needed; in fact they are best left alone until after their first fruiting. They bear fruit on the previous season's growth. Enjoy its ornamental foliage because the tree won't begin fruiting until at least its fifth year and could take up to ten years to really come into its own. It will bear clusters of small yellowy white flowers in late spring, and fruit in late autumn. Harvesting takes place from April through to August.

Fruit is harvested according to the colour of olive required. For green olives, pick the fruit when it's full-sized and has turned from deep green to a paler green or yellow, depending on the variety. For black or ripe olives, pick the fruit when it has become dark blue or purple. After harvesting, the tree would appreciate a feed of citrus food. Olives usually fruit more abundantly every other year.

'Manzanilla' is the world's most popular table olive. It produces medium to large fruit, which usually ripens early so there's less risk of frost damage. It is a heavy bearer and the tree has a low, spreading habit that facilitates picking. Both 'Barnea' and 'Mission' will fruit relatively quickly — in five years. The former will produce quite large fruit while those of the latter are small. 'Mission' is very resistant to the cold. 'Sevillano' will produce an abundant crop of large fruit if given a long, cold winter. 'Verdale' provides good green table olives. These varieties are all self-fertile. There are many others, however, that require a pollinator. New varieties are arriving all the time from Spain, Italy, Algeria, Israel, Turkey, and Australia,

Previous page: Capsicum, beans, tomatoes, artichokes, eggplants, courgettes and a decorative bunch of sage have all found their way from the garden to sit colourfully with our olives and a selection of sausages for this 'meal of tastes'. You can find out how to grill the capsicum and slow-roast the tomatoes in the Kitchen Garden section.

Centre: Although we may consider growing olive trees very 'now', this stand was planted in Cornwall Park in the 1870s by Sir John Logan Campbell when he returned from an inspirational extended visit to Tuscany.

Processing home-grown olives

The length of time olives take to shed their bitter juices depends largely on the size of the fruit. If you have a reasonable haul it will pay to sort them into small, medium and large groupings before you start, and it is best to discard any blemished fruit to avoid contamination during the curing process. Green olives take longer to cure than black ones.

Very ripe black olives can have the bitterness salted out of them. In a ceramic, glass or stainless-steel, but on no account alumin-ium, bowl layer the olives with a liberal showering of sea salt. Cover the bowl from the glare of the sun. You will be astonished at the amount of bitter juices emitted by the olives. This should be drained off each day for about two weeks — or even longer — until you are happy with the taste. Then you have to rid the fruit of the excess salt. Rinse them well and return them to the cleaned bowl and cover with water, changed daily, for several days until you are satisfied with the saltiness — again it's up to the cook to act as guinea pig. The olives can then be drained and spread on a tray to dry for a few hours. These olives are now eminently edible. They can be tossed with a well-flavoured olive oil in a bowl and enjoyed then and there. Any left-overs should be packed in sterilised jars, topped with oil, sealed and stored in the fridge to be used in the not-too-distant future.

Olives that have been soaked in water then stored in brine will enjoy a longer shelf life. Both black and green olives can be done this way. Cracking the skins first by gently rolling them with a rolling pin will speed the process. Soak the olives in water for 10–20 days, depending on the size and colour of the fruit, rinsing and refreshing with fresh water every day. That should eliminate the inevitable scum that appears. It also helps if the container is kept airtight with some sort of lid. After this time, place in sterilised jars and cover with brine. The basic brine mixture is made up of 1/3 cup of sea salt, 1 cup white vinegar and 4 cups water — you may need to increase the quantities if you have a particularly fruitful tree. Bring this mixture to the boil and

let it cool before filling the jars to overflowing. Seal and leave them for four to six weeks. By then the olives will be ready to eat, although they may be too salty for most tastes. Another day-long soak in water should make them palatable. They can then be drained and stored in fresh sterilised jars with a more flavourful brine. For this, use the same basic mixture and add a few goodies, such as bay leaves, whole chillies, peppercorns, garlic, orange or lemon zest and, lest we forget, some herbs. Once opened, these little beauties should be stored in the fridge. Unopened they will sit quite happily on a shelf for a good year — but chances are they won't. If they do, or if they look a little lack-lustre, drain your olives from the brine, put in a jar or bowl and cover with a good olive oil. You can add to this a peeled clove of garlic, sprigs of thyme, rosemary or marjoram, a chilli or two, bay leaves, strips of orange or lemon peel — whatever takes your fancy. Cover and let the flavours mingle for about a week. When you have received due praise for the fruits of your labour, you can use the remaining oil from the marinade to liven up your everyday cooking.

and we are propagating some to call our own. If you are considering your own grove, it would pay to contact the New Zealand Tree Crops Association for information on what varieties are best suited to your area.

Olives are quite inedible in their natural state. The mind boggles as to how exactly those ancient civilisations worked out how to make them edible. A foul substance called oleuropein has to be leached from the fruit. Most commercial ventures use an alkaline solution, such as a potash lye or caustic soda, to remove the bitterness. The fruit must then be leached of the lye residue and the whole process may have you wondering why you bothered in the first place, with supermarket varieties suddenly regaining their appeal. However, there are straightforward ways to home-cure your olives without resorting to chemicals (opposite).

GO GRAVEL

For those of us who would rather not lug hoses or brimming buckets round the precious plants in the hottest months: be smart — go gravel.

It's a Mediterranean theme but has all kinds of interpretations around the world. They call it xeriscape in California, with desert-look-alike gardens planted out in xeriphytes — plants that thrive in dry conditions. English plantswoman Beth Chatto has transformed an old car park into an outstanding gravel garden inspired by her visit to a New Zealand river. Once established, you won't be troubled by too many weeds, the selection of plants for this type of garden are hardy and the gravel acts as a mulch, retaining moisture in summer and offering protection in winter: a low-maintenance syle of gardening well suited to New Zealand conditions.

Plants for the gravel garden

ARTEMISIAS have feathery leaves with a sheen of silver that sparkles in the sunlight. Few plants can trace their journey from their Mediterranean origins with such clarity. It was planted by the roadsides by the Roman army so that soldiers could put a fragrant sprig in those famous sandals to soothe their aching feet. So wherever the legions marched, the artemsias were there first. *Artemesia*

How to make a gravel garden

Gravel gardens are best located in an open, sunny situation. To prepare a site you must first remove all the weeds. If the soil fertility is poor, add some good compost. If the ground is heavy, spread a 3 cm layer of gravel and fork it into the top 10 cm of soil. This is also your chance to rake in a light dressing of fertiliser, before the lid is put on with another 2–3 cm of gravel.

If the garden is on a slope, the soil can be held in place with pieces of stone and the gravel can sweep around them. Rocks are also useful to break up dull flat areas. Planting is best undertaken in spring, and the plants should be thoroughly watered when put into the ground. If possible, plant as much as you can before spreading the topcoat of gravel. For any later planting, scrape the gravel to one side, set the plant in place with a little extra gravel mixed in for good measure, and smooth the 'mulch' around it.

Silver and grey-foliaged plants grow naturally in harsh, drought-prone regions. Their colour comes from a layer of white hairs on the surface of the leaf. These little hairs reduce the amount of water loss and help the plants cool off by reflecting the sunlight. Clusters of shrubs and perennials, making mounds of silver, grey and grey-green, many capped with soft clouds of flowers, will make a most harmonious carpet around the olive trees. Well, more of a very accommodating, downy cushion really.

When planting your gravel garden, be generous with the clusters. Three lavenders will provide a more effective drift of purple haze than one lonely specimen, no matter how generous it is with its flowers. There's a golden rule (perhaps silver in this case) that planting in groups of odd numbers is always more agreeable to the eye.

arborescens will quickly form a nicely rounded bush of 1.5 metres with fine, silky, silver foliage. It has small insignificant yellowish flowers in summer. This plant requires perfect drainage and can't compete with the frosts over winter. *A. absinthium* is hardier, growing untidily to 1 metre. It has one cultivar that is neater in habit, 'Lambrook Silver', which also has masses of pale flowers in summer. *A.* 'Powis Castle' is thought to be a hybrid between the two species. This one is perfectly behaved, making a compact bush of 80 cm. It rarely flowers and will stoically tolerate drought and rain. Like most of the grey plants, artemesias can be cut back after flowering. If they become too straggly over the autumn and winter months, they can be cut back again in spring. I treasure my shapely little 'Powis Castle' because it looks superb all through the year in my Wairarapa garden.

ERYNGIUMS (sea hollies) provide an ethereal mood. Eryngiums have a metallic lustre to their cone flowerheads, which are surrounded by a spiky choirboy's collar, or bract, some grievously prickly. *E. giganteum*, commonly known as 'Miss Wilmott's ghost', comes to life in a dry garden with the palest of stems holding dazzling light blue-green cones ringed with silvery green bracts. This plant is biennial; it will last just two seasons, growing during the first (to over 1 metre) and flowering in the second year. I forgot to stake mine with the unsatisfactory result that it flopped over like some sort of vicious groundcover, its branches snapping off the main crown. Stake it when you plant it to show off to best advantage. Like most biennials, it self-sows freely. Miss Wilmott herself was apparently very generous with her eryngium seed. Hers was a charmed life for a gardener. In her garden in Essex she had a hundred helpers. She would take her favourites with her on sojourns to her other garden in France. I've visited French gardens where legend has it that the sea holly plants growing today are descendents from original seed scattered by the determined woman herself.

PENNISETUM SETACEUM, the dusky-pinky, deciduous African fountain grass, makes a wonderful arching clump with coppery pink flowers. Unfortunately, it can make its presence felt too much in the garden by self-seeding far too freely. It has become quite invasive in parts of Australia. Best to stick to the Asian fountain grass, *P. orientale*, which will form equally attractive clumps that reach a metre when its silvery pink plumes flower.

LAVENDERS are ideally suited to a gravel garden as they require a well-drained soil and little else, though an occasional side-order of lime — a handful per plant

Top: Grey-foliage plants are a good complement to a stone wall in this gravel garden.

Above: The bonus with planting Pennisetum setaceum, *or any ornamental grass, is that the slender leaves will rustle in the wind as well as sway, offering sound and movement to the garden.*

worked into the soil — wouldn't go amiss. They also benefit from pruning: lightly after their first flowering to promote a second flush; then hard pruning at the end of the summer, but never back to the old wood. *Lavandula angustifolia*, the most fragrant of lavenders, is called English lavender, although it also comes from the Mediterranean. It is quite hardy but hates wet weather. *L. dentata* seems to flower all the year in many northern gardens and is well suited to coastal areas. The showy-winged French or Italian lavenders, *L. stoechas,* are hardy except where winters are severe, though they will come back after frost and are good in humid conditions. One of the better known cultivars is 'Marshwood', named after the Invercargill garden where it was discovered as a chance seedling. Its extra-long wings are mauve. The deeper purple 'Helmsdale' is from the same garden. To prevent your plants from becoming too woody and to encourage bushy foliage, you should ruthlessly remove all the flowers for the first year.

PACHYSTEGIA INSIGNIS is also content in a dry, rocky environment. The leaves of the Marlborough rock daisy plant are thick and leathery with a white hairy underside that seems to curl slightly over the top of the leaf to give it an edge in more ways than one, emphasising the leaf's becoming curves. The pale grey flowerbuds look like suede and make a good show for months before the white daisy flowers actually open for a short time in December.

MACLEAYA CORDATA takes up rather a lot of space, but it's worth making room for a good clump of the plume poppy. It's a striking plant with large heart-shaped leaves that look like those of the fig, grey-green above with white undersides that shimmer in the light summer breezes. The stems will reach an impressive 2 metres and are crowned with feathery plumes of creamy flowerheads through summer that turn a smoky bronze by the end of the season. The plant spreads by rhizomes that have invasive tendencies and should be lifted and divided each autumn to keep the clumps confined to more reasonable bounds for the average garden. Their colouring and size make them a perfect back-of-the-border plant, where they'll need about a metre's width to feel and look at home. The tall sturdy stems can make an effective screen against a wall or garden shed. Macleayas need some protection from cold winds, although they are frost-hardy. They like a moist but well-drained soil and prefer full sun — the leaves tend to lose their shimmer when the plant is partially shaded. *M. microcarpa* is a slightly smaller version with the same good looks but even more keen to take over the whole garden.

The dusky plumes of Macleaya cordata *place a check on some of the more glaringly luminous plants, such as artemisia, which can be a bit too brilliant for their own good in the height of the summer.*

One of summer's great delights must be the sight of the dazzling white flowers of Cistus landanifer, *each petal kissed with a crimson beauty spot.*

Opposite: Salvia madrensis, *the forsythia sage, will grow to 2 metres, presenting a striking display of sunny yellow blooms from late summer to early winter. It shows up well here behind the purple spires of* S. tesquicola.

ROCK ROSES (*Cistus* spp.) have astonishing flowers. The buds look like crumpled balls of crêpe paper and slowly unfurl to expose radiant blooms that have all the beauty of an old-fashioned single rose, hence the name. These treasures last only a day but the shrub is a reservoir of continually unfolding buds and resplendent flowers mainly in spring and early summer, although some varieties perform for most of the year. They come in white, cream, lemon, pink, purple and magenta — all with a sunny centre of yellow stamens and most kissed with a dark crimson or chocolate blotch. These beauty spots are their *pièce de résistance*. There are varieties with pure white flowers and spots removed, but they almost look too clean for the garden. *C. landanifer* has blooms as big as the palm of your hand, white splashed with deep crimson. It grows to a large (2 metres) spreading bush. *C. salviifolius* has smaller flowers on a smaller bush that are pure white except for a redemptive splotch of orange at the tip of each petal. *C.* 'Silver Pink' has pale clear-pink flowers with even paler centres. Cistus will grow quickly and without protest in full sun and a well-drained poor soil. They love to be around rocks and rubble where their roots can seek out deep moisture, hence the other part of its common name. They will withstand desert and coastal conditions, but not frosts, although the popular *C.* x *purpureus* 'Brilliancy', with its deep pink flowers splashed with crimson, is hardier than most.

HELIANTHEMUM, the sun roses, little cousins of the cistus, do well in the same conditions. They will grow to 30–40 cm. There is quite a range of hybrids — some with silver foliage, others a mid-green. Flowers are generally brighter — yellow, pink, red or orange — with and without those endearing splotches.

TEUCRIUM has been used extensively for hedges but if allowed to grow naturally it'll form pleasantly rounded silvery grey bushes. If left unpruned, *Teucrium fruticans*, the bush germander, will eventually attain a 2 metre spread, and, even when clipped, it will soon regain its former height. It bears pale-blue lipped flowers for most of the year and it will grow just as well in the shade of trees as in the full sun. The smaller wall germander, *T. chamaedrys*, will grow to just over 50 cm, if allowed. This one spreads with underground runners and, as its name suggests, is quite suitable for steep banks and walls. The tops of its leaves are a glossy deep green and look like tiny oak leaves; their undersides are grey.

LYCHNIS CORONARIA is another glittering prize. Its shapely branches will form a good-looking mound of silvery-white downy leaves topped continually over summer with cerise flowers. These flowers are small enough not to look out of place in a soft border, and have a special charm. To pacify gardeners with quieter tastes there's 'Alba' with white flowers, and 'Oculata' is soft pink. Tough as it is, this brave plant can exhaust itself after a couple of years' hard flowering. It self-seeds readily, so there should always be a colony.

HELICHRYSUM PETIOLARE is also a great spreader. This liquorice plant from South Africa has grey, heart-shaped leaves on stems encased in a cobweb of fine white hairs. There is the occasional, insignificant pale-pink flower. It will obligingly form mounds up to 50 cm and sprawl a couple of metres. It looks good trailing out of containers, or left to spread over a wall or path. 'Limelight' has bright lime-green foliage that ignites all manner of thrilling associations with euphorbias, *Alchemilla mollis* and the rich, velvety violet-blues of some of the salvias. *Helichrysum bellidioides* is one of ours. A native groundcover whose stems will develop roots as they touch the ground, it will cascade down a wall or provide a cool undercover for surrounding shrubs. Its spoon-shaped leaves are grey-green on top with a web of white hairs beneath and its small white strawflowers provide a good show from spring into summer. Even though preferring to bake under the full glare of the sun, this plant is surprisingly cold-hardy.

So far in our gravel garden we have the silvers, greys, bleached whites, blues, purple-blues and mauve-pinks, which all reflect the skies and seas of summer. Yellow is the colour of the sun and it will take the chill off the blues and whites and put a bit of life into what could be rather a bland landscape. Even the imperiously discerning Gertrude Jekyll remarked, 'To pass from the cool quiet of lavender and pink into a golden garden is like stepping into sunshine.' A considerable number of grey-foliaged plants are adorned with yellow flowers. It seems a futile task to hide their lively blooms. Sit back and enjoy them rather than making extra work for yourself. You could well discover how clever grey foliage is, having the ability to temper the brighter flowers and link an assortment of colours, making for a more harmonious arrangement.

SANTOLINA CHAMAECYPARISSUS, the cotton lavender, has mustard-yellow button flowers, which are often not seen in gardens. Those who grow it for the aromatic, finely cut but heavily felted, silvery leaves usually find the spicy yellow blooms offensive to their softer colour schemes, and the little buds are unceremoniously beheaded before flowering. A better choice for the pastel border is

Salvias

Salvias produce the bluest blues and most scarlet scarlets imaginable. There's one for almost every situation — mind you, there should be, for there are over 900 species originating from the Mediterranean, North Africa, the Balkans, the Middle East and others from Mexico, South America and South Africa. Generally, those from Europe are better in colder areas and the American species are best further north. They thrive in gravel soils but require regular watering in summer.

The most well-known salvia is *S. officinalis*, the culinary herb, sage. It forms a compact bush of velvety leaves of pale slivery green that look good all year round. Its summer flowers are soft shades of lavender-blue and mauve-pink. *S. argenta*, the silver sage, is grown more for its large silvery white leaves that form a ground-hugging rosette. *S. officinalis* 'Purpurascens' has dusky green and purple leaves that mix gently with grey foliage. It also makes an interesting filler between pink, purple and blue flowers, where it will add subtle texture. Its strong purple flushes stand up well to the bright reds and oranges towards the end of the summer. These sages can be increased by earthing up the soil at the base of the plants and replanting the rooted cuttings that form. For some sage advice for the kitchen, turn to page 160.

The tall spires of Echium pininana *are often used 'architecturally' to add a very definite point of interest.*

S. 'Bowles Lemon', which has pale grey-green foliage and small flowers the colour of creamy butter.

BRACHYGLOTTIS GREYII (the plant formally known as *Senecio greyii*) has bright yellow daisies that are hard to hide. This tough plant has soft grey-white leaves to temper the impact. It forms a lovely mound before becoming a bit straggly, although it soon smartens up with a good prune. One of the remaining senecios, *S. cineraria*, sometimes called dusty miller, has fantastic jaggedly cut leaves that look like silver coral. It comes from the Mediterranean, where it grows naturally in sandy coastal areas. It doesn't like too much humidity but, given a dry spot, it will form a mound the same size as lavender.

CENTAUREA CINERARIA is another plant called dusty miller, and the two are often mistaken for each other when not in flower. *C. cineraria*, the perennial cornflower, has the same jagged silver foliage. This plant thrives in drought conditions. Its flowers are like thistles in hues of lilac and pink which would augment the purple haze we're trying to achieve. Centaurea has a species with rich yellow flowers, *C. macrocephala*, that look like a bright golden thistle sitting on a rich brown pine-cone bract atop dandelion leaves.

Now that the arid desert of gravel is covered with a background chorus, you could add a few highlights to contribute to the performance with their bolder, more dramatic presence.

ASTELIAS must have first billing for combining bold leaves with gracefulness — rather like a strong, handsome dancer. *Astelia chathamica* 'Silver Spear' will form a large clump similar to flax, but tidier, as its old leaves will wilt away. Its grey leaves curl around to reveal, yes, a silver lining. Originating on the Chatham Islands, it is well used to weathering drying coastal winds, growing in sun or shade. There are separate male and female plants, both bearing flowers, but the female's become showy orange fruits.

ARTHROPODIUM CIRRATUM, the rengarenga lily, is a hardy alternative to hostas, which can also boast marvellous foliage. Its strong leaves arch elegantly from a solid clump that's crowned with sprays of starry white flowers over early summer. This is another plant to be found naturally tumbling down cliffs and rocky faces but, besides standing up to droughts and harsh coastal conditions, this one will grow anywhere — even in the shade. Town planners, aware of its versatility, have stumbled on yet another talent — it doesn't mind car fumes — but don't be put off by its prevalence in traffic islands. Rengarenga lilies are not found alone in nature and are best grown in groups. Once established, these treasures are easily divided to facilitate large drifts. Slice up the clumps with a spade, cutting the leaves back like you do with leeks. Trim the roots and replant. Water well and mulch with gravel to help conserve the moisture.

ECHIUMS are another bold performer. Few plants can reach the exalted heights of the tapering spires of *Echium pininana*. In just the right conditions plants can grow to 5 metres, but most have less lofty aspirations. This majestic plant sends up columns of lilac-blue flowers in early summer. They self-seed freely (they're biennial) and grow in relaxed, natural drifts. They are also quite used to tumbling down cliff faces in their native Canary Islands. Their chubbier, shrubbier cousins, *E. candicans* (syn. *E. fastuosum*), are the ones called pride of Madeira. From rosettes of furry grey leaves rise spires made up of hundreds of sapphire-blue flowers with crimson stamens. Some days the plant looks on fire. These perennials will grow to 2 metres and their spread will be wider. Occasionally one of these echiums will cross pollinate with the other and before too long you may have a colony of beauties with the height of the former and the deep, rich blue of the latter.

Another echium from the Canary Islands is *E. wildprettii*, a biennial which will form a rosette of silvery leaves the first year and send up imposing spires of rich coral-red flowers the next. This is sometimes befittingly called tower of jewels. Echiums are tough plants that enjoy warm, sunny gardens. They thrive in the same semi-arid coastal conditions from whence they came.

VERBASCUMS are stately soloists that could rise above our gentle background. They fit in to the gravel scene very well, with their need for a well-drained sunny position. *Verbascum bombyciferum* is another biennial, spending its first year forming a magnificent rosette of beautifully felted pale grey foliage. In the second year the plant sends up tall spikes (to 2 metres), which hold golden-yellow flowers over summer. *V. olympicum*, although perennial, is not long lasting. It will form a large (3 metre) rosette of silvery white leaves and its flower columns will soar to 2 metres, holding a great branching candelabra, supporting woolly buds that become yellow flowers. *V. phoeniceum* is the purple mullein with rosettes of dark, glossy leaves and shorter spires of soft purple flowers. *V.* 'Pink Domino' is a cross between the last two species and has rose-pink flowers. If its spikes are cut back after flowering, you may see a second flush in late summer.

A planting of Verbascum olympicum *can exude an elusive, slightly mysterious air in the garden.*

Alliums will grow in most conditions.

BEARDED IRISES ask for very little in the garden, apart from a well-drained soil. They prefer cold winters and long hot summers and wouldn't say no to a dressing of dolomite lime in autumn and another of bonemeal just before they flower in spring. They come in three sizes. Dwarf bearded irises start flowering in August, the medium varieties in September and October and the taller ones in October and November. By planting a few of each you could have an extended period of colour. And what a range of colours will burst on to the stage in sumptuous costumes of indigo and violet, copper and bronze, creamy yellows and mahogany reds, all velvety and bejewelled and fit for a medieval pageant. When they shed their fine robes their grey sword-like leaves fit conveniently into the Mediterranean setting. So they should. *Iris germanica* 'Florentina' has been grown commercially around Florence for hundreds of years. When its roots are dried they produce orris root, highly valued in the perfume industry. Rhizomes are best planted out in the summer months; the top of each should be left exposed above the soil so that it can bake in the sun. The plants will flower much better. The rhizomes should be divided every four to five years.

ALLIUMS are also willing to stick their heads up above the rest. The ornamental onions will grow in miserable soils but will look all the better with a good feed. The appropriately large mauve globes of *Allium giganteum* will stand 2 metres high, each globe holding hundreds of starry flowers. This allium tends to be far too liberal with its seeds and is considered a bit of a pest, but some species are better behaved. *A. christophii* is the most impressive, with good-sized heads of silvery pink stars. When flowering commences in early spring its foliage dies back and is discreetly concealed by the cushiony underplanting. This is a plant that knows how to exit graciously; its delicate stem remains purple and the seedheads dry in perfect spheres, continuing to add interest and height in the garden and useful for dried arrangements later on. *A. cernuum* is a wild onion from the mountainous regions of North America. It is smaller, with dainty, nodding flowers which look fantastic in a light breeze. These can be pink, white or an intriguing amethyst and look effective when planted with purple sage and other violet salvias. *A. moly* is from Spain and is quite different again, with upturned bright yellow flowers. It doesn't have the distinctive onion smell, so it can be picked for the vase. Of course, the vegetable-garden varieties of allium — leeks, garlic and chives — will also set an ethereal mood in the dry garden.

KANGAROO'S PAWS, or *Anigozanthos*, grow in grassy clumps of sword-like leaves and curious felty flowers. There's quite a range in the height of various cultivars — from 25 cm to 2 metres. Anyone who has seen them growing wild in Western Australia will vouch for the fabulous spectacle they make flowering en masse. The flowers come in a dazzling array of lime-green, orange, pink, terracotta, golden yellow, brown and, as Aussies would put it, flaming red. Some of the stems are also brilliantly coloured. There is one that is absolutely stunning: *A. manglesii* has blue-green leaves and its flowers are deep green. These contrast vividly with the red bases and stems they sit on. The only trouble with this species is that it's probably the hardest to grow, requiring just the right shingly soil and a long, dry summer. It also succumbs to inkspot disease without putting up a fight. Most paws suffer from this disease — it doesn't kill them, but the plants are severely weakened by it. Several years ago an Australian scientist admirably decided to make this problem his retirement project. He planted thousands of the seedlings of the various species and ruthlessly culled any that showed signs of affliction. The remainder then bred a new strain called the 'Bush Gems'. Any paws that bear the prefix 'Bush' are resistant to inkspot. 'Bush Dawn' grows to 1.5 metres with bright-yellow flowers in summer and autumn. 'Bush Glow' reaches 70 cm with bronzed red and yellow flowers in spring and autumn. 'Bush Noon' has orange flowers on a bronze stem at the same time of the year. It will grow to 2 metres. All these gems need to be planted in the sun in a well-drained soil. Watering is necessary in really dry conditions. Snails can be rather partial to their leaves.

POPPIES. It may sound a bit Irish, but I'd plant some Californian or oriental poppies in my Mediterranean garden. There's that great feeling of anticipation as each bud warms to the day and finally splits open to show its true colours. The shades of silvery pink and scarlet would go well with the flowers of cistus, both having similar crepy blooms with dark markings. The seedpods are decorative long after the fragile petals have blown away in the warm summer air. I'd also include some opium poppies (*Papaver somniferum*) for their toothed foliage and showy blooms, but beware the poppy thieves: it might pay to plant poppies away from where passersby can see them.

Orange, like yellow, goes well with blues and white, and fortunately this once-reviled and misunderstood colour is back in fashion. Some oriental poppies

Other plants suited to the gravel garden

- Rue, *Ruta graveolens* 'Jackman's Blue', has lustrous blue lacy leaves.
- The globe thistle, *Echinops ritro*, will grow to 80 cm with leathery grey-green leaves and round balls of blue, some the deepest, most beautiful blue you'd ever see.
- The Russian sage, *Perovskia*, is actually from the Himalayan region. 'Blue Spire' will grow to 1–1.5 metres in three years.
- The sea lavender, *Limonium latifolium*, can be the mainstay of the garden as well as florist shops over the hottest months.
- *Eryngium bourgatii* has numerous silver-blue flowers held in a spiny silver bract. *E. alpinum* has bracts of purple-blue and requires a better soil. *E. maritimum* is the toughest of the bunch.
- Some of our hebes are suited to gravel conditions. *H. pimeleoides* 'Quicksilver' has spreading bronze stems that hold leaves of silvery grey. It also has spires of violet-blue flowers over summer.
- The Californian lilac, *Ceanothus*, is heavily clad with foliage and masses of flowers in spring. 'Blue Cushion' will grow to 1 metre and has flowers of soft lilac-blue.
- *Buddleja davidii* has many cultivars with grey-green foliage and panicles of cream, pink and mauve flowers. The blooms of 'Empire Blue' are a rich violet-blue with an orange eye. 'Ile de France' is dark purple and 'Black Knight' darker still. *B. fallowiana* has deciduous felted grey leaves and thin panicles of pale lavender flowers with pale orange throats which are intensely fragrant. The popular 'Lochinch' is a cross between these two species.
- *Convolvulus cneorum* will grow to 1 metre in a sunny dry position, producing a long succession of white flowers throughout the summer.
- *Stachys byzantina* (*S. lanata*) does extremely well in dry soils under a hot sun. 'Silver Carpet' is flowerless.

Stately cypress

Sentinel rows of pencil-thin cypress standing to attention along the highways and byways of Italian roads provide some of my more enduring memories of travelling through Europe. Back home, if your landscape calls for a formal feature with that authentic Mediterranean atmosphere, the upright, dark green columns of *Cupressus sempervirens* could be just what you're after.

In the wild, a cypress can top 40 metres, but fortunately most cultivars on offer in New Zealand are destined to stay within the 3–10 metre range. Native to Crete, Rhodes, Turkey and Iran, most species hail from mountainous areas or very low rainfall regions. Armed with this knowledge, it's not difficult to work out cypress are best planted in a dry, sunny spot, tolerating light shade and preferring a well-drained, preferably limestone soil. Their foliage, made up of small, erect branches, is easily damaged so will need some shelter from harsh winds.

When it comes to pruning, a light tidy-up trim in autumn and spring is really all that's needed. Cuttings, which are easy to strike with a little help from a rooting hormone, can be taken at the same time. Be very wary about tampering with the main growing tip of a cypress because if you cut the central leader by mistake, you'll throw the tree into confusion and it will sprout out plumply from the base, losing that slim, pointed, pencil shape.

Incidentally, the best way to ensure absolute uniformity if you want an avenue or row of look-alike cypress is to take cuttings from the same 'mother' tree — or buy all your plants at the same time from a reputable grower.

A top variety for local conditions is the New Zealand-raised *C. sempervirens* 'Gracilis', attaining a height of around 3 metres and growing about 35 cm wide. Dense and compact, with fresh green, thread-like foliage, this cultivar retains its perfect columnar shape, guaranteed not to 'sag' or collapse as other cypress are inclined to do.

Another cultivar inclined to keep to the straight and narrow is the dark green *C. sempervirens* 'Stricta'. Taller than 'Gracilis', it can be expected to reach 5 metres high and 70 cm wide after ten years. At 2 metres by 35 cm, the more compact-growing *C.* 'Totem' is a reliable accent plant, featuring neat, vertical rows of coarse-textured, needle-like foliage.

The slow-growing *C. sempervirens* 'Swane's Golden' is a compact, boldly yellow Aussie import that can be counted on to keep its looks and figure. On paper, this conifer is supposed to grow to 3 metres, with a girth of 35 cm, but I have seen it reach a stately 5 metres in sheltered conditions . . . so be warned.

have hints of orange and the hint is at its least subtle in the flowers of *Papaver pilosum*, a perennial found wild among the rocks in the mountainous parts of Turkey. Better still is the orange of the sea poppy, *Glaucium flavum*. This short-lived perennial grows naturally around Mediterranean shores, is very hardy and thrives in sunny places. It forms a rosette of grey leaves from which spring glowing golden yellow and orange flowers all summer long.

ROSEMARY is another of that tough breed of sun-worshipping plants from the shores of the Mediterranean. It flourishes in dusty, dry places and relishes life by the sea. It grows so luxuriantly on the islands of Corsica and Sardinia that fishermen can smell its wafting fragrance far out at sea. Its Latin name, *Rosmarinus*, means 'dew of the sea'. There are a large number of varieties to choose from these days — some with deep-blue flowers, some pale or pink or white. Some have even traded their dark-green needles for golden ones, while others have lost their silver lining. For the time being, though, I'm sticking with the tried and true *R. officinalis*, with its familiar dark-green and silver foliage and pale-blue flowers. It has never let me down, growing healthily in the sun in well-drained ground. It makes a very neat uniform hedge in the herb garden and it could make an effortless transition into more formal surroundings with its compliant attitude towards clipping. It can be shaped into a good standard 'lollipop' and even tied to look like an upright conifer. It requires little attention save for trimming to retain its dense foliage. Prune like lavender, never going all the way back to the old wood. Rosemary strikes easily from cuttings so a line-up to make a hedge is not going to empty the coffers. The prostrate rosemaries will also spill over walls and banks with enthusiasm as long as the site is warm and sunny and will make a wonderfully aromatic groundcover.

THE IMPORTANCE OF THE VESSEL

The way I see it, there are pots and then there are pots. There are those that are beautiful in themselves. They can stand alone and are best planted simply so that their own loveliness of colour, shape or pattern is not lost. These pots dictate their own terms: a square tub asks for a neatly clipped round ball of box; a shallow glazed bowl begs for a clump of ornamental grass; a simple, boldly

How to make hyper-tufa pots, tubs and troughs

Tufa is a type of porous limestone that is soft enough to be scraped or dug out yet hard enough to hold its shape. It is an excellent medium for the likes of alpines and lime-loving ferns, and the stone blends in well in the garden. These good looks can be mimicked with a made-up mixture called hyper-tufa, which makes a durable container of very natural appearance, after a bit of weathering. It's a style of container that has all the attributes we both look for: we give it top marks because it's not only easy to make but fulfils the criteria of minimum effort for maximum effect. It is a good idea to start off making a pot before graduating to the likes of a trough.

The hyper-tufa is made with **1 part sand, 1 part cement** and **2 parts coarse peat.** These are combined well and water is added until the mixture is pliable and moist but not too wet — rather like concrete. Fill the base of **a large plastic nursery bag** (say, size PB18) with the hyper-tufa mixture to a thickness of about 3 cm. Place some **3 cm long pieces of cut hosepipe** downwards through the base for drainage. **Fill a smaller plastic bag** (say, size PB6.5) with **sand or gravel** to stabilise it and place this inside the larger bag to mould the inside of your pot. Leave it all to set for about two days, then gently remove the inner bag and cut away the outer one. The outside of the pot can be scuffed with a wire brush or an old file to expose some of the peat and give it a rough texture. Moss and lichen will eventually grow over the pot to further enhance its character.

Square shapes or troughs can be formed by using two sizes of cardboard box. The cardboard should be reasonably sturdy and can be kept in place with bricks placed around the outside of the larger box and something like polystyrene packing blocks inside the inner box. (Sand would be too heavy and awkward.) The base and edges should be made thicker as the size of the container is increased — 7.5 cm for a standard carton. If you use big boxes, the base and sides need reinforcing by first placing a sheet of chicken wire over a 2 cm layer of hyper-tufa. Stick your bits of hose in between the wire and then cover the bottom with a remaining 5–5.5 cm layer. It is hard to be this precise around the sides; just make sure that the wire is roughly in the middle and is well covered. Larger containers will take up to a week to dry.

shaped pot demands the same from a plant like a hosta, an agave, astelia or even an evergreen azalea.

Ornately decorated pots don't need the distraction of a trailing plant to steal their thunder. Quite often the colour of the container leads you to plant in similar tones, or contrast with an opposing shade like red on green or yellow on violet-blue. Other games can be played with shapes. A long narrow container or one sitting on top of a pedestal will make a tall, willowy grass or miniature flax look like a fountain of water. The rustling sound when a breeze blows will heighten the effect.

Then there are the ordinary garden variety of pots that rarely call for a second glance. These pots are better served by staying well in the background and letting the plants do the talking. They can be planted flamboyantly with startling shapes or colours to divert attention from themselves. They can also be filled up with a medley of plants, but sometimes they tend to lose the plants in a clutter and the result is visually exhausting. These everyday pots are best gathered into groups where they'll find safety in numbers. Their uninspiring bases can be concealed by their neighbours' flowers and foliage and together they'll put on a show which they have no hope of sustaining individually. Again, it may pay not to plant too diverse an assortment or the profusion becomes a confusion.

There is the great temptation each year to plant an explosive range of spring bulbs, cheerful mixes of red and pink tulips, bright yellow daffodils and blue irises in a single pot. The planned riot of colour becomes a mishmash at flowering time with each container looking like nothing in particular, and yet when spring bulbs are planted in single colour groups, they can sing the joys of the season. This is a more natural look that takes you back to days when drifts of bluebells covered the ground beneath the apple blossom and daffodils enveloped the front paddock. We may not be able to fit such drifts into our court-yards but by planting a lot of the same in containers we can allude to the same expansiveness. This planting can't be stingy — nothing spoils the glory of spring as much as mean-spirited planting.

Many of the new concrete and terracotta pots can look just that — new — and can stick out like a sore toe in what could otherwise be a very harmonious grouping. They eventually assume a weathered look with natural growths of moss and lichen. This can be hurried along by smearing yoghurt over the surface of the

Following page: The narrow lanes and small houses of Córdoba leave little room for gardens, so for centuries the inhabitants of this Spanish town have specialised in decorating their patios and flowerpots are arranged on any available horizontal space. Pelargoniums predominate (mostly P. peltatum *and* P. zonale*) and are the perfect foil for the traditional lime-washed walls. I made a point of visiting Córdoba in May during their annual festival known as* Cruz de Mayo *when prizes are awarded to the best patios.*

pot. I've heard that a mix of manure and water also hastens the aging process — the things we do for appearances. Liquid plant food might be a more acceptable alternative. Vita Sackville-West recommended a coat of whitewash for harshly coloured pots, but avoid a stark white. A little raw umber mixed in the whitewash will give the pot the look of stone.

PELARGONIUMS MEDITERRANEAN STYLE

With a few pelargoniums in a terracotta pot, you don't really need a handsome Italian or a whitewashed wall to conjure up that Mediterranean atmosphere. Although of course, if the personable continental happened to be able to garden too . . .

Synonymous with hot bright summers, pelargoniums were made to be in pots and actively prefer cramped quarters as opposed to the luxury of a big container all to themselves. What's more, they're happy to stay put in the same old pot for years, flowering obligingly for months and yet demanding little attention in return. Their needs are simple: as much sun as you can give them and a well-drained soil. Waterlogging is often the cause of any fungal diseases they may contract. Little wonder they've been so popular for so long.

Pelargoniums were first introduced to Europe from South Africa by Dutch traders in the seventeenth century. They and many other 'novelty' plants needed winter protection in their new homes and it was for their benefit that increasingly elaborate greenhouses were built. After two centuries of tampering in the form of hybridisation, four distinct breeding lines began to emerge. They remain with us still:

ZONAL PELARGONIUMS are probably the best known and most popular of the four groups. Bushy plants, they have round or kidney-shaped leaves that more often than not have a deeper colour just inside the leaf margin. Carried aloft are the big heads of single, semi-double and double flowers in shades of red, pink, lilac and white. Zonals also include varieties with rosebud blooms — their central petals remain unopened like the bud of a rose — as well as a cactus-flowered group with twisted petals.

The miniature and dwarf varieties of the zonals, which stay at about 20 cm in height, are the ones that took Europe by storm. In Spain, Greece, France and Italy, every nook and cranny that sees the light of day seems capable of sustaining these vibrant, tenacious little plants. Some are stuck in old tin cans or plastic bottles, but in their humble containers they flower just as flamboyantly as the more carefully cultivated urn-bound specimens. Their colours mix surprisingly well together too, agreeing to disagree without clashing. That's more than can be said for the next group of pelargoniums.

REGAL PELARGONIUMS have large bell-shaped flowers in a wider range of colours. These are the ones with the mauve-lavenders and the fiery oranges and scarlets. There are also mahogany-browns and crimson-blacks. There is even one, 'Quantock', that is salmon flushed with orange, with purple marks on the upper petals – there must be a home for it somewhere. Regals require more watering than other pelargoniums, usually once a day over summer. They also like some shade in the afternoon.

IVY-LEAVED PELARGONIUMS, the third group, consist of trailing varieties that are fantastic in containers and hanging baskets. The leaves alone would make them worth growing, but they'll also flower for months and don't mind dry conditions and they can be trained to trail up a wall or trellis. The original ivy-leavers have succulent stems and glossy leaves that always look fresh. Some hybrids have variegated leaves which even those who are not fans of variegated plants could not help but be impressed by. They are very refined. Some have cream or silver margins that catch the light, good for illuminating an otherwise dull area. The flowers tend towards subtle, their delicate shades of pink, white and mauve harmonising well with silvers and greys.

SCENTED PELARGONIUMS are the last of the species the Victorians very kindly grouped for us. These are grown for their fragrant leaves rather than their pallid flowers. There are leaves that smell of roses, lemons, oranges, peppermint, apples, spices, pine and even coconut. The leaf shapes vary, some deeply cut and lacy, some rounded. The dark green oak-leaf pelargonium (*P. quercifolium*) has a spicy fragrance, while *P. tomentosum* has large grey-green downy leaves and a strong peppermint smell. 'Attar of Roses' has tri-lobed leaves and purple flowers as well as the delicate rose perfume.

Pelargoniums are among the easiest of plants to grow from cuttings. Take a 5–10 cm long stem from a well-grown plant. Slice the cutting free about 3 mm

Topiary

There are two ways to tackle a topiary. The old method was to grow the plant and gradually clip it into shape. This can take many years. The densely clad evergreens that are amenable to constant pruning — yew and box — are slow growers. Our own *Podocarpus totara* is also a good topiary plant with dense needle-like foliage. It reacts well to clipping if it is started when the tree is young. *P. totara* 'Aurea' is a slower grower with gloriously rich golden needles. It is readily pruned to any size and shape. The main time to prune is in spring when there is sufficient new growth to shorten. This forces the plant to branch out. Another clipping can be undertaken in early summer. This process of pruning to encourage more branching continues until you've achieved the desired shape. From then on, you just prune to keep it tidy. As its natural inclinations are constantly thwarted, the poor tree could do with some compensation. Extra rations of food and water help make amends.

For the impatient, there is a cheat's way to faster topiary. You simply make a frame of the required shape, out of an old wire coathanger if you like, then plant a climber to cover it. Ivy has a justified reputation of being invasive, but there are less vigorous, small-leaved forms that would make a dense cover over the frame. 'My Love' and 'Ivy Lace' are both good. Regular clipping would make for denser foliage. The small dark-green leaves of *Trachelospermum jasminoides*, star jasmine, make a lush cover and there are sweetly scented little white flowers in early summer. For a bit more fun, imagine two long cones covered with the sunny *Thunbergia alata*, or black-eyed Susan. It produces those orange trumpet-shaped flowers with bold black centres almost all year round.

below a node, where a leaf is joined to the stem. The cut needs to be clean and close to the node, which produces a hormone that encourages root formation. Remove the leaves except for a couple at the tip. At this stage, take a well-deserved breather and leave the cuttings to seal and dry out naturally for a few hours. Later you can plant them either into a free-draining potting mix or straight into the ground. The rooting takes places within two to three weeks. Promise.

INDESTRUCTIBLE SUCCULENTS

Another group of plants that never say die are the succulents. They need sunlight and a well-drained soil, so add pumice, sand or gravel to the soil mix, but they will adapt to the most miserable conditions. Despite their ability to withstand droughts, succulents in containers will benefit from consistent watering over summer. Soak the plants thoroughly each time the potting mix is nearly dry. They should be repotted in fresh soil every two to three years. That said, I've seen succulents growing on roofs, on the outskirts of compost heaps, by the beach and even in the gentlest of curves in an upturned roofing tile. The tile looked superb and could have easily graced a coffee table.

Succulents come in all sorts of odd shapes and sizes, and some shapes are odder than others. The bushier types suit tubs, while many of the groundcovers are a fine complement to shallow glazed bowls. These low-lying succulents are grown for the shape and colour of their leaves, so experiment with mixing and matching combinations with different containers for startling results. The other great advantage of these plants is that most are quickly and easily propagated from cuttings. Cut off the best of the crowns, leaving about 8 cm of stem, and put these in a shady place to dry out for a couple of days before poking them into a sandy soil to grow.

MEXICAN ECHEVERIAS. The familiar rosettes of the hen and chick plants, are reasonably hardy to the cold. *Echeveria elegans* will form a dense mound of rosettes, frosted blue-green with red margins. It has reddish pink flowers. The smaller *E. secunda* is perfect for containers. Its leaf margins redden as the plant matures and there are small red and yellow flowers.

SEMPERVIVUMS, or houseleeks, come from the Northern Hemisphere and are much more cold-hardy. They'll grow anywhere (in fact they were traditionally grown on roofs to ward off witches and lightning), although some northern New Zealand areas may prove too humid for them. Many rosettes have subtle shades of bronze and pink, others red and grey. The foliage of 'Lavender and Old Lace' is fringed and is a lavender-blue colour over summer, turning grey towards the end of the season. That of 'Pacific Red Rose' is a rich burgundy. All these rosettes produce 'chicks' or offsets that can be broken away from their mothers and replanted to raise families of their own.

HAWORTHIAS come from South Africa and they look like miniature aloes. *Haworthia attenuata* is called the zebra plant for the white stripes that appear on its dark green leaves. The leaves of *H. fasciata* stand upright in neat clumps, and each leaf is edged with a row of little white dots. Both have white flowers, either in spring or early summer, and both are quite frost tender and require a little shade over the hotter months. *Senecio serpens* also comes from South Africa. It grows to about 30 cm and its fleshy leaves resemble very thick blades of steely blue grass, which look refreshingly soothing on a hot day.

SEDUM KAMTSCHATICUM is a prostrate stonecrop that will grow to about 20 cm, even in the driest conditions. *S. k.* 'Variegatum' has leaves flushed with pink and cream and looks great tumbling out of a pot of pretty pale pink plants.

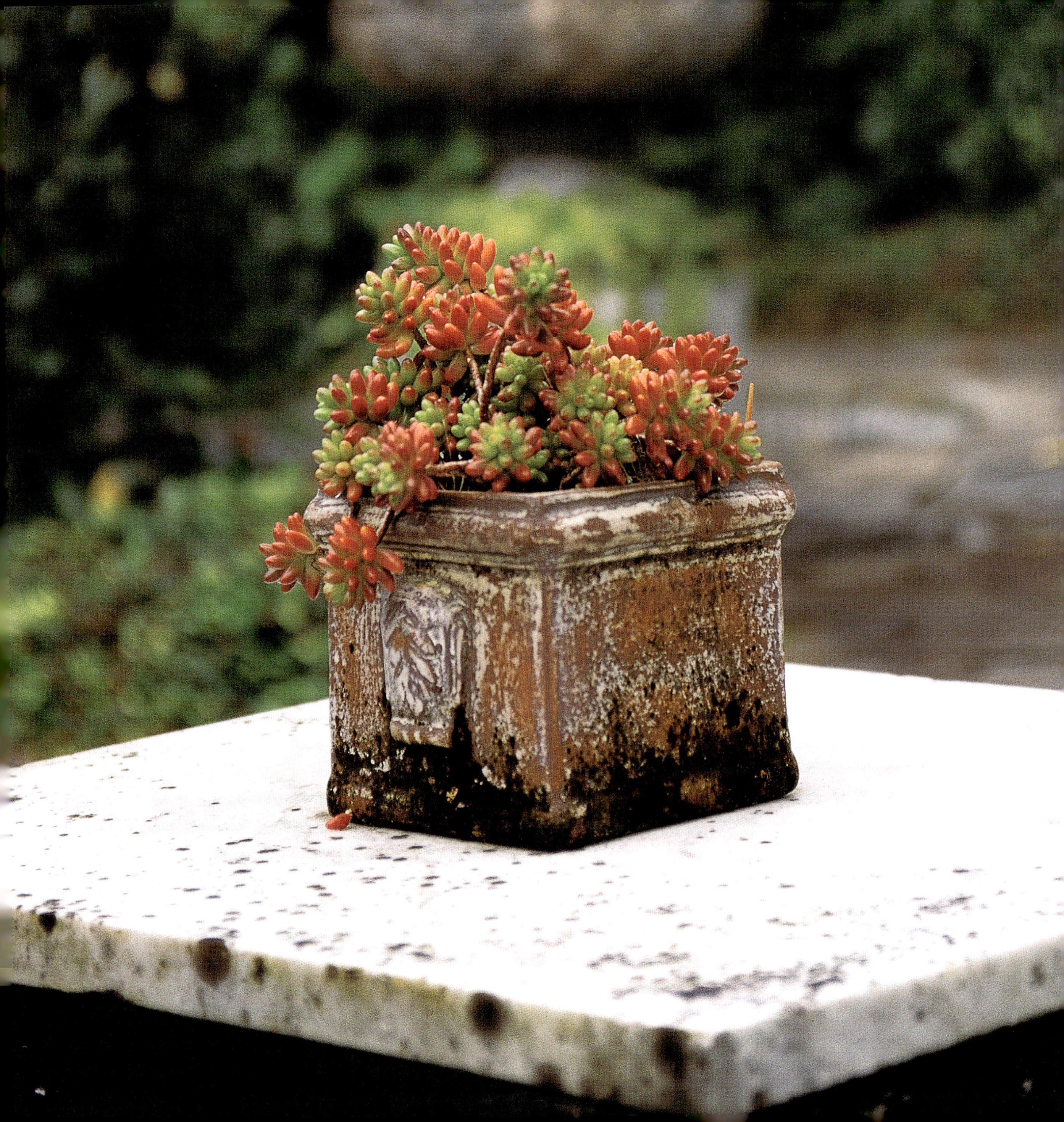

S. rubrotinctum and *S. pachyphyllum* are the jellybean sedums. The former will take on reddish tones as conditions become drier while the latter has blue-green jellybean leaves that are sometimes pink or red at the tips. Both have yellow winter flowers. For a real acid yellow, there's the almost too reliable *S. acre* or common stonecrop, which only grows 35 mm high. It looks like a moss for most of the time until spring, when it's covered in a mass of tiny blossoms of the sharpest yellow possible in a flower. It looks fantastic sitting in a stone-coloured bowl.

These low-lying succulents make wonderful groundcovers, prepared to spread over hot spots that most respectable plants would only be seen dead in. They make a very effective 'living mulch' that will help more fragile plants retain their cool composure over the hotter summer days. The most prostrate succulents can perform the same service when used as underplanting in containers. They can also make their own contributions of boldness and intrigue to the lush subtropical garden.

Sedum rubrotinctum is also known as the jellybean succulent, for obvious reasons.

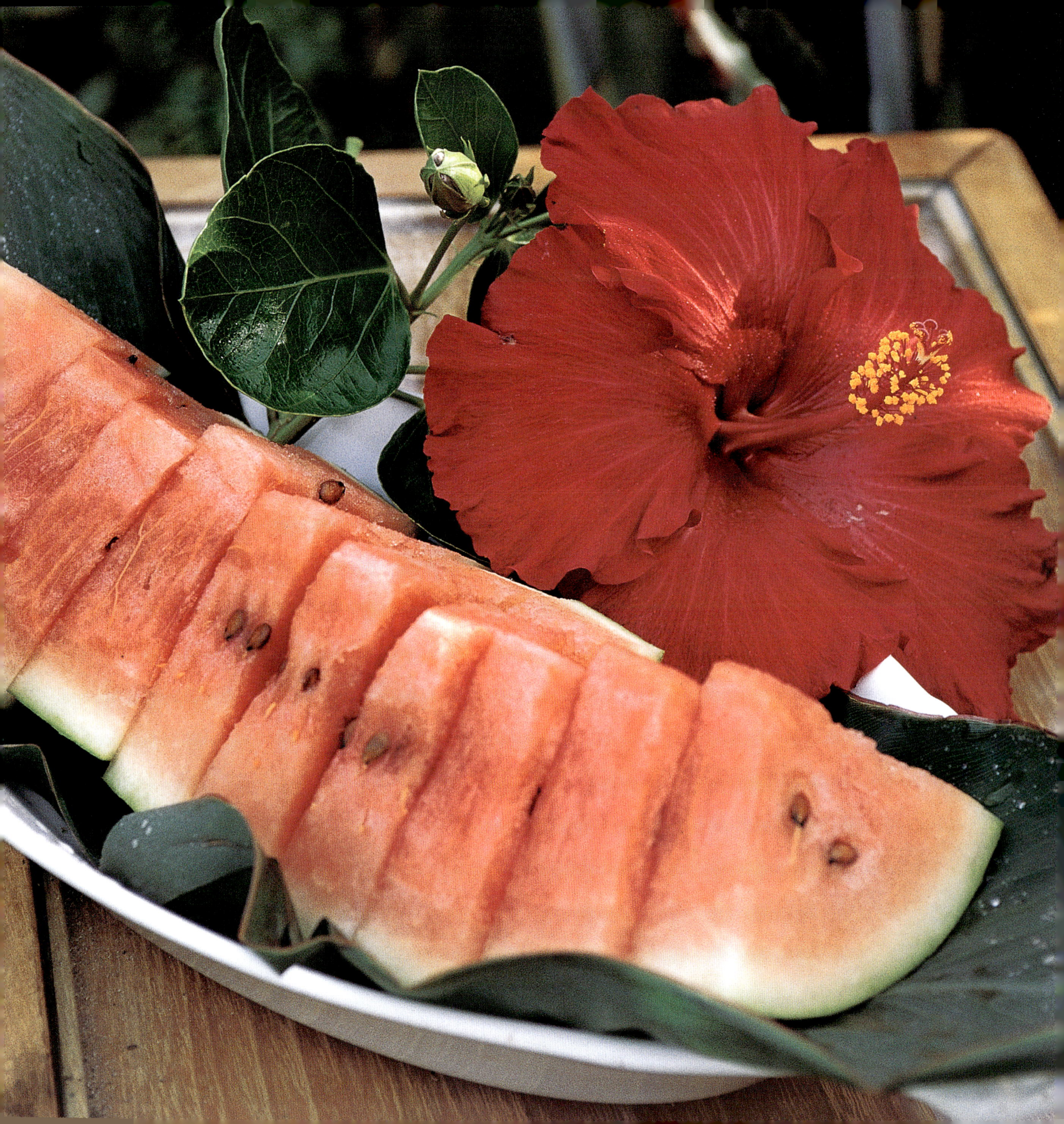

Tropicanna

Maggie: I've always thought New Zealand gardeners have a very healthy attitude to international trends. With a 'why reinvent the wheel' approach we've tended to take the best and leave the rest.

Traditionally, we've looked to Europe for inspiration but perhaps because we've grown tired of the chaotic cottage garden or box-edged formality, a distinctive Pacific-based flavour is starting to emerge. I've dubbed this vibrant, fun style 'Tropicanna' and even in colder climates it's easy enough to achieve this hot, new look.

HOT HIGH FASHION

Who among us is unmoved by the notion of a good-looking garden that requires very little maintenance and no sacrifice of style? A 'Tropicanna' theme is currently 'hot high fashion' with hardy alternatives to recreate the mood for cooler climates. Always lush, the luxuriant foliage and showy flowers of these gardens makes them wonderfully sumptuous places to linger. This is a look that's very successful in city gardens because it doesn't take many plants to convey a tropical ambience. Limited space limits the spectrum — too many colours can look far too busy and overwhelm a small garden or courtyard, but while too much of the same colour can look very ordinary, careful deployment of shades of green can definitely enhance a small area.

When selecting plants for this theme, you need to think about their texture and combinations. By planting delicate palms and ferns, upright reeds and grasses alongside bulky flowering plants, it's possible to get an airy, tapestry effect. The long, lean lines of a palm's trunk, the elegant swerves of its fronds, the fascinating symmetry of a cycad and the shapely curves of bromeliads all have their place here. Other useful designer tools include the bewitching forms of various aloes and the bold leaves of agaves.

Palms provide a lush subtropical look.

Subtropical plants are associated with warm, sheltered northern areas, although many can cope with cooler temperatures. Some are suited to containers, which allow you to give them some protection from the vagaries of the weather. It also means that you can give each the type of soil it requires; some like it moist and others very dry.

PALMS are an easy way of establishing a subtropical character. Despite their usual image of fronds swaying by the water's edge of some sweltering South Sea island, there are many that can take a few knocks and a certain degree of coldness. They all require a moist but well-drained soil. Traditionally the old favourite is the phoenix or Canary Island date palm (*Phoenix canariensis*), whose shallow fibrous rooting system allows it to be easily lifted and transplanted. The phoenix will rise to 15 metres high, with a palm spread of 9 metres. Even the trunk is a metre wide, so these palms are not for the ordinary courtyard. Many palms cannot tolerate full sun when young but this palm enjoys sunlight right from the start. It needs a mild climate.

One of the most cold-hardy palms is *Trachycarpus fortunei*, the windmill palm from China. Its trunk will grow to about 9 metres and is swathed in a brown fibre. The fronds are a rounded fan shape with fingered margins. Other palms to consider are the popular *Washingtonia robusta*, the Mexican fan palm (apparently the most planted palm in the world), the Australian fan palm, *Livistona australis*, and the smaller *Chamaerops humilis*, the European fan palm. These are reasonably hardy to a little cold. The queen palm, *Syagrus romanzoffiana*, and *Butia capitata*, the jelly palm from Uruguay, are also hardy in most sunny situations. The latter is a very good-looking palm with arching foliage of silver-green flushed with blue and a trunk the colour of honey. If you are contemplating a palm for the garden, it would pay to visit the little known Alberon Reserve in Parnell, Auckland, where they have a considerable planting of palms to explore.

CYCADS are primitive plants that were flourishing when dinosaurs roamed the plains, reaching their peak in the Mesozoic Era, 150 million years ago. Many of them have trunks topped with waving fronds and look very palm-like although they're not related. Other cycads prefer to hide their trunks underground, sometimes 2 metres down. They will grow in tropical, subtropical and many temperate areas but they are frost-tender. They do well in pots, and you don't need ridiculously deep containers to accommodate those underground trunks initially, because cycads grow very slowly and are easily transplanted. Their propagation and early cultivation can be difficult and this is the main reason why they seem so darn expensive. They are, of course, extremely long-lived, having evolved ingenious methods of survival over their long tenure on this planet. If the big bomb blows they'll still be around, if that's any consolation when you're digging deep into your pocket.

BROMELIADS are not as difficult to grow as their appearance might suggest. They like to be kept moist and thoughtfully have a central water 'cup', which lets you know when they need more liquid. In fact they're living vases, made up of brightly coloured tubes holding the water, then supporting their flowers, some inconspicuous and others showy, and later containing the berries of certain varieties. Counting the pineapple, there are over 2000 bromeliad species, which give rise to all sorts of shape and colour combinations. Most are epiphytes, squatting on the branches or trunks of other plants. They don't take nourishment from their host, just space. Such lofty accommodation suits bromeliads as they need to be protected from frost and sunburn. It also suits gardeners with not much room, as they can double up on available space. Many of these plants will grow directly in the ground under the shade of a tree, preferably deciduous. Here water should still be poured into the plant's vase, not the soil. Bromeliads like good light and warm temperatures over winter.

TREE TOMATOES or tamarillos *(Cyphomandra betacea)* belong to the same family as the tomato. They form an elongated shrub that can look regal with a crown of large green leaves, fragrant flowers of princely purple tinted with green, followed by egg-shaped fruit, the heavy colour of an aged claret, that hang so elegantly from the branches. These well-bred good looks demand a little indulgence. Tamarillos like a warm environment with no threat of frost. Their large leaves, brittle stems and shallow roots call for the best possible protection from strong and not-so-strong winds. Even then they are not long lived and replacements should be planned every five to seven years. The two main types of tamarillo bear red and yellow fruit. The more popular red fruit has a sharp acidic taste and the yellows tend to be rather bland. In recent times, hybrids of these two have appeared with a reddish-orange skin and red pulp with lower acidic levels. The fruit ripens over several months and harvesting starts in autumn and continues right through winter and into spring. The fruit should be cut with the stalks attached and can be stored for up to a month in a cool place. We've included a few methods of tarting up your tree tomatoes on page 160.

TARO PLANTS can look outstandingly ornamental in the subtropical garden. Both the species you can eat, *Colocasia esculenta*, and the one you should keep well clear of the kitchen, *Alocasia macrorrhiza*, have great leaves. Those of the former are a bold heart shape, usually dark green and they sit horizontally from their long stems and look very like the leaves of waterlilies without the water. There are varieties with black and purple stems that give the impression that the flat leaf is suspended in the air, hovering above the ground like a gentle crash pad for the 'little people' to land on. (*Colocasia esculenta*) 'Fontanesii' has dark purple stems and leaves tinged with bronze. The leaves of *Alocasia macrorrhiza* are shaped like a broad arrow, and a big one at that — the stems grow a metre high and the glossy green leaves themselves are also a metre long. All taro like a sheltered position with rich, very moist but well-drained soil; none will stand up to frost.

ALOES are a group of succulents mainly from South Africa and include small spreading groundcovers and large trees. They are grown for their often strange shapes and flowers that look very like red hot pokers. The unusual forms are distinctive in that they all have a rosette of sword-like leaves growing either from the base or at the ends of stems or branches. Leaves vary in colour from a dull green to a blue-green, often with purple, orange or reddish sheens brushed across their edges or tips. They like a warm, dry climate and a well-drained soil. Once established, they can tolerate a little frost. A frost-tender exception is *Aloe plicatilis*, one of the most striking species, with pale blue-green leaves fanning out from the tips of the shrub's many branches. It flaunts scarlet-orange flowers in spring. This shrub will slowly grow to about 1.5 metres high and wide in a sunny position, although it may need some protection from very fierce sun.

A. saponaria is perhaps the most easily looked after as it can go for an awfully long time between drinks. Its dark green leaves are mottled with white flecks through them. The sap from these leaves foams to a lather in water and is often used as an alternative to soap. *A. bainesii* is the tree aloe. It will grow to around 20 metres but it will take fifty years to do so. It's a sculptural tree with long slender leaves forming a rosette at the tip of each branch. There are rose-pink flowers in late spring and summer. With such a tropical appearance, one would expect this tree to be very intolerant of colder conditions but it will

Aloe arborescens is one of the better known aloes. It will grow into a reasonably solid clump about 3 metres high with the same spread and brightens up the winter months with bright orange blooms. The tree in the background is *Senecio grandifolius*.

Agave attenuata.

withstand moderate frosts and strong winds and can even take the full glare of the sun over summer. It also has an unadventurous rooting system, which means it can be planted close to a building without too many repercussions in later years.

AGAVES, originally from Mexico and tropical America, have been widely adopted by Northern Hemisphere gardeners as well as those Down Under. Their artistic stature, with large rosettes of bold sword-like leaves, has seen these succulents embraced by landscape designers everywhere. Mind you, the sharp-toothed edges of many of the leaves discourage too close an embrace. *Agave americana* is a definite case in point, with really sharp tips and teeth that edge its striking stiff grey leaves. The leaves of *A. a.* 'Marginata' are framed in yellow while those of *A. a.* 'Mediopicta' have a broad yellow stripe running down the middle. They can grow to 2 metres high, with the same spread, although an old clump may sprawl much wider. When this species is ten years old it will flower impressively, bright yellow on a 6-metre stem, but with grave consequence, as the plant then dies. Other species can take between five and forty years to flower. Most leave upcoming young plants to continue the family tradition.

The commonly grown silver agave (*A. attenuata*) is a less prickly customer, even a little, you could say, spineless. But individual specimens have been known to show great strength of character. I couldn't bear to give away my urn overflowing with prime *A. attenuata* when I shifted from Auckland to the Wairarapa. I put it on a sheltered verandah draped with frost cloth, but Jack Frost got the lot . . . or so I thought until spring. Literally dozens of new tiny plants emerged, most of which I removed and gave to friends in warmer climates. I've kept a few if only to prove how stubborn I am. *A. attenuata* produces a clump of symmetrically spiralling broad pale-green leaves, and it eventually flowers on a long arched spike that gives the plants its nickname, the swan's neck agave. Unlike most agaves, *A. attenuata* will grow in the shade, which could afford it some protection against the species' worst enemy, the cold. This threat can be assuaged by planting them in containers that can be moved out of frost's reach.

Agaves make fantastic subjects for containers with their sculptured shape and undemanding natures. They like a gritty, well-drained soil, full sun, and once they're established, they only require water over summer, although they can adapt to survive long dry periods. Very humid conditions can cause them some strife.

YUCCAS make up our trio of bold rosette plants. Their leaves resemble long thin bayonets rather than the swords of the others. Their tips can be just as lethal, so they may not command pride of place in the border. They look very impressive, though, with their arsenal of grey-green, deep-green and variegated leaves and long erect spikes holding masses of creamy flowers over summer. *Yucca gloriosa* is most handsome. It starts life with a greyish cloud over its foliage which clears to a deep green in time. For most of its life it's a spiny clump, but as the plant matures it develops a trunk as long as 2 metres and from its top the rosette of leaves branches out. The flower spikes grow out of the rosette and can reach 2.5 metres into the sky. Extremely tall people can see easily that the flowers are quite beautiful, stained purplish brown in bud and opening out to ivory white bells.

Y. elephantipes quickly attains the size of a small tree with a thick trunk, characteristically swollen at the base, with several branches each bearing a cluster of glossy green leaves. It looks a little like a cabbage tree but its flowers are typical of the yucca family, creamy white blooms growing in metre-long panicles. This plant strikes easily from cuttings; cut off a side shoot or a piece of the stem and leave it to dry in the sun for a few days before poking it in the ground. *Y. elephantipes* prefers a mild climate and is quite tolerant of dry conditions, making it a good tub plant for a while anyway — in their native Central American environment these 'trees' can reach 10 metres. Yuccas prefer the hot sun and a sandy soil but can adapt to ordinary soil without enrichment.

FLOWERING SUBTROPICALS

HIBISCUS come to mind automatically when tropical shrubs are being spotlighted. For blazing colour at the height of summer, and well into autumn, few can eclipse their flamboyant flowers, particularly the Fijian and Hawaiian cultivars of *Hibiscus rosa-sinensis*. The Fijian hybrids are the older, more common hibiscus found in our gardens. They form evergreen bushy shrubs and, naturally enough, thrive best in a sunny position and don't mind summer dryness. The Hawaiians are a little more precious and require very warm conditions and adequate water through their flowering season. A retired Auckland nurseryman, and the driving force behind Eden Gardens, Jack Clark, crossed both these hibis-

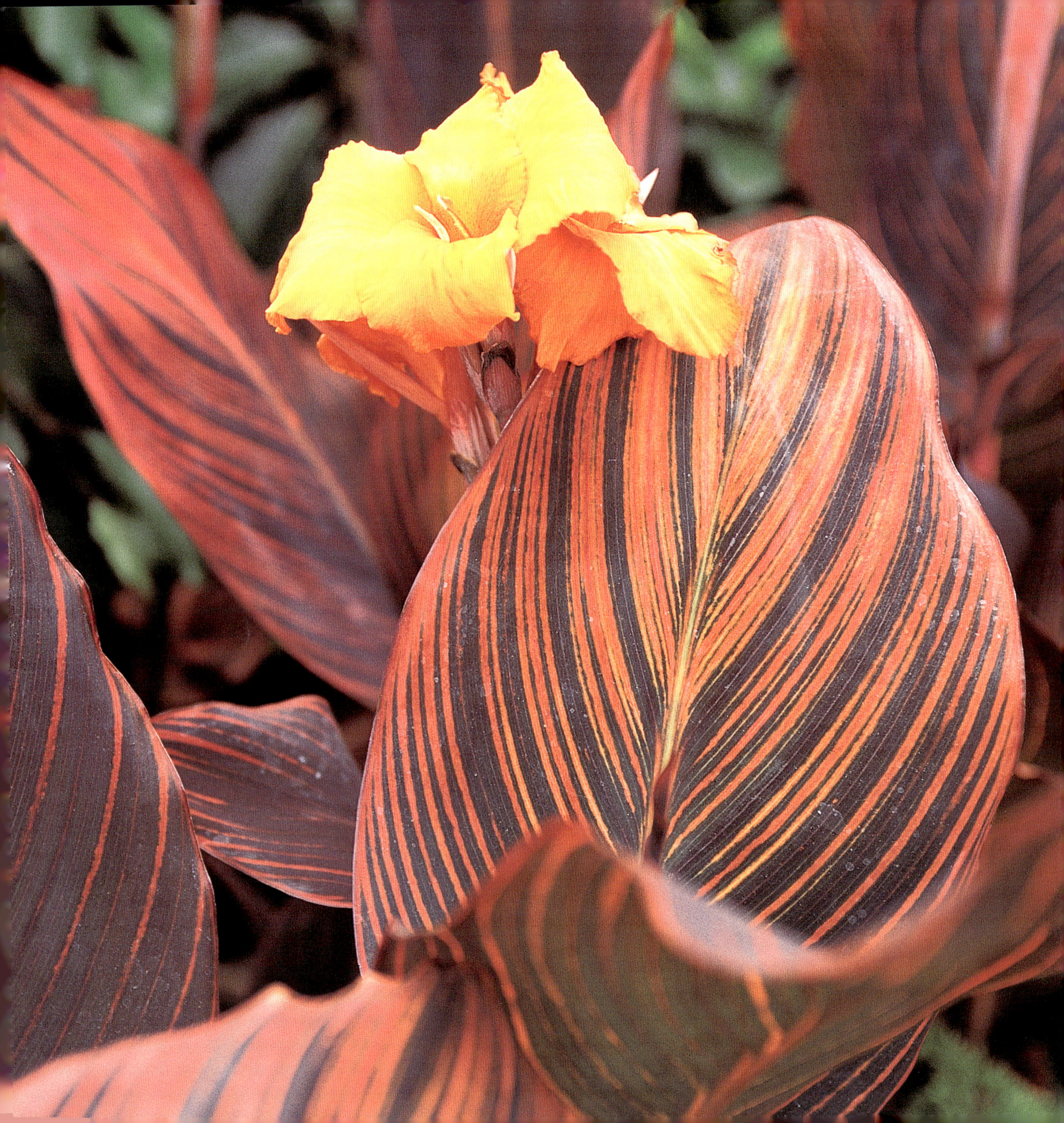

cus and came up with the Clark cultivars that are well suited to mild areas. With all of these hybrids there are single, semi-double, double and even ruffled blooms.

Hibiscus require pruning to encourage new growth, which in turn supplies the best blooms. This should be done when the weather warms up in late September–October. Remove roughly a third of the stems all over. Leggy plants can be cut back harder.

For those in cooler climates, *H. syriacus*, the Rose of Sharon, looks very tropical and likes sun, but is very hardy indeed. Planted in any reasonable, well-drained soil, it will survive both very hot and very cold seasons and flowers continuously through summer and autumn. It bears classic hibiscus blooms in various shades of pink, mauve and purple; there are also soft-red and white-flowered varieties. Left to its own devices, this deciduous shrub will grow to a straggly 3 metres, but a good pruning in spring, back to three or four buds a branch, will keep both bush and flowers in order.

Our two native hibiscus, *H. trionum* and *H. diversifolius*, both have pale lemon flowers with purple centres, but will thrive only in the subtropical regions of the Far North.

CANNA LILIES vie with hibiscus for chutzpah, but are less demanding. Modern hybrids of *Canna* x *generalis* come in a kaleidoscope of warm colours, also cream and paler shades; in blooms that are plain, spotted or streaked; and in heights ranging from dwarf (75 cm) to giant (2 metres or more). The imposing leaves, half sword, half shield, are very dramatic, and coloured purple, reddish, bronze, variegated or plain green. They look striking in legions of the same colour in mass plantings at the beach or along the drive, but small clumps will also shine in the courtyard or small city garden. Two for such use are 'America', which will stand very tall at 2 metres, with bronzed foliage and deep crimson velvety flowers, and the smaller and intriguingly named 'North Star Coral Belle'. Its flowers are that warm coral-rose colour of lipsticks and tracksuits in the 70s and, just like the plant itself, slightly tacky but great fun.

Cannas are sunlovers but appreciate water at their roots year-round. They respond to heavy feeding and need to be cut back after flowering. Propagate by division in the spring.

VIREYA RHODODENDRONS are well suited to northern climates where normal rhododendrons are hard to grow. They like a warm sheltered environment

Many people grow Canna tropicanna *solely for its striking foliage, though, as with 'Fantasia' pictured here, they also have stunning flowers.*

with protection from all but the lightest frosts. They require good light and sun for part of the day, preferably a site that receives morning and afternoon sun but not the strong rays around the middle of the day. They also need adequate moisture and excellent drainage. At Eden Gardens in Auckland, vireyas have been planted in open-ended ponga pots that have been sunk into the ground and, judging by the prolific flowering, this arrangement suits them well.

There is no set pattern to the flowering times of these rhododendrons. Many will bloom three or four times a year, with each display lasting about two months. Spent flowers should be removed so as not to drain the energy from the plant itself. Vireyas come in various sizes from 30 cm high to 5 metres; the taller ones can be kept manageable with pruning. 'Tropic Glow' will grow to a metre, with yellow trumpet flowers that are flushed with red and orange; 'Simbu Sunset' will grow taller, to 1.5 metres, with the same vibrant tones. 'Java Light' will attain a similar height, with large orange blooms. There are many more varieties with apricot, iridescent pink, coral and red flowers. And there are white varieties that have the added quality of fragrance.

Vireyas love containers, which would suit gardeners in cooler climates who can protect them from frosts, then carry the plants on to centre stage when they are in bloom. Vireyas don't have a large root system, so their watering requirements are not extensive. They will survive on little moisture for reasonable periods but can't be allowed to dry out completely. In hot weather they will need deep watering twice a week. Some compact varieties that would fit nicely into a pot include the red-flowering 'Littlest Angel' and 'St Valentine' and the yellow 'Kisses'. These three would also suit hanging baskets, preferably lined with coconut fibre.

CLIVIA (*Clivia miniata* and *C. m.* 'Firelight') have strappy leaves of glossy dark green that accentuate the lushness of a subtropical planting. Coming at the tail end of winter, their flaming orange-red trumpet flowers are a stand out in the shade where they prefer to grow. Plant them in drifts under trees where they will also get much needed frost protection. Preferring a reasonably rich, well-drained soil, these plants resent having their roots disturbed; the older the clump, the better it will flower. Because they don't mind root restriction, clivias make good container plants, once again useful for gardeners in cold regions who aspire to a hot look.

THE POOR KNIGHTS LILY, *Xeronema callistemon,* will also bring a brilliant splash of colour. Completely unknown until the 1920s, when it was discovered growing on the rocky terrain of our offshore islands and found to be the only species of its genus, this plant was very rare indeed. It can also be very hard to grow. The conditions must suit it down to the ground. It needs a fairly rich soil to which pumice or sand has been added to ensure good drainage. It likes an open sunny situation without a whisper of frost. To comply with these demands, it is a lot easier to grow it in a container. A handsome pot specimen it forms an elegant fan of sword-like leaves, like irises but leathery. It may take a few years to flower, but it's worth the wait. The stems rise from the fan of leaves and a mass of gleaming red flowers cluster at the ends, reminiscent of bottlebrushes but jutting out horizontally to accommodate any birds who may wish to perch and try the nectar. It could be called an uncommonly thoughtful plant.

THE NON-SUBTROPICAL TROPICANNA LOOK

There are ways to evoke a subtropical mood without having either the exotic plants or the sultry climate — and without taking out a second mortgage.

NEW ZEALAND'S NIKAU, *Rhopalostylis sapida,* has the best of all palm shapes. Its arching fronds are gently held like a feathery crown in the swollen shaft at the top of the trunk. Nikaus look all the better growing in stands of three or more. If there is any dispute over how to group the trees, it can be settled with a throw of marbles. Toss them in the air and plant where they land, which should bestow a naturalness to the siting, as if that's just where a bird dropped the seeds as it happened to fly by. Wherever they are planted should be reasonably sheltered, although mature palms are happy in sun or shade and can take the odd light frost. It is the world's most southerly palm and even grows on the Chatham Islands. Nikau palms are very slow growing. It will take many years to reach 10 metres and the first flower takes around thirty years to appear. The Norfolk palm, *R. baueri*, is faster off the mark. It has the same great shape as the nikau but is slightly more colourful, its leaves have a slight reddish tinge to them when young, and the round shaft they are held in is a soft pale green.

CORDYLINES, despite being essentially temperate, provide an exotic tropical quality to any landscape. This talent has made them the envy of many a European gardener. Cabbage trees always put me in mind of home even when they're flourishing in an Irish garden or gracing the red border at England's 'Hidcote'. *Cordyline australis* is a magnificent tree grown for its strong, distinctive shape. Eventually it will bear a bonus of trusses of sweet-smelling, starry flowers early in summer, but it can remain for many years in its juvenile state, when it looks more like a flax, before forming a trunk and ultimately stretching out to 6 metres. Cordylines grow well in tubs at the early stage. There are colourful purple-bronze and reddish varieties, and variegated forms streaked with cream, pink and gold. These native plants do not mind the cold, will grow in dry or boggy soils, and can hold their own in windy and coastal situations. *C. indivisa*, the mountain cabbage tree, which many consider even better looking, is more particular, growing well in cool places with a steady rainfall. If you have but a balcony for a garden, you can still raise a cabbage tree. *C. pumilo* is a dwarf variety, its ultimate height being not quite a metre. Admittedly its thin brown leaves look more like grass, but it has fragrant flowers over summer.

POHUTUKAWA or *Metrosideros excelsa* is truly glorious, but it may not sit comfortably in the average garden — a mature tree can reach 20 metres. It will feel more at home clinging precariously and sometimes precipitously to a cliff by the sea. There are several new hybrids, though, that are more suitable in the smaller garden. Many hybrids occur naturally with the equally colourful northern rata, *M. robusta*. One of these, 'Mistral', from Great Barrier Island, will grow into a medium-sized tree that will present you with deep scarlet blooms in November. The southern rata, *M. umbellata*, will provide the festive scarlet-red touch for South Islanders. The Kermadec pohutukawa, *M. kermadecensis*, is a smaller tree again and will flower erratically throughout the year. There are cultivars of another Pacific Islander, *M. collina*, that make excellent smaller plants in frost-free areas. 'Tahiti' will form a compact shrub about a metre high and wide. It will produce dazzling orange-red blooms in late winter and spring and sits very nicely in a container.

PUKAS, *Meryta sinclairii*, have extravagant foliage that would enhance even the most lush of tropical gardens. The paddle-shaped leaves are a glossy dark green and strikingly veined, while the undersides are a paler green. They look as if they've been pampered every day of their precious lives and yet they require little attention other than some protection from frosts when they're young. Mature trees will be more tolerant in that regard. Pukas don't grow very high — usually between 2 and 3 metres — so they would fit neatly under the canopy of a bigger tree which could offer some frost protection. They don't mind light shade and are very tolerant of dry conditions. There is a variegated puka, 'Moonlight', which has a broad yellow band edging each leaf and is a very effective way of illuminating a dark corner of a garden.

TREE FERNS are the ultimate designer plants, growing tall and elegant, with some of their lush green fronds arching towards the sky and others away from it. *Cyathea medullaris*, the mamaku, is the tallest and the fastest growing. Its black trunk will rise 15 metres, while its arching black stems, holding drooping dark green fronds, can span 5 metres. This fern needs a bit of space, preferably in a sheltered, ideally damp situation where it may need the trunk and, when you can reach it, the crown, to be watered in really dry times. That prized icon, the good old silver fern, *C. dealbata*, is slower-moving towards the long white clouds. Once established, it will put up with both dry and cold conditions. *Dicksonia fibrosa*, the wheki-ponga, will fit snugly into a small garden. Its slow-growing, thick trunk holds its mid-green fronds upwards to the sky. *D. squarrosa*, the wheki, has a slimmer trunk. Both are reasonably cold-hardy but do best out of the wind and require water over a prolonged dry spell.

Ponga trunks provide a good home for bromeliads. The fronds tend to sit on the tree for ages after they have turned brown and can be cut off when accessible to keep the scene nice and green. If it's at all possible, plant these ferns where you are able to look down on and enjoy the fresh baby fronds, the koru, uncoiling from their familiar curled state. All tree ferns can be underplanted right up to their trunks, which allows more room for interest in a small space. An underplanting of other ferns would weave a luxurious green carpet on the subtropical garden. *Asplenium bulbiferum*, the hen and chickens fern, will grow to 50 cm. Ferns grow more lavishly when planted in a well-drained soil that's sheltered from wind, hard frosts and, ideally, shaded from the sun. They should never be planted too deeply; their crowns should sit up above the ground.

FLAXES offer a wide range of exhilarating colour for any garden, as they'll grow in almost any soil or situation, although cultivars of *Phormium cookianum*, the mountain flax, prefer a well-drained soil. Colours range from apricot, pinks,

Tree ferns can make superb focal points for a New Zealand Tropicanna theme.

soft oranges, flaming reds and bronzes to creamy and bright yellows, purples, almost black and, strangely enough, green. Sizes also vary from a grass-like 30 cm to robust specimens nearly 3 metres tall.

Flax forms a beautifully self-contained clump that requires little augmentation. A solitary specimen in a pot looks picture perfect. The clumps of harakeke (*P. tenax*) stand stiffly erect, while those of *P. cookianum* weep elegantly. Many of the colourful array available today are hybrids between these two species. Their leaves tend to stand erect initially and start to droop as they get older. Like most of us, flax looks better with a little grooming. Dead or dying leaves can be cut off with some sharp secateurs or scissors as near to the base as possible. With so many conglomerations and variegations of colour and leaf, hybrids can revert back at times to the colouring of one of their parents. These reverted clumps tend to be more vigorous and can crowd out your designer stripes, so should also be cut off.

THE BIRD OF PARADISE plant (*Strelitzia reginae*) gives the impression it's a very tender treasure from tropical climes. In fact it's South African and, like most South African plants, does well in all but the coldest areas of our country. Strelitzia will grow in sun or partial shade, in poor or rich soils and in dry or wet conditions. Their slim paddle-shaped leaves reach heroic lengths of more than a metre and will live for about a year. The imposing stems, holding the 'bird' in all its glory, can extend a further metre and a half. The only drawback is that the roots are just as venturesome going the other way, so this bird is not one to be cooped up in a container or planted close to the house.

CLIMBERS are useful in a small garden, taking advantage of every centimetre of available space. There are legions of climbing plants that will convey the feel of the tropics: the dazzling papery blooms of bougainvilleas; the soft pink and yellow-toned trumpet flowers of mandevillas from South America and the Australian pandoreas; and the louder solandra blooms from the Caribbean. *Tecomanthe speciosa*, once on the point of extinction, is a vigorous New Zealand climber, decidedly tropical looking with large shiny dark evergreen leaves. It is not particular about soil types and will grow in full sun or partial shade, but anything more than a light frost will cause some strife, so a sunny position under the eaves is an ideal situation. The flowers appear in autumn on the old wood and will linger for at least a couple of months. They come in clusters of up to 20 blooms and each lustrous creamy white flower is about 6 cm long and shaped like a slightly ruffled trumpet. These imposing clusters tend to hang down, so it's a good idea to drape them over a pergola on a terrace where it's easier to appreciate their loveliness.

Passionfruit is considered to be one of the best of all tropical fruits, mainly by those in countries where it is impossible to grow and where they wax lyrically of the pulpy ambrosia. Perhaps in New Zealand we tend to take this luscious fruit a bit too much for granted, expecting them to make the annual summer appearance on top of the pavlova. The orange and golden fruits of new passionvines receive much praise, but they don't come anywhere close to the familiar purple fruit for exquisite flavour.

Strelitzia reginae.

Passionfruit syllabub

In a bowl combine **the pulp of 8 passionfruit** with **2 tbsp each of lemon juice, white wine and brandy**, and **½ cup caster sugar**. In another bowl beat **1 cup cream** until it forms firm peaks, then gradually whisk in the passionfruit mixture. Pour into 4 long-stemmed martini glasses and refrigerate until required.

Although *Passiflora edulis*, hailing from the tropical climes of South America, requires a well-protected, warm, sunny situation, it can withstand the occasional light frost. Colder weather could prompt the vine to drop its evergreen image over winter but it will return in spring, along with the exotic-looking purple and white flowers. It prefers a rich, well-drained soil, which may involve raising its bed, as well as a reasonably long, warm summer to initiate and then ripen its fruit. When fully mature the fruit turns purple and can be harvested when the skin is still smooth. It can then be stored to develop wrinkles, which indicate that the fruit is sweetly ripe and at its best for eating.

Passionfruit vines are relatively short lived and will need replacing about every five years. Planting a grafted variety will reduce the risk of collar rot, to which passionfruit are very susceptible. Both 'Robinson's Black' and the larger fruiting 'Crackerjack' are pretty resilient varieties. The best time to plant is in spring after any danger of frost has passed. Let the vine grow straight up until it reaches the top of the trellis or support it is growing on, then pinch out the top and it will produce lateral growths which can be trained along the support. Prune in the growing season to avoid die-back, keep the vine in line and produce better fruit. In warmer districts this can be done in late summer, but it's better to wait until spring further south. Fruit are borne on the current season's growth.

Passionfruit pulp can add its sweet perfume to fruit salads, ices and creams, also mixed into cake batters — if the seeds are unwanted, put the pulp through a sieve first. It also makes a good icing for the top of plain cakes, and a creamy syllabub that will end a meal on a high note. The pulp is easily frozen; spoon it into ice-cube trays and later transfer the frozen cubes to a plastic bag. These can be added to a large jug of orange juice for a tropical taste.

TROPICANNA ACCESSORIES

Many find the backdrop of the various forms of lush green foliage give more than enough pleasure throughout the year, but there are additional flourishes that might add some extra interest. Paths of crushed shell will support the tropical theme. The shell can be contained with wooden boxing or bricks, or striking coloured tiles would give the path an extra edge. Seats can be just as vibrant, such as sturdy Cape Cod chairs painted in bright colours. Lazy, hazy days are also facilitated with the classic safari chair, and the accommodating cane and wicker numbers, which recall those balmy Somerset Maugham days when the sun would start to set about midday.

There is also an exhilarating array of coloured pots to choose from. Deep sumptuous glazes are a good match to the bold luxurious foliage. Ultramarine blues, tomato reds, and forest and emerald greens would all cast a rich complexion on the planting. Pasty pastel shades have no place in a Tropicanna garden, and this is a place to be brave with shapes as well as colour. A piece of chiselled stone or moulded clay would sit well with the voluptuous leaves of a puka, and a contorted artifice of steel or corrugated iron would make an interesting companion for an agave. A brightly painted or mosaic-finished birdbath would create a focal point with a splash.

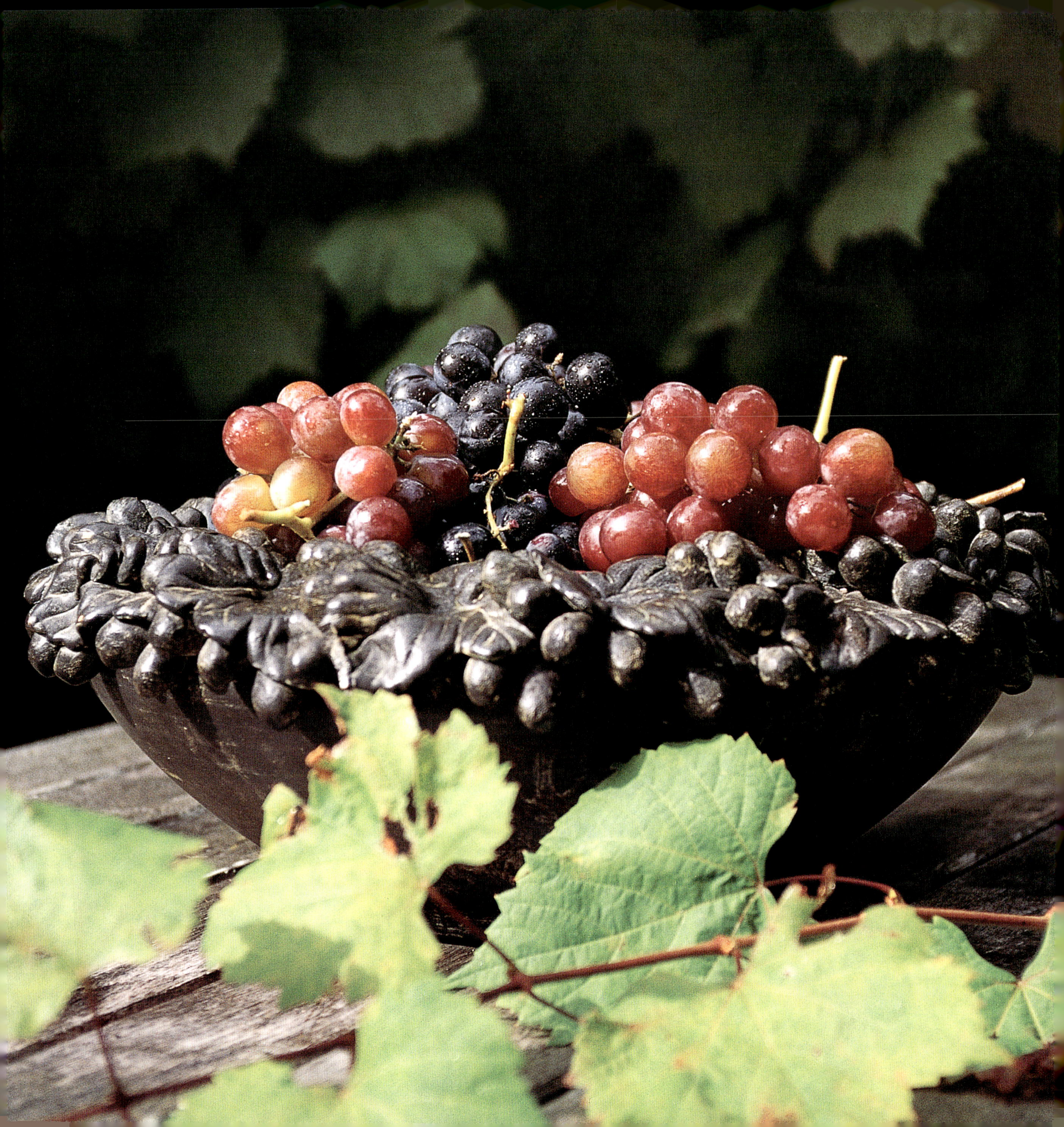

Fruit of the Gods

Mary: As Maggie found when she visited the Villa Gamberaia, fruit trees can make an elegant statement in the garden, but I'm also attracted to their wonderful contribution to the table. We're all familiar with apples and pears, so I've chosen instead a few unusual fruit trees that can add something special to your garden as well as your plate. But I couldn't go past our trusty citrus and grapes, so I've included some unusual ideas for using them in the kitchen.

THE STUFF OF LEGENDS

Some fruit are tremendously ornamental — appealing in flower and leaf and as one season unfolds to the next. Three in particular — the fig, pomegranate and persimmon — have long been valued, their origins reaching back to ancient times and civilisations — from Greek and Roman Empires, from the Middle East and from the dynasties of Asia. Having been part of these cultures for thousands of years, these fruit have become the stuff of legends, and by planting them in your garden, you will have your own living legacy from times long ago.

The Pomegranate

The pomegranate (*Punica granatum*) is glorified in the rich still lifes of the Flemish masters, where the fruit often shares canvases with pheasant, hare and those magnificent heavy old roses that seem to be forever unfolding. Shaped like apples, pomegranates have thick grainy skin in hues of gold, orange or russet brown. Often these were painted open to reveal their treasure: a deep-red pulp holding countless seeds that sparkle like rubies. Maybe it was the excess of precious booty as much as the brilliant complexion of the vessel itself that captured the imagination of so many artists.

The pomegranate tree can also shine in the garden setting. Originally from the Middle East, it likes a hot, dry climate. In spring the tree will give you dazzling red-orange blossoms and in autumn glorious foliage will frame your fruit. The tree won't bear for the first five years but will remain productive for many subsequently — pomegranates are long livers. The fruit is produced on two-year-old wood or older. This means an espaliered specimen needs to be supported by a relatively permanent structure. Pick the fruit in autumn before the rain sets in. If it isn't mature don't worry because it will obligingly continue to ripen indoors. Place the pomegranates in a blue or violet bowl and you'll have a wonderful table decoration over the colder months.

When the fruit is ready, the flesh can be eaten, seeds and all, with a little salt and sugar. The little jewels of seeds make a princely garnish on top of other less noble fruits, soups, couscous and those fragrant chicken and almond dishes from the Middle East.

The juice from the pomegranate gives another dimension to chicken dishes.

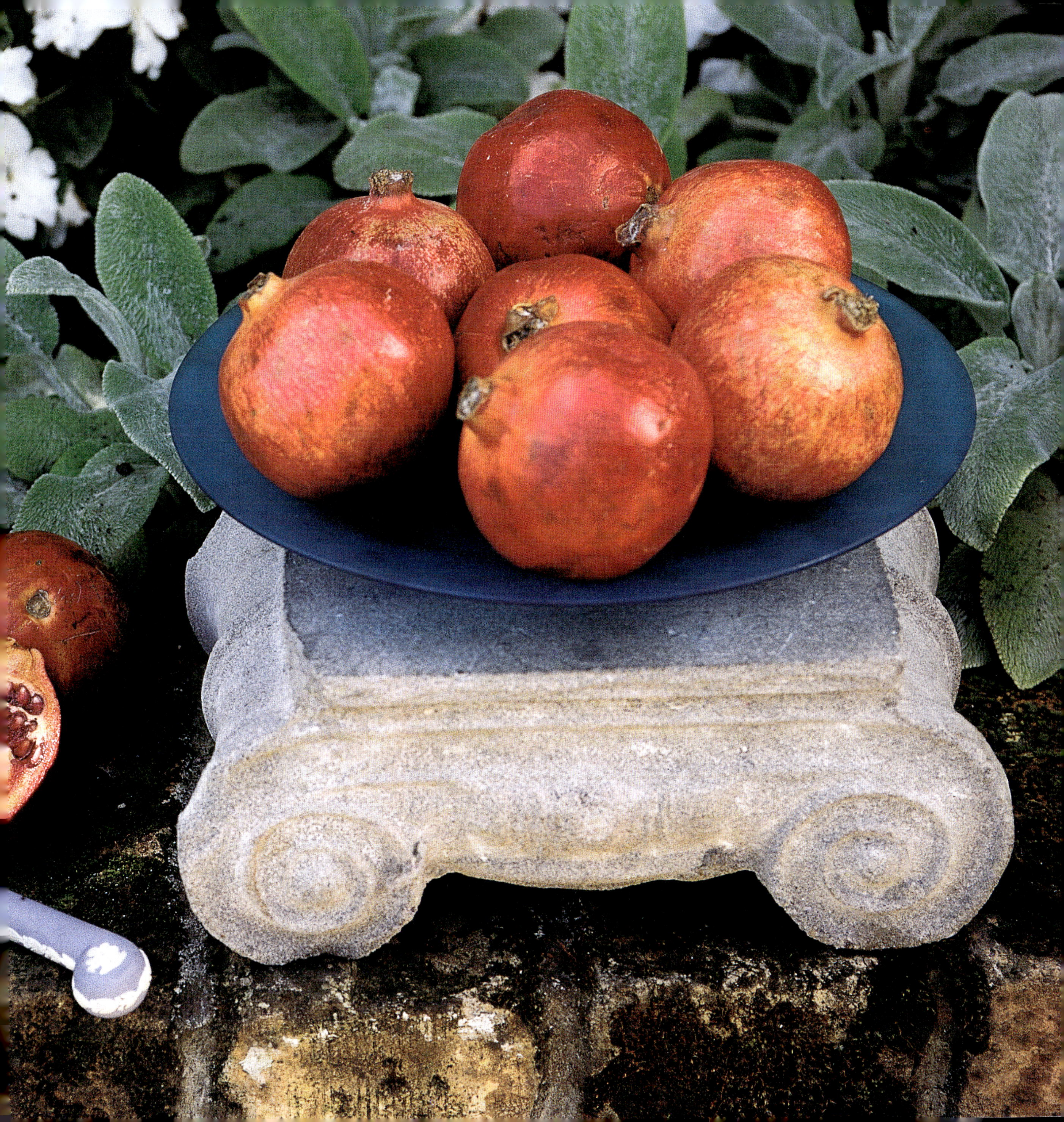

Sweet and sour at the same time, the juice also makes wonderful jellies. It is the main ingredient in the syrup called grenadine, which is used to flavour and colour drinks. To extract the juice, scoop out the seeds and remove any pith, which tends to be bitter. Crush the seeds in a blender, then put them through a sieve. Be warned! The juice stains something chronic — in fact both the skins and juice were used to dye the bright vermilion strands through those sumptuous old Persian rugs.

The most common variety available in New Zealand is 'Wonderful'. The fruit is large and glossy, with purplish red skin and crimson flesh. Note that dwarf varieties produce inedible fruit.

The Fig

Having survived the Ice Age, the fig (*Ficus carica*) reportedly featured in the Garden of Eden and the Hanging Gardens of Babylon and has graced many an illustrious table since. It hides its blossoms within — a fact that has probably given rise to its sexual allusions and added to its mystery. The distinctive leaves have been borrowed from time immemorial to cover all sorts of bits and pieces. These bold leaves, along with the natural, well-balanced shape of the tree, make the fig a very graceful addition to the garden. The luscious fruit makes its inclusion compelling.

A fig tree will flourish in mild areas and, although it will prove reasonably hardy, would perform better against a warm wall in cooler climes. There are a couple of good reasons for espaliering figs. They bear a better crop if their roots are constricted, and a wall or pathway would curtail wandering roots. This also makes them suitable for growing in a container. Figs bear their fruit on the new season's growth, so once the main stem of the tree is established, the fruit-bearing laterals can be renewed each year. The tree's own inclination to branch out facilitates the espalier procedure — this tree's a natural. Picking the figs is that much easier, too, if you can get the timing right. You may just get there before the birds, which seem to know when the fruit is at its succulent best. Can you blame them? When ripe, beads of sweet nectar burst from the opening of the fruit.

The most versatile type of fig to grow in the garden is the Adriatic or common fig. It's self-fertile, so you'll need only one. (The most notable variety, the Smyrna fig from Western Turkey, requires a special tiny wasp to enter a small opening in the fruit to pollinate the flowers within.) Varieties to look out for include: 'Brown Turkey' with large, pear-shaped fruit, purple-brown skin and yellowy, red-tinged flesh; 'Black Ischia', a rounded fruit with dark purple skin and deep-red flesh; 'Brundswick' which is large and pear-shaped, with russet skin and amber flesh; 'Sugar' a large pear-shaped fruit with green and purple skin and deep-pink flesh; 'White Adriatic' a medium rounded fruit with yellowy-green skin and strawberry-flavoured flesh; and 'White Genoa', which is hardy for cooler areas and has bronze skin and amber, pink-tinged flesh.

The Persimmon

The botanical name for the persimmon, *Diospyros*, is literally 'food of the gods' in Greek. When perfectly ripe — or overripe — this fruit's smooth, rich taste was thought to be straight from heaven. The persimmon's impressive lineage can be traced back along the dynastic lines of Asia. It is, in fact, a staple fruit to millions of people, a bit like the apple in the West. There are hundreds and hundreds of varieties. We are still becoming acquainted with the delights this tree can bring.

From the fresh greens as the fruit forms in spring, to the deep glossy summer foliage that turns vibrantly autumnal, we are left with the glowing orange fruits hanging alone on the leafless tree over winter. This is indeed a tree for all seasons. It is also a well-behaved species, tolerating most soils and climates, and it will slowly grow round and shapely, providing abundant fruit from the third year. Fruit is produced on current wood, so it is an obliging tree to espalier, needing only a light prune to encourage the growth.

There are two types of persimmon: astringent and non-astringent. Non-astringent persimmons require mild temperatures and are ready to be picked when their skins turn colour, from yellow to orange. The fruit is edible at this stage, when it is firm and crisp. With these you can make the perfect winter salad. Simply toss together slices of the crunchy persimmon and young spinach leaves with a dressing made of walnut oil and cider vinegar. Garnish with freshly picked violets. The deep purple colour against the orange and fresh green, together with the nutty, earthy tones of the vinaigrette mixed with the flowers' sweet perfume will transport you far from the bleak winter weather outside.

Astringent persimmons have to be left to soften before they can be eaten.

When they look their best, firm and with gleaming skin tone, they are a very bitter disappointment. One has to wait until the skin sags and almost becomes translucent for the soft, pulpy flesh within to lose its astringency before it can be eaten. A good frosty snap will speed this process. This means that astringent varieties prefer colder areas. After the frost, or, if you like, a short sojourn in the freezer, they can be brought indoors to ripen fully. Set out on an equally colourful platter or stand, the bright orange balls make a long lasting and very practical alternative to flowers.

When your table arrangement is starting to look sad, you can find compensation by turning it into sweet, soothing desserts. The soft pulp, much tastier than the non-astringent flesh, combines smoothly in sorbets and creams. These can look impressive if you serve them in the fruit's frozen, hulled-out cases. A simple but delicious treat at the end of a meal is to serve the ripe persimmon with a drizzle of lemon juice and some lightly whipped cream. The gods would be very happy indeed.

Although many persimmon varieties are considered self-fertile, it may pay to plant a good pollinator at the same time, just in case. Non-astringent varieties include 'Fuyu' (the most well-known); 'Matsumoto Wase Fuyu'; 'Maekawa Jiro'; and 'Ichikikei Jiro', which is a smaller, more compact tree. All could use the services of a pollinating companion like 'Gailey' or 'Omiyawase'. Astringent varieties include 'Hirtanenashi' and the small 'Tanenashi'.

WINTER ASSETS

Their generous endowments of fruit, dense and glossy foliage and fragrant flowers ensure that citrus reign supreme all through the year but particularly in the winter when their fiery oranges and glowing yellows provide warm colour to the garden and kitchen.

Citrus trees are cheerful growers, although most prefer a mild winter. The order of hardiness ranges from the lime (the least hardy) to most lemons, to grapefruit, then oranges, mandarins, the Meyer lemon and kumquats. You can beat the cold by planting your trees in containers which can be moved to a sheltered spot for the worst months. The Italians have done this for centuries — they even make

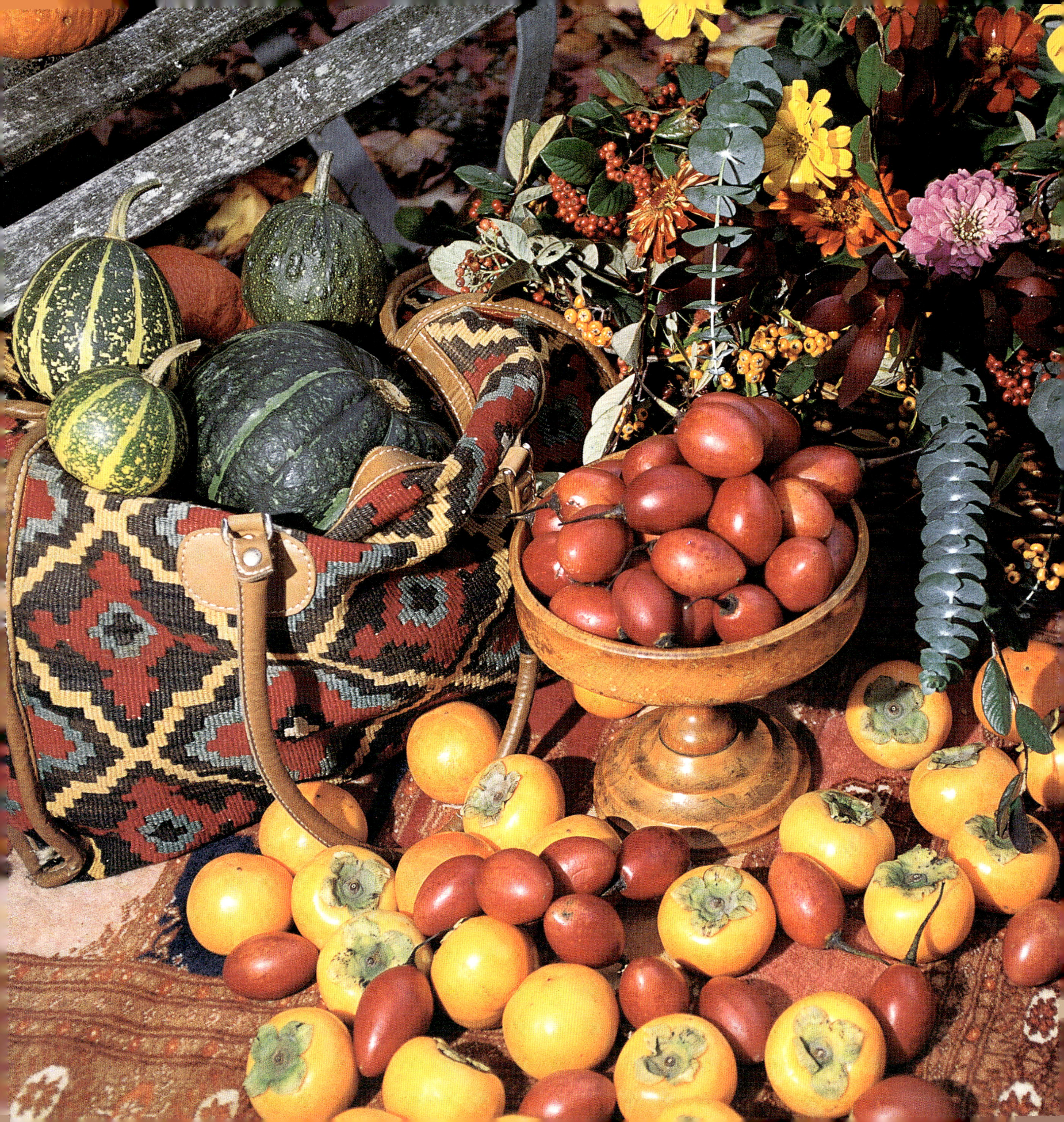

Villa Gamberaia

Italian gardeners are well aware of the aesthetic value of citrus and traditionally have gone to an enormous amount of trouble to ensure their survival. Laid out on a terraced hillside overlooking Florence, the Villa Gamberaia has devoted a large area of precious flat space to growing its lemons. At the beginning of September, for the past 200 years, the lemons in their stylish terracotta containers are carefully carried into their winter quarters. This labour-intensive operation is essential if the plants are to survive the harsh winter temperatures and be returned in full health to their outdoor plinths in spring. The cherished lemon terrace is located in the sunniest part of the garden, overlooking a mosaic grotto and a long bowling avenue leading to an elaborate nymphaeum.

Gamberaia was the first garden I ever visited in Italy, and it will always be high on my list of favourites. Its seduction begins on the short stroll from the village of Settignano. A convent garden is tantalisingly visible through a tall hedge and the lane takes you past tidy vegetable plots and olive groves underplanted with red poppies, then narrows, ending at the imposing formal entrance of the villa.

Begun in 1717, Gamberaia has had many influences, and two owners in particular have left an indelible mark on the gardens. In the early 1900s, Princess Ghika of Romania, a descendant of the Queen of Sheba, went to live there and, in a daring and brilliant move, replaced the traditional flowerbeds of the parterre with limpid pools of water. It's said that when the Princess lost her beauty to old age, she would leave the house only at night to bathe in the waters of her enclosed garden.

During World War II, the garden was extensively damaged by the retreating German army. Its salvation came in the form of a Spanish doctor who, remembering the garden from his childhood visits there, restored the features, retaining the original eighteenth century layout. The family of the late Dr Marchi still live in the elegant villa, while three gardeners keep the garden immaculate according to centuries-old traditions. Given the back-breaking nature of much of the work, I had always felt sympathy for the staff who laboured to keep the formality and geometric lines sharp. On a recent revisit to Gamberaia, I was relieved to see that modern equipment has its place, with the miles of cypress and box hedging benefiting from a twice-yearly trim in the spring and autumn with motorised trimmers.

special terracotta pots for their oranges and lemons. The trees in the famous Orangerie at Versailles have survived over 300 winters under cover.

By growing citrus in containers you are better able to pamper them with their own particular requirements, though, on the whole, they are pretty easy to look after. Citrus like a sunny, sheltered position and in well-drained, slightly acidic soil. Mulching will benefit both light and heavy soils. They have a fine, surface-feeding root system. Grass and weeds — or any underplanting — will compete with these roots, so the area beneath the tree's canopy is best kept clear. Because of their shallow root system, citrus shouldn't be planted too deeply. Try to plant the tree at the same level as it was in its container or nursery bag.

Citrus are great eaters and drinkers. They like to be watered regularly throughout the year and they shouldn't be allowed to dry out. They require more nitrogen than other plants and there are specific citrus fertilisers which take this into account. Citrus in pots will need more frequent watering and feeding.

They don't require a lot of pruning, other than a little trimming to keep them in their naturally good shape. Some old trees may need cutting back to encourage new growth. Oranges and grapefruit bear their fruit at the end of their branches, so you will sacrifice some fruit when you prune. (The fruit growing in clusters — like oversized brunches of grapes — gave grapefruit its name.)

Mandarins and lemons can take pruning as the fruit is produced along the branch. When picking the fruit, always cut them with secateurs, leaving a couple of centimetres of stem.

The main diseases to afflict citrus sound worse than they actually are. Melanose appears as small, dark-brown raised spots on leaves and fruit. Verrucosis, or citrus scab, affects mainly lemons, appearing as corky blisters on the fruit. If you like, a copper spray in early spring, late spring and again in early summer will help ease these afflictions, although both are considered cosmetic diseases only. In any case, it seems almost improper to spray the fruits when the zest from the skins is so useful in the kitchen.

The worst thing that can happen to your citrus is a visit from the dreaded lemon-tree borer. Its arrival will be announced with telltale piles of sawdust. The borer is extremely difficult to control — best to cut off the infected branches and burn them.

Home-made lemonade

Cut **two dried figs** in half and boil them with 1 litre of water for 15 minutes. **Drop 2 sliced lemons** and the **zest** of yet another **two** into the pot and boil for a couple more minutes. Pour into a heat-proof jug, cover and chill. Then strain the mixture into the jug you're to serve it in and stir in **2 tsp of honey**, or a little more to taste. Add **ice and mint leaves**.

Limoncello (lemon liqueur)

From a **1-litre bottle of vodka**, remove about 1 cup of the spirit and leave aside.

Peel **the skin from 8 lemons** with a potato peeler. Cut this into thin strips and add to the bottle. Cap and shake the bottle to disperse the lemon. Set aside for a week, shaking the bottle daily. On the seventh day, combine **3 cups of caster sugar** with **1 litre of water** in a saucepan and stir over a medium heat until the sugar has dissolved. Let this syrup cool and then pour into a large pot or jug. Add the lemon-vodka mixture and the reserved vodka and combine well. Allow this mixture to sit for a few hours before straining it through a funnel lined with cheesecloth into two 1-litre bottles — you've just doubled the volume! Seal bottles and set liqueur aside for at least 3 weeks before using. At this stage the bottles can be put in the freezer, where they'll keep for ages, if permitted. There is a great selection of interesting bottles around which, if filled with the limoncello, would make very acceptable Christmas presents.

Preserving lemons

If blessed with a surplus of lemons, salting them is an excellent way to preserve them. There are several recipes for preserving: they all start the same, cutting and salting the bitter fruit, but then some top the jar with olive oil, some with water, others with lemon juice, and there's a school of thought that you should leave them 'as is'. I've tried two of the methods and was happy with letting the lemons sit in oil and delighted with those in lemon juice. Those exposed to the air developed a crusty film that washed off but was hardly a good look on the shelf.

Wash and dry **10 lemons**. Cut into quarters, but not all the way through — leave the whole fruit attached at the stem end. Toss with **1 cup flaky sea salt** in a large bowl and push into a sterilised preserving jar with a skewer or wooden spoon — don't use your hands. **Place a bay leaf** here and there as you go. Top the jar with **1–2 cups oil or lemon juice** (the quantity depends on the size of jar), cover and store in a cool place.

After 2 days the lemons will have softened slightly and more can be added. They will be preserved in about 4 weeks. Once opened, the jar can be topped up with olive oil or juice and kept in the fridge. The lemons should last a good 4 months. When used, discard the pith and pulp and cut the skin into fine strips.

Use sparingly — a little gives a lot of flavour. Slivers can be sprinkled over barbecued eggplant or zucchini. They will add a bite to toast rounds topped with smoked salmon. They'll slip very easily into spicy chicken and lamb dishes or will add life to a bowl of couscous. Bring **1 cup of chicken stock** to the boil in a pot and **add 1 tbsp of olive oil** then remove from the heat and stir in **250 g couscous**. Cover and set aside for 2 minutes before stirring in **40 g butter, a tbsp of chopped parsley and 2 tbsp of chopped preserved lemon rind**. Check for salt, although it probably won't be necessary.

HARDY LEMONS

If you were going to plant just one citrus, it would have to be the Meyer lemon. The most hardy of citrus in colder climates, it grows into a good-looking shrub, about 2.5 metres tall, resplendent in bright green foliage. It's thornless and throughout the year will produce golden fruit of mild, sweet flavour. The perfect lemon for a smaller garden or balcony, it will provide the trimmings for the long, cool drink. Pick the lemons when they are fully ripe (completely yellow) because they tend to lose flavour if left on the tree.

Apart from tarting up drinks, there are many ways lemons can add zest to your cooking. The lemon has to be one of the essentials of the kitchen — along with good olive oil and fresh herbs. With them you can make magic.

Adding a mixture of finely chopped parsley, garlic and grated lemon rind to various dishes has an astonishing effect. This mixture is called cremolata (or sometimes gremolata). The ratio is 1 teaspoon of chopped garlic to 2 tablespoons of finely chopped parsley and the grated rind of a large lemon. You can simply sprinkle the mixture over a casserole, risotto or soup before serving. The same mixture can become a tangy marinade with the addition of a little oil. It will also make steamed vegetables come alive, and it is wonderful mashed into potatoes with a little cream and butter.

Chermoula is a hotter version from Morocco, usually spread over fish or chicken as a marinade. Combine the rind of a fresh or preserved lemon and 2 tablespoons of lemon juice with a cup each of chopped parsley and coriander leaves, 2–3 cloves of finely chopped garlic and red chilli to taste. For a 'wet' marinade you can add $\frac{1}{2}$ cup olive oil to the mixture. Combine with fillets of fish or chicken pieces and allow the flavours to develop for at least two hours before grilling the meat or fish in a pan or on the barbecue. A little cream added to the pan at the end of the cooking will make a sauce. Another way to enjoy your lemons is to mix up a jug of old-fashioned lemonade, laiden with ice and sprigs of lemon verbena and mint. A recipe for a refreshing lemon drink flavoured with figs and another for a more fortifying liqueur can be found on page 81.

Perhaps the easiest way to bring the sweet tang of citrus indoors over winter is to toss the dried skins into a glowing fire. You could also throw in a cinnamon stick or star anise for good measure. Your living room will smell delicious.

GRAPES

The well-defined seasonal changes of the grapevine make it a particularly attractive prospect to cover a fence or a pergola. The fresh pale-green leaves in spring give promise that's fulfilled in the darker leaves of summer, their shapely shadows providing relief from the sun. Then there's the plump fruit — first green, with some changing to yellow, purple and black. By late autumn the fruit is ripe for the picking and for a few bright weeks the leaves take on all the mellowness of the season before falling to make a blazing carpet at your feet. Even the gnarled trunks and twisted vines add their interest to winter.

Grapes will grow anywhere it's sunny. The soil must be well drained, keeping in mind that with wine the best flavours are siphoned from poor, stony ground. Grown on a pergola near the house, a grapevine will provide shade in the summer and in winter let through what sun there is. An open frame will enable the warm summer air to circulate freely. Grapes will happily grace a wall, but a solid wall reflects a lot of heat and the wee bunches of fruit could be scorched or even stewed. Mind you, this reflected heat could be an advantage in cooler climes, enabling the grapes to ripen before the first frosts.

In humid areas you will probably be faced with more than your share of fungal diseases. Powdery mildew thrives on hot nights and dewy mornings. A spray of copper in August and again at bud swell, followed by a dose of sulphur and, if you feel you must, fortnightly sprays of fungus and mildew preventives will all help. Never spray within a month of harvesting. To save spraying seek out some of the newer varieties which are more resistant to fungal diseases.

'Concord' is a large blue-black variety that's resistant to powdery mildew. If you prefer green (white) grapes, there's the vigorous 'Niagara', which will quickly cover a large pergola, and the small-growing 'Diamond', which would be ideal for a town garden. Less disease-resistant is 'Albany Surprise', which is found in many an established garden. But if you've seen it you'll know it's very robust with delicious juicy black fruit.

The fruit is produced on the current season's growth. In the first few years it's best to establish a framework of five or six main branches. Each winter cut back the side growths, leaving two buds on each. These buds will grow into fruit-laden branches the next summer. If the vine is becoming a little crowded, remove

Verjuice

If the grapes from your vine are a little on the sour side, disregard something I once read about burying a dead sheep where you intend to plant your vine, but consider making your own verjuice, which is just that — the green or sour juice from unripe grapes. It is good for deglazing a pan after roasting meat, to make a quick sauce. Its subtly sharp flavour also enhances salads, and chicken and game dishes, where you'd use it as you would a vinegar.

Holding on to the stem, dip the grapes into boiling water for a few seconds to kill the surface yeasts. Drain grapes in a towel, then dry them and discard any blemished fruit. Put the grapes in a blender and purée for 10 minutes, then strain juice again, preferably through cheesecloth. This can be frozen in ice-cube trays.

Butter sauce, made with verjuice, is particularly good with steamed fish or vegetables and is very simple to prepare. In a saucepan over a moderate heat cook **2–3 chopped spring onions** with **250 ml verjuice** until it is reduced and syrupy. Don't boil. Gradually whisk in **250 g butter**, cube by cube. Add the **juice of a lemon** and some **freshly ground pepper** and keep the sauce warm until you're ready to serve.

Another useful sauce involves reducing verjuice with a couple of spoonfuls of either a grape, quince or apple jelly until the mixture is reasonably thick and syrupy. Some fennel or caraway seeds can be added — great with roast pork.

Fruit of the Gods

Crimson glory

The occasional flourish of fruit from *Vitis coignetiae*, the crimson glory vine, is so horribly bitter that it's hardly fit for a god, but come autumn, its leaves assume such heavenly shades of deep red and purple-brown you could call it de-vine. It is strong-growing and will easily cover a wall or scramble down a bank. It also makes a particularly useful and decorative camouflage for pergolas and trellises close to the house, providing shade when it's most appreciated over the hot summer months, followed by a glorious show in autumn, and then it bows out for the winter allowing what sun there is to find its way inside. It is best kept in line by pruning when the plant is dormant over winter. The long side-shoots can be cut back to the main framework. You could prune the odd shoot ahead of schedule in the name of art to make a wreath: entwine some of the long shoots with their sumptuous foliage still attached. Its radiance will be fleeting, but you are left with a permanent base to add dried flowers or festive touches for Christmas.

some of the side branches completely. In any case, it's good practice to take out one of the main branches each year to allow new ones to develop. That way, there'll always be a semblance of youth about your vine. Prune when all the foliage has dropped and before the new growth commences, otherwise the cut tissue will bleed and greatly reduce the vine's fruit quality and vigour the next season.

If you have an old vine that's not fruiting so well, prune it back ruthlessly — yes, you can go all the way to the ground. There'll probably be no fruit the following year, but there will be a good flush of healthy new growth which you can lightly prune at the end of the summer. You will be well pleased with the ensuing harvests.

Grapes are best eaten fresh. They go particularly well on a cheese platter and with other fresh fruit. You can dress them up for dessert very simply by frosting them. First you brush the fruit with lightly beaten egg white, then you dredge them in caster sugar. Let them dry on a cake rack in a sunny spot. The sugar coating will stay crunchy for about ten hours.

Many recipes using grapes ask for the fruit to be peeled and seeded. To peel grapes, ensure you choose ripe ones, then put them in a bowl and pour boiling water over them. When the skin looks like coming off easily, pour off the water and get skinning. Once skinned, cut them in half to remove seeds with a sharp knife.

Balsamic vinegar has been made the same way in Modena, Italy, for hundreds of years. Fresh grape juice is boiled in an open pot over a fire for at least a day, then put into wooden vats to age. The liquid starts its journey in a large oak barrel, moves into a smaller chestnut one, then cherrywood, ash, and finally the revered wood of the mulberry. The liquid is left in the vats for a couple of years for the cheaper vinegar and up to fifty years for the most expensive. The older the vinegar, the darker the colour and the sweeter it is. Most of the balsamic vinegars available to us are blends of mainly younger brews with a little of the older concentrate. Pavarotti hails from Modena and proudly sings the praises of the local brew, volunteering the veal dish on page 161 as one of his all-time favourites.

The leaves of the grape vine can also find their way into the kitchen. Apart from being a wonderful base for platters of cheeses or fruits, you can also use them as a wrapper, Greek-style, for spicy concoctions. You need to use tender, pale leaves which have been dipped in boiling water for a few seconds. To preserve grape leaves, layer them with sprigs of thyme in a wide-mouthed jar and cover with olive oil. A blanched leaf placed on top of pickles will help your preserves stay clear.

For an impressive show, you could try grilling a round of goat's cheese in vine leaves. Lightly season the cheese with salt, pepper and a drizzle of olive oil. Top with a couple of sprigs of marjoram or thyme and wrap in three or four overlapping vine leaves. Cook for 5 minutes and serve with crusty bread. The inner leaves will be tender enough to eat.

The list of the many wondrous ways to harness the grapevine goes on: prunings from your vine will provide aromatic smoke to give your barbecued food a pleasant flavour. The dried fruits give us currants, raisins and sultanas, according to the variety of grape. The seeds give us oil. Even that pinch of cream of tartar we put into our pavlova mix is a crystalline salt extracted from the residue of pressed grapes, known as 'marc', and from the sediment in wine barrels.

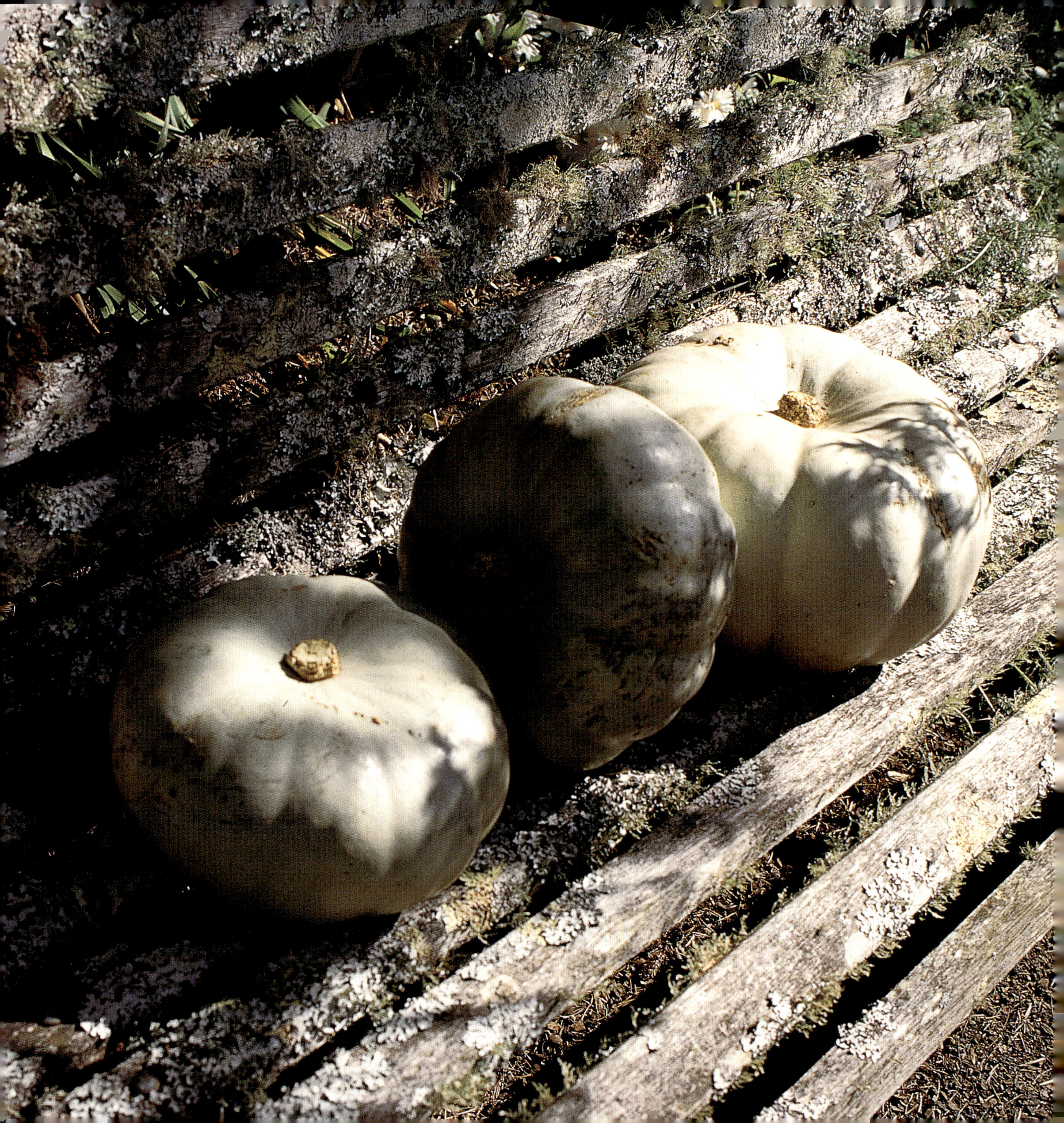

The Kitchen Garden's Comeback

Mary: This section is where I indulge my passion for fresh produce for the kitchen. But as Maggie's description and snaps of Villandry indicate, even the humblest of vegetables can be an integral part of the garden design. Our separate visions come together most aptly with the potager.

LE POTAGER

The past ten years have seen a quieter French revolution — no heads have rolled, just turned to take a closer look as vegetables have moved into a more prominent position in the garden. A few decades ago, few people found themselves with either the time, room or inclination to grow their own vegetables. Some herbs and a lemon tree usually satisfied any urges to emulate that ever-so-nice TV couple on 'The Good Life'. Along the way, gardeners banished vegetables to a corner, forgetting many are highly decorative, with handsome foliage and pretty flowers. But in the eighties, as adventurous and talented cooks tempted us to broaden our culinary horizons, we were frustrated that many 'exotic' vegetables weren't available in the shops: peppery arugula (rocket), chartreuse cauliflowers, purple broccoli and beans (that reverted to a disappointing green when cooked), chocolate capsicums, and golden and red beets. There was nothing else for it: we had to get out there and grow them ourselves.

The potager garden at Villandry.

It became trendy to harvest the greens at their baby stage, so our patience wasn't stretched, and with the advent of 'no dig' gardens, our backs weren't either. A renaissance of 'heritage' or 'heirloom' vegetables followed. These old, once-popular varieties that had long been forgotten, were rediscovered, such as tomatoes that tasted like tomatoes, and the purple striped beans and cultivars of garlic first brought to Northland by the Dalmatian gumdiggers last century. Now, in the nineties, the kitchen garden has made a comeback worldwide. The English cottage, the Italian l'orto and le potager of France are all making a contribution towards an eclectic new style of growing vegetables.

The French have always known how elegant an ordinary vegetable can look when suitably displayed, perhaps enclosed by a formal parterre. They are also keen on the romantic garden, where full-blown roses bow their heavy heads towards emerging garlic shoots, and marigolds skirt around lettuces. Capsicums, eggplants and zucchini are all encouraged to clamber over wigwams and obelisks wrought of iron or wood, erupting among the perfumed trumpets of lilies and a haze of blue lavender. Scarlet runners compete with clematis and espaliered fruit on trellises. All of which make us realise that you don't really need the luxury of a 4 metre square (or more usually oblong) plot to plant orderly lines of cabbages and silverbeet – vegetables can fit anywhere. Within reason, of course.

RHUBARB has such large decorative leaves, some don't see the point of growing ornamental rhubarb when you can grow the real thing. *Rheum* x *cultorum* prefers a sunny, moist but well-drained soil, although it can take a little shade. You can raise it from seed but for fast results plant crowns, pick sparingly the second year and enjoy a good crop thereafter. Considered ripe once the stems have turned from green to red, they are at their most tender in spring. Although watering isn't usually necessary, the rhubarb stems taste better if they get adequate moisture over prolonged dry periods. The leaves are highly poisonous and should be discarded at the kitchen door.

SILVERBEET OR SWISS CHARD (*Beta vulgaris* var. *cicla*), on the other hand, has glossy dark-green leaves that hold no such peril. They're the ones we were always told were good for us, being full of vitamins and minerals, especially iron. These wholesome leaves are appealing on the plant, especially the rainbow chards with their brightly coloured stems of pink, crimson, yellow and orange. They make a

Le Potager at Villandry

It's known as the kitchen garden in England, the vege patch in America, l'orto in Italy, but in France they have elevated le potager to work-of-art status.

Villandry, in the Loire Valley, must surely be the most ornate and elaborate vegetable garden in the world. The scale is staggering: the potager covers a total of 12,500 square metres, consisting of nine separate plots, each identical in size but unique in design. Those beds take a lot of filling, and the seven full-time gardeners work hard. A total 120,000 seedlings are raised at Villandry each year, with the first seeds sown in March for the big spring display. The planting out and resowing for summer carries on for a further five months, while the weeding, all done by hand of course, is ongoing. September must fly by as the staff hurry to trim the 140 shaped yews and box hedges in the ornamental flower garden. There's still the wooded park to maintain and the citrus to be moved indoors before winter sets in. Then, after a brief respite, it's time to start the two-month task of pruning the eleven hundred lime trees.

With a work schedule like that, you'd need a few perks, and that's where the bountiful harvest comes in. When the ten chateau staff and their families have eaten their fill, the surplus is not wasted but combined with rotted cow dung and reinvented as compost and mulch to nurture the next season's crops.

bold association with the fiery flowers of rudbeckia and bergamot, alstroemeria and nasturtiums. Make your own rules: try combining scarlet-stemmed beets with tall red long-flowering antirrhinums. If your playing with fire results in a garden from hell, you can always harvest and eat the culprits.

On page 161 you will find the recipe for a terrine I often make for a lunch or picnic. You can use spinach instead of silverbeet, but the sturdy leaves of the latter hold their shape better while cooking. The stems, however brilliantly coloured, are not used in the terrine but can be cooked separately in a white sauce or the like, but be warned, their blazing hues fade when the heat's applied. (The Swiss, who gave their name to the chard, only use the stems in the kitchen and discard the leaf altogether.)

ASIAN MUSTARDS can make dramatic foliage plants, especially the giant variety with large green leaves with purple veins and the giant red type with deep burgundy leaves whose undersides and veins are the brightest chartreuse. These mustards (*Brassica rapa*) develop a tall flower spike resplendent with acid-yellow flowers which are followed by unusual seed pods. The plants self-sow freely. They are crops for the cooler weather when very young leaves can be added to salads and slightly older ones cooked like spinach. Age and hot weather tend to make them less palatable.

CHINESE SPINACH (*Amaranthus gangeticus*) enjoys the summer heat and its decorative red-tinged leaves can be eaten raw when very young and cooked as they age. Plants will grow to a metre in a warm sunny spot, where they must be kept watered. Later in the summer they produce red flower spikes that look like candle flames.

LETTUCES offer more rich shades of red, also purple, copper and smoky bronze, looking surprisingly at home in the flower garden. They also appreciate the dappled shade offered by close neighbours over the hotter months. Beautifully sculptured rosettes of radicchio would give bergenias a run for their money with their glorious bronze and russet tones over winter. These foliage colours all have a wonderful affinity with blue and pink flowers and can also prove a great foil to bright oranges and yellows.

OPAL BASILS (*Ocimum basilicum*) 'Red Rubin, and 'Purple Ruffles' have stunning dark purple leaves, and the more muted tones of purple sage (*Salvia officinalis* 'Purpurascens') would snuggle in comfortably among flowering plants. Perhaps the best mixer in these circles is the bronze fennel (*Foeniculum vulgare* 'Purpurascens'). The purple and bronzed tips of its feathery new growth will fit like a smoky haze into most settings, and like all the fennels, these fronds will lend their anise flavour to many a fish dish.

FLORENCE FENNEL or finocchio (*Foeniculum vulgare* var. *azoricum*) is by far the best fennel for the kitchen. It develops a bulbous root at its base that boasts the same delicious anise flavour as its leaves. Seeds can be sown in spring or autumn on a warm, sunny site. 'Albaro' is a good variety. Plants need to be watered over dry periods or they could easily go to seed. As the bulbous root starts to swell to golf-ball size, soil can be earthed up around it to encourage more development and also stop it from discolouring (or rather colouring, as they should be a pristine white) and turning bitter. The aromatic bulb is ready to be harvested when it reaches the size of a tennis ball — any bigger and it may become coarse and stringy. The outer layer usually is too stringy in any case and best cut off. This can be popped into fish stocks along with the hollow stems. The bright green feathery leaves can be chopped and sprinkled over the top of a dish, so none of the plant is wasted. Even the aromatic seeds are used in cooking and baking.

The crisp inner bulb can be cut into slivers for a salad. They're particularly good with orange segments and black olives, tossed in a dressing of olive oil mixed with fresh orange juice, a little honey and salt and pepper. The bulbs, sliced, can be served with a strong cheese like parmesan at the close of a meal, just like celery. In fact the bulb is interchangeable with celery in many recipes. Bulbs can be halved or quartered, and steamed or braised or baked with cheese and cream.

BROCCOLI is another Italian designer vegetable, coming in green, purple and white varieties. The one to grow for a stunning show in the garden is 'Romanesco', which forms conical heads and are a pale, almost lime-green, that look like minarets. Seeds can be sown in summer for a late autumn and winter crop. The plant must have cold weather for the heads to develop. Like other broccolis, the spears must be picked before they flower and cooked soon afterwards if their flavour is to be best enjoyed. Unlike some of the other broccolis, 'Romanesco' will not send out side shoots for a repeat performance of spears, so the plant is best lifted once the head has been cut.

Don't ask me why but broccoli and anchovies make a great marriage. For a pasta for six, roughly chop two heads of broccoli and cook until just tender in

The leaves, seeds and bulbs of the Florence fennel, Foeniculum vulgare, *can all be harvested for the kitchen.*

salted boiling water. In a pan cook a couple of cloves of garlic in 3 tablespoons of olive oil until soft, not browned, Add 6 anchovy filets and a little chopped chilli and mash into the oil. Mix through the broccoli. Meantime cook 500 g farfalle (little pasta bows) until al dente. Drain and add to the broccoli mixture and serve with wedges of lemon.

GLOBE ARTICHOKES (*Cynara scolymus*) are for those who like to mix their vegetables with their flowers. Growing to well over a metre tall, its large divided silver leaves make a perfect backdrop for pink and blue flowering plants within the mixed border. They also look spectacular when planted en masse. Globe artichokes like plenty of space — allow a square metre per plant — and a sunny situation. They can be grown from seeds sown in spring or from autumn offshoots from the parent plant. These suckers need to be kept firm and well watered until they're established. Only one or two flowerbuds will form in the plant's first year but there'll be considerably more the following season. After the third year it's probably better to discard the parent plant in favour of the offshoots.

'Green Globe' is the best-known variety but recently we have been introduced to 'Purpurea de Jesi', 'Purpurea Romanesco' and 'Camus de Bretagne', whose names better reflect their Mediterranean origins, where although the vegetable is widely grown, it is still considered a delicacy. The flowerbuds of 'Green Globe' are an attractive deep green while the petals of 'Purpurea de Jesi' are tinged with red and purple.

It is the thistle's immature flowerhead that is the epicurean's delight. These are cut when the bud is fleshy, still green at the base, and while the scales are still shut. Once the scales open, revealing a purplish tinge at the base, the head is inedible. Don't worry if you can't eat all your buds because you'll be rewarded with a stunning show of large pink-purple flowers over summer.

Globe artichokes are notorious for attracting every possible garden insect, so it's not a bad idea to soak the heads in salted water — for at least an hour — before tackling them in the kitchen. The thorny outer leaves are best removed and you can either cut the globe in half and remove the hairy centre at this stage or that can be done once the bud is cooked. This part, the choke, becomes the purple of the thistle flower if the bud were allowed to develop.

Artichokes can be braised with wine and fresh herbs in the oven or plunged into boiling water and cooked until tender (about 20 minutes). You'll need a

The large silver leaves of Cynara scolymus *(middle right) would be equally at home in the vegetable or flower garden.*

little lemon juice on hand as they discolour very quickly when cut. Their shape makes them wonderful receptacles to stuff with all manner of goodies. They're great served whole. You simply remove the leaves, one by one, dip the broad ends into butter or vinaigrette and prise off the flesh with your teeth. Inside the leaves is the special part — the bottom or 'fond'. (Artichoke 'hearts' are the bottoms with some of the tender baby leaves attached). The cooked bottoms are often dressed in a little olive oil and served as part of an antipasto platter. They can also make a wonderful addition to pastas and risottos.

Beware of the vigorous growing habits of Jerusalem artichokes. Once you have them, they're the devil to get rid of. They'll even grow from skin peelings, so be careful with composting any part of the plant. They belong to the same family as sunflowers (*Helianthus* spp.), and their common name has nothing to do with the holy city but is a corruption of the Italian word for sunflower, *girosole*. Each plant will yield a bumper crop of tubers that are versatile enough to make into soups, delicate soufflés, potato substitutes and crisp winter salads. They can be eaten raw but discolour if not rubbed with lemon juice. Their flowers like a warm sunny site and their height may require some protection from strong winds. The tubers can be set into well-drained soil to a depth of 5 cm and spaced about 25 cm apart. Then just wait for the giant stems to dry off towards the end of summer and cut them back to about 30 cm from the ground. The nutty flavour of the Jerusalem artichoke is improved by a good cold snap — cooler areas produce a better quality choke.

The joy of this vegetable is that you don't have to lift the tubers all at once; they are better left in the soil and dug up just as you need them. Dig them up as close to cooking time as possible as their flavour deteriorates in the open air. Their only drawback is their knobbly shape, like ginger root, that makes peeling an arduous and wasteful task. In most cases it may quicker to scrub them well, cook them for about ten minutes, then cool and peel them before proceeding with the recipe. A purée of the tubers is delicious with barbecued vegetables or with bruscetta as part of an antipasto platter. Take 2 kg Jerusalem artichokes, peeled to begin with or when cooked, and cook until tender, about 15 minutes. Drain and put in a processor with 50 g butter and slowly blend in 3–4 tablespoons of olive oil while the motor is running. Season to taste with salt and pepper.

CELERIAC is another versatile tuber that's usually hard to buy. Its leaves and

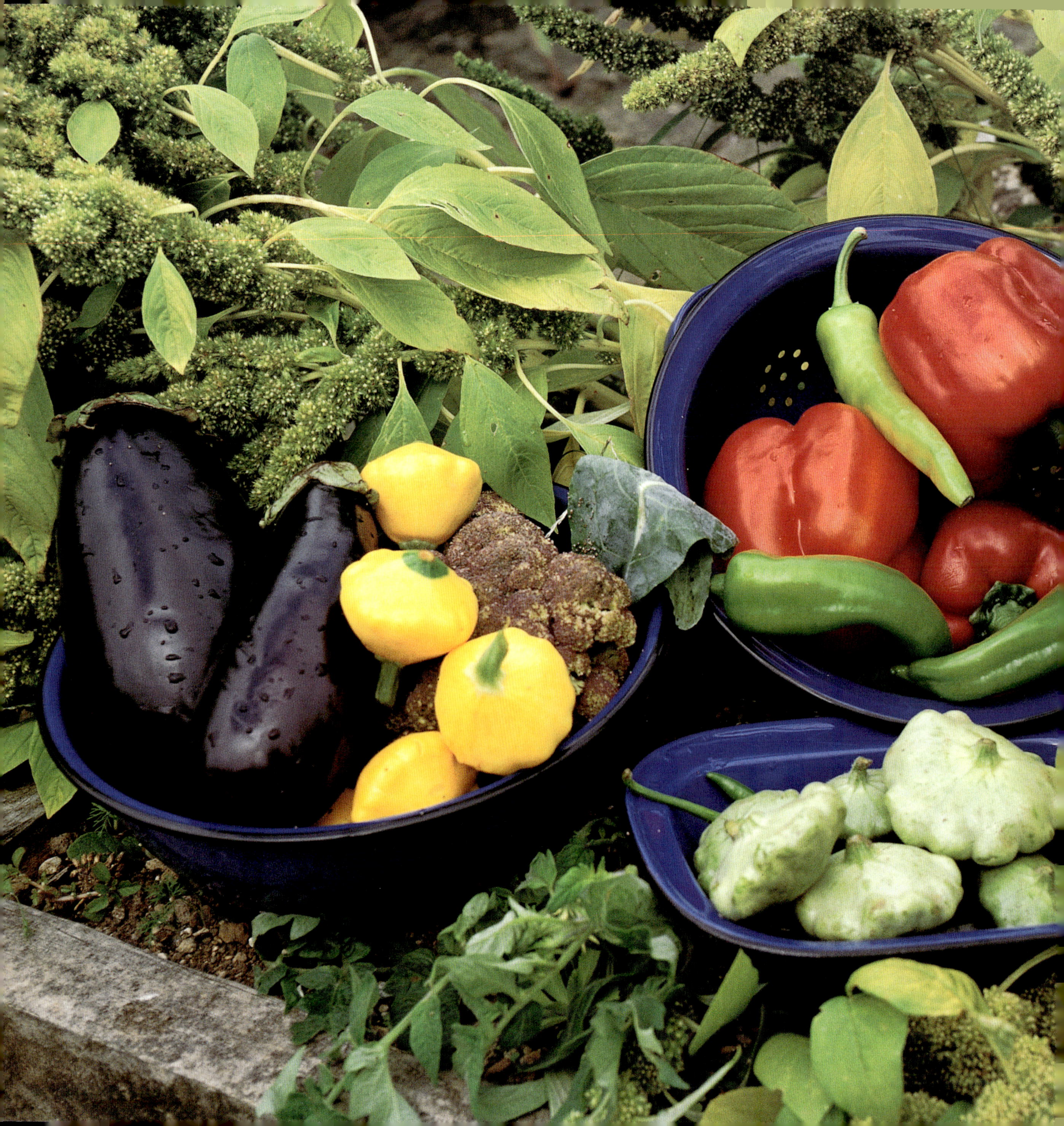

stalks taste like a crude celery and can be added to stock with a very light hand — a little is more than enough. The root itself has an ugly brown skin, white flesh and is often misshapen but, despite its rough appearance, has a taste more refined than either its better-looking half or celery itself. Celeriac is not as fussy as celery about where it grows and is less susceptible to disease. Seed can be sown at the end of September and it takes so long to germinate that you'd be forgiven for giving up hope or having forgotten about the plant by the time the first little leaves emerge. The more you feed the plants, the larger the roots, and they will require watering over dry spells. Try to keep the soil away from the base of the stalks and top of the root and cut off any side shoots that sprout, to redirect the growth into the root. Roots can be harvested when they are about 5 cm in diameter, which is roughly five months from planting. They can overwinter in the soil, like the Jerusalem artichokes, and be dug up as required. It may pay to cover the plants with straw or a mulch to protect them from harsh winter frosts.

Again, like Jerusalem artichokes, celeriac discolours quickly when it is peeled or cut and will need to go into acidulated water (which is water with some lemon juice or vinegar added) while it is being prepared. The root is used in much the same way as Jerusalem artichokes in the kitchen, making lovely soups and purées. You could cook the root in place of the Jerusalem artichokes for the above purée and serve it in much the same way. Or you could try boiling the diced root with potatoes, half of each, then mashing them together with a little butter, cream, salt and pepper and a grate of nutmeg.

TOMATOES are one of my favourites. Nothing quite compares to that first bite of a warm, just picked, vine-ripened tomato. It is reason enough for growing your own, particularly as many commercially grown tomatoes seem to be less tasty by the year. It's understandable — we demand that produce looks good on the shelves, and to survive the rigours of handling and transportation, the poor vegetables now have to be really thick-skinned. There's now an impressive range of tomato seeds to choose from, including 'heirloom' varieties. As well as the familiar red and yellow there are pink, purple, orange, green and striped ones, of all shapes and sizes, from tiny currant-like dots to whoppers that weigh in at well over 1 kg (the world record is nearly 3 kgs).

Old and new tomato varieties all love warmth and sunlight. Seeds can be sown anytime indoors but require reasonably warm day and night temperatures

Gazpacho

In a large saucepan put **4 kg skinned and chopped ripe tomatoes** and **1 or 2 crushed cloves of garlic**. Cook until the mixture has reduced by half. Add 1 litre of chicken stock. Season with **salt and pepper**. Allow the soup to cool, then add **a good bunch of basil leaves**, chopped. Chill gazpacho for 3–4 hours. Just before serving, add **ice cubes**.

Garnishes to serve with this soup could include bowls of **diced sweet peppers**, **cucumbers**, **olives**, finely chopped **Spanish onion** or **spring onions**, **diced yellow**, **green** and **orange tomatoes**, and **croutons** or **slices of toasted bread** rubbed with **garlic**. Other less scrupulous versions of this traditional soup replace the chicken stock with water and add **vodka** to give a somewhat wholesome twist to the 'liquid lunch'. Serves 4–6.

An icy pitcher of gazpacho makes for easy summer entertaining.

to germinate in the ground. Labour Weekend is the traditional time to plant out seedlings but these could come to a premature end with a sudden cold snap. There are 'determinate' plants that grow into bushes and produce most of their crop at the same time and then there are the 'indeterminate' vine tomatoes that bear fruit throughout the season. Both need some form of support — either stakes, trellis or a tomato cage.

Pruning depends on the type and variety of tomato. Tall varieties need pruning to aid air circulation and let light into the plant. It also allows the plant to concentrate its energy into fruit development. As the plant grows, the lateral growths can be removed — these are found between the leaf and the main stem. When the plant has six or seven good trusses of fruit the growing tip can be pinched out. Dwarf varieties and little cherry tomato plants don't require pruning — just let them fruit their little hearts out. Grafted tomatoes are different again. The growing tip can be pinched out when it reaches 30 cm and the resulting tangle of stems reduced to about ten goodies. Leaves can be clipped to let the air and sunlight filter through as you think it necessary.

Tomatoes must never be allowed to dry out over the growing period. The soil should be kept moist but not overwatered, which can cause the plants to rot. If you are growing a bush plant that produces most of its fruit at the same time, you may be brave enough to try an age-old method used by Italian farmers. They reduce the watering as soon as the fruit begins to colour. This causes stress to the plant which could lead to it rotting and burning up in the sun but it also results in a wonderful concentrated flavour, which in turn makes for perfect summer fare.

With so many differently coloured tomatoes available, salsas can become a kaleidoscope of sunny shades if you grow your own ingredients. It's worth analysing just what you require of your crop before you buy seed. Some varieties make better sauces than others, for example. These 'paste' tomatoes are usually red 'Roma'-shaped fruits. 'Amish Paste' and 'San Marzano' are particularly good. For a simple tomato sauce, sweat a diced onion and a couple of cloves of garlic in 50 g butter until it is soft. Add 1 kg skinned chopped tomatoes and as the mixture starts to get watery, turn up the heat and cook for 5–10 minutes until most of the juices have evaporated and the sauce is chunky. Season with salt, pepper and a handful of chopped basil.

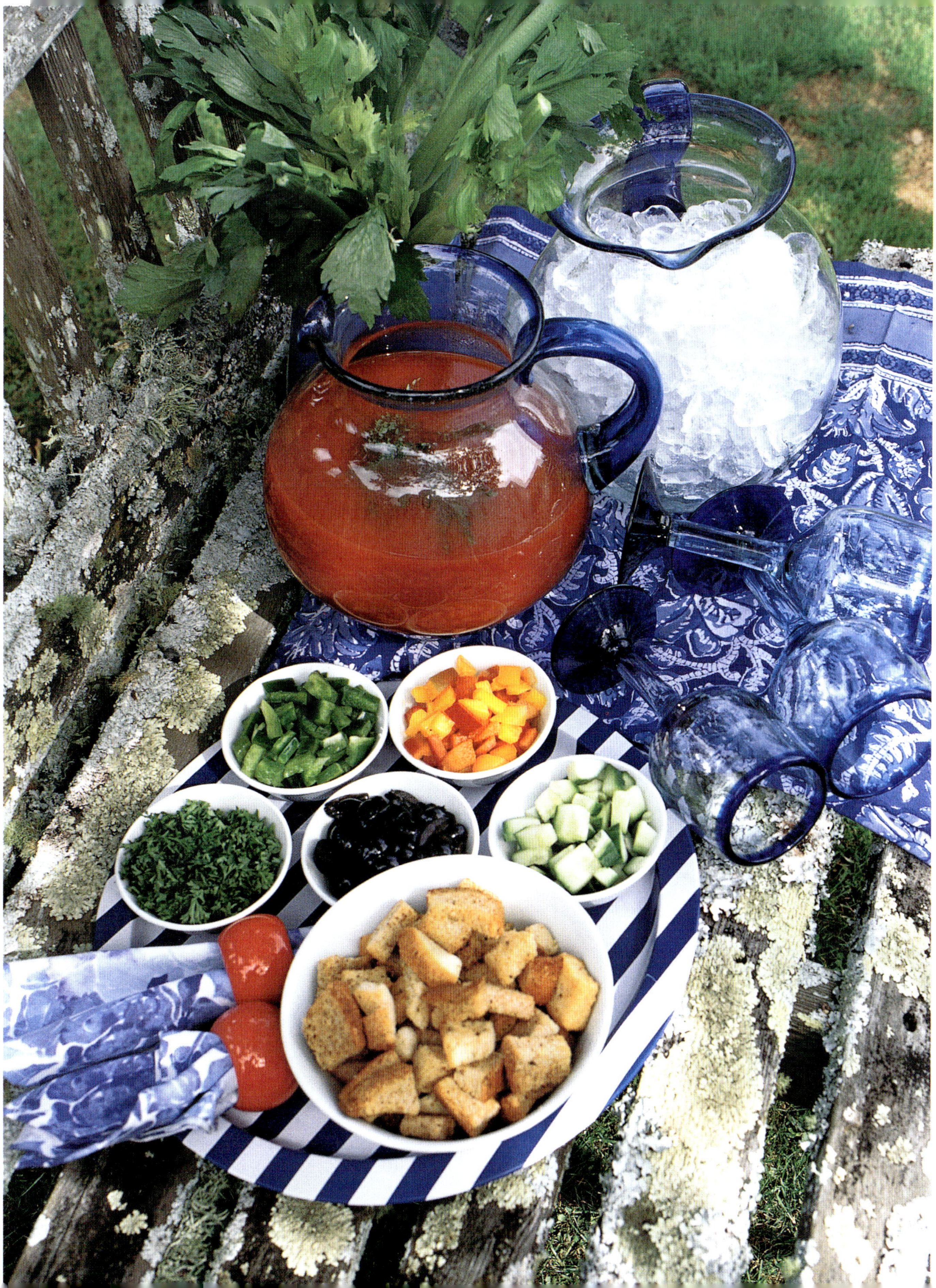

Many recipes ask for tomatoes to be skinned and deseeded. The skinning part is easy — just cut out the core and mark an 'x' at the tomato's base before tossing them into a pot of boiling water for no longer than 20 seconds, then revive them in very cold water. The skins simply give themselves up.

We've become a bit lazy about the deseeding and rightly so — a few pips aren't going to hurt anyone. There are varieties which list very few seeds among their assets ('Amish Paste' is one). A quick way to get rid of the seeds is to put the skinned tomatoes in a blender and then pass this through a sieve. The resulting juice can be heated until almost boiling and then some good olive oil can be whisked in to make a rather nice sauce. A spoonful of pesto can be added at the end for even more flavour.

Cherry tomatoes can benefit from a leisurely bathe in a herbed and seasoned marinade of good olive oil and balsamic vinegar before being served. Marinate the tiny tomatoes for at least a couple of hours — they should just be starting to burst as you serve them, with plenty of bread to mop up the juices.

Perhaps the best use you can make of the many coloured tomatoes is in the form of a large jug of gazpacho, the traditional cold soup for which there are probably as many recipes as there are types of tomatoes to make it with. For a summer lunch, fill a tall pitcher with the chilled liquid and serve a selection of diced vegetables, in separate bowls for your friends to help themselves. This way you can make the most of the various hued tomatoes and whatever else is ripe for the picking from the garden.

Pull the tomatoes out of the garden before the first frost and hang the whole plant, with ripe and unripe tomatoes still attached, in a cool dark place. The fruit will ripen slowly, extending your supply for weeks. Don't ripen any stragglers on the windowsills, where they'll tend to rot; it's much more effective to put them in a paper bag and leave them under the bed for a few weeks. Another tomato 'no-no' is storing the fruit in the fridge where they will loose their wonderful flavour.

If you are lucky enough to have more tomatoes than you can use at once, cook them into simple sauces, adding the last of the summer herbs, then freeze for the colder months. If you are assured of four sequential hot fine days, you could dry some of your harvest in the sun. 'Principe Borghese' is a great variety for drying. Cut the tomatoes in half and place on a tray, cover with cheesecloth to keep the insects away and leave in a sunny spot to dry. These should probably be kept in the freezer or at least frozen for a little while after they have dried, in case any little creatures found a gap in the cheesecloth. It is less risky and a lot more hygienic to dry them in the oven. Again, cut the fruits in half, place on an oven rack above a tray to catch the juices and turn the oven on to its lowest setting, leaving the door slightly ajar, and let them dry overnight. Some of the not-so-flavoursome fruits would benefit from a sprinkling of sea salt and a little sugar before going into the oven. If you have a glut of baby cherry tomatoes, you could oven dry them, cutting them in half first, and pack them in jar with olive oil perfumed with a sprig of thyme or oregano. They will take a lot less time to dry.

Another delicious way to cook tomatoes is slow roasting. Cut tomatoes in half lengthwise. Remove the core and place cut side up in a shallow oven dish. Sprinkle with salt and pepper and a little olive oil. You can also drizzle a few drops of balsamic vinegar if you wish. Bake in a moderately low oven (150°C) for about an hour — or until they're cooked but not mushy. The tomatoes should just have started to lose their shape. These are great just like this but for some dishes it's better to remove the skins when they are cool enough to handle. The long, slow roasting intensifies the flavour of the tomato. These are lovely with crusty bread. They can last in the fridge for up to a week but they probably won't.

CAPSICUMS (bell or sweet peppers) grow in similar conditions to tomatoes, requiring warm sunny days, although they need a lot more of them and it can seem like an interminably long wait from the time you sow the seeds until the fruits are ripe for the picking. You can try to get a little ahead by sowing seeds under shelter in early spring and then setting the seedlings out once the last whispers of cold air have expired. Capsicums don't take too kindly to transplanting, so the seeds would be best sown in peat pots that can be planted directly into the ground, but make sure these don't dry out.

Given a sunny position with moist but well-drained soil and the assurance of water, especially around fruit-setting and development times, the plants should be quite happy. They form good-looking bushes with lush glossy leaves that add depth to the garden and, once the fruits start to ripen, they will add a bright cheerful note among the summer flowers. Most sweet peppers start life green (don't we all) and change colour when they reach their prime. Different varieties will turn yellow, red and orange. 'Marconi Red' and Marconi Yellow' produce extremely long, tapering fruit — some will grow to 30 cm. 'Mandarin' turns an amazingly rich deep orange. 'Long Sweet Yellow' is a tapered banana pepper which is lime-green at first and turns yellow, then red with splashes of violet. The purple and 'chocolate' capsicums are so coloured at their immature stage and turn deep red as they ripen.

Capsicum can be picked at any stage, depending on how you wish to use them. The glowing warm colours indicate the sweetest fruits and they're the ones to roast with other summer vegetables and to purée for delicious sauces. The difference that comes with skinning the peppers is too wonderfully flavourful to forgo.

The peppers can be popped on a hot barbecue grill until the skin is blackened and blistered, then put in a plastic bag, or bowl covered with plastic wrap, and left to cool. The skin comes away very easily. Alternatively, you can cut them in half and place them, skin side up, in a shallow oven-dish, drizzle over a little oil and bake in a hot oven (220°C) for about 15 minutes. Take the dish out of the oven, cover it with tinfoil and, again, let the peppers cool before removing the skins, seeds and core. The sweet flesh that you are left with is perfect sauce material. You can purée it and slowly incorporate some olive oil, then add some finely chopped herbs to make a sauce for meats or a dressing for salad greens. The skinned peppers can be cooked a little longer in chicken stock, then puréed with the stock to make a sauce. The addition of a little cream gives this a smooth finish. Puréed peppers can be incorporated in a homemade mayonnaise to give it flavour and a fantastic colour, whether bright red, yellow or orange. Try serving a dollop with a fan of avocado slices. The skinned peppers can be left sitting in an oil marinade for a few hours and served as part of an antipasto platter.

AUBERGINES (*Solanum melongena*) are worth growing just for the look of them, for you'll never grow enough to keep body and soul together. Considering their large felted leaves and corpulent fruits, it comes as a surprise to see an eggplant actually growing in the garden, because the plants are not nearly as big as you'd expect, but rather on the short and stocky side. The leaves and purple flowers would not look out of place in a grey-blue Mediterranean-style garden, or the plants can be grown in pots where you can position them to best view the developing fruits, for they are a sight to behold. Eggplants are sponges that soak up whatever sunlight comes their way — they need even more hot summer days than tomatoes or capsicum and have similar growing requirements.

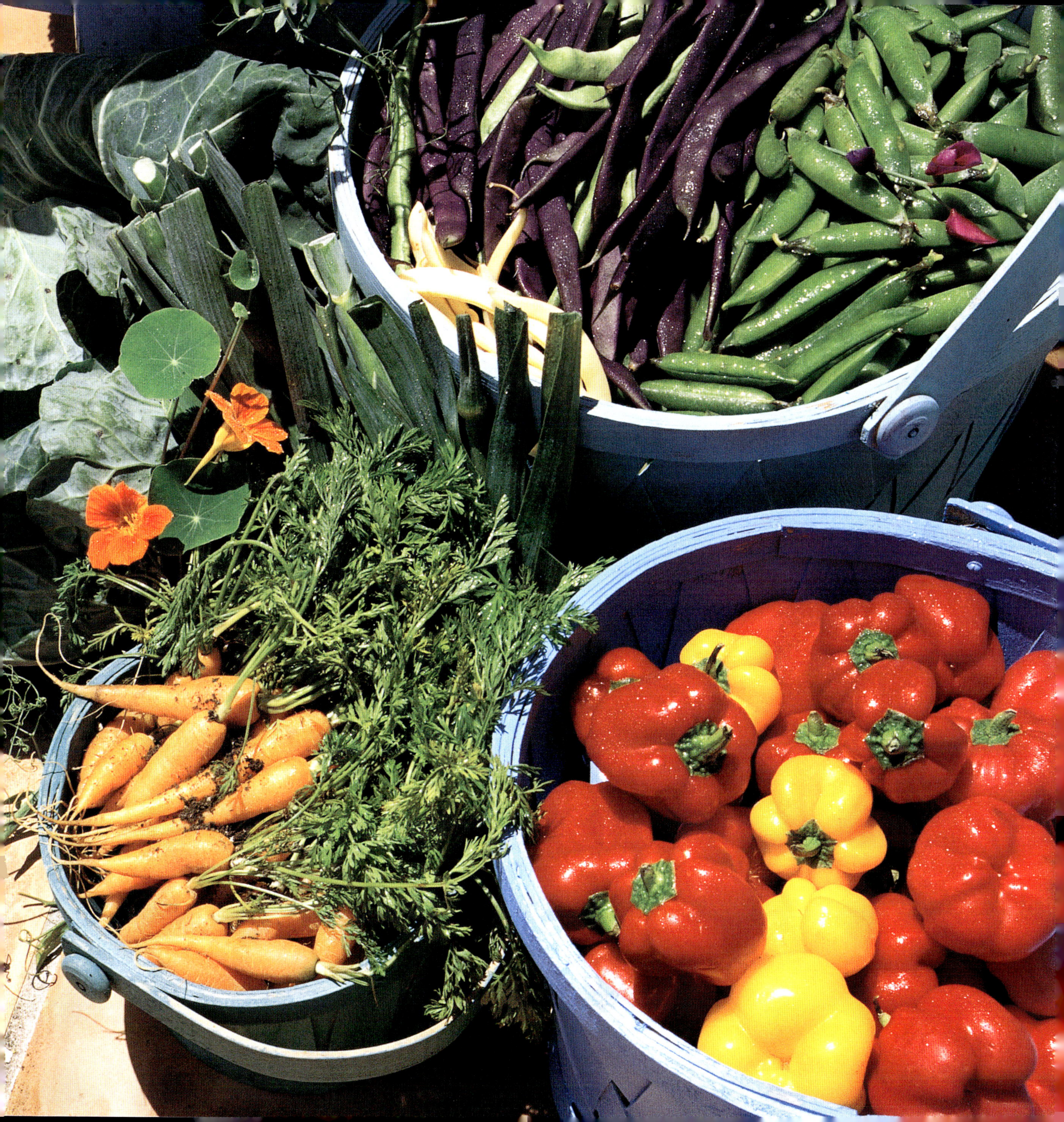

Aubergine dip

Prick **1 large or 2 medium aubergine (eggplant)** in several places with a fork. Cut the top off **1 bulb of garlic**. In a baking dish put the eggplant and garlic, then drizzle over **3 tbs olive oil**. Bake both in a moderate oven (180°C) for ½ to ¾ of hour or until the flesh of eggplant and garlic is soft. Scoop the flesh of the aubergine into a food processor. The cloves of garlic should pop out of their skins when you press them. Add these to the blender with **juice of 1 lemon**, a little **chopped chilli**, to taste, **2 tbsp tahini** (sesame paste), some chopped **parsley**, **basil** or **mint**, and any oil left in the baking tray. Process until smooth. Add **salt** and **pepper** to taste. Just before serving, stir in **1 cup unsweetened yoghurt**.

This purée can be 'Italianised' by omitting the tahini and yoghurt and adding a little **fresh tomato** and lots of **chopped basil**. You could also add a couple of **anchovy fillets** and **rinsed capers**. Some **cream** or **créme frâiche** will make it into a sauce.

Nowadays we can grow aubergines of all shapes and colour, which add even more interest in the garden and on the table. There's the very small and ornamental 'Bambino' and the beautiful sounding 'Violetta de Firenze', which produces rounded fruits in a deep lavender with creamy streaks. There are also the long narrow Asian eggplants in various shades of pink and violet and the small white oval fruits that gave the plant its name. Alas, the sheer beauty of aubergines can be to their detriment, because we are quite happy to leave the exquisite fruits on the bush or in a bowl for our visual pleasure, loathe to cut into them until they're well beyond their use-by date — hence the bitterness associated with the fruit. An aubergine should be harvested when it flaunts a rich colour and shiny skin — once eggplants lose their sheen, they become quite unpalatable. By harvesting often, you encourage more fruit, but don't be disappointed by the size of these — they are much smaller than the giants found on the supermarket shelves.

Aubergines are a joy to cook as they are very responsive to whatever flavours you add. The only dilemma a cook faces is whether to degorge or not. This sounds horribly uncomfortable but is basically salting aubergine slices to drain off the bitter juices. Most varieties offered these days as seed, and even those from the supermarket, have a lot of bitterness bred out of them, so the need to degorge is not as urgent as it once was. A good gauge is whether the fruit has little black seeds showing when you slice it. If it has, it's best to degorge.

Aubergines are also sponges in the pan and will soak up every drop of oil that comes their way. If you degorge the fruits you will lessen the quantity of oil they absorb during cooking by about two-thirds. If you are frying cubes or slices of aubergine, make sure both the pan and the oil are hot before you add the eggplant, as this also cuts down on their oil intake. Baking or roasting aubergines whole circumvents the problem happily.

The cooked aubergine flesh can be puréed with roasted garlic, some sesame paste and yoghurt to make either a dip or sauce, which is delicious with barbecued lamb.

COURGETTES (*Cucurbita pepo ovifera*) will bring colour into the potager through their bright yellow flowers and later their fruit. There are varieties that bear fruits of the darkest green and the sunniest yellow, as well as some striped pale and dark green. Some are cigar shaped, others patty-panned and scalloped around their edges. Like the other summer revellers, they enjoy a sunny situation in a well-drained soil, and, like the others, you can give them a head start by sowing the seeds under cover and setting them outside once the weather warms up. The plants should be kept adequately watered during their fruiting period.

The fruit is at its most delicious when very young and can be picked when it reaches 5 cm in length. By growing your own, you have the luxury of enjoying courgettes at this sweet stage. These pets need little cooking or embellishment and can simply be tossed with butter and a little lemon zest for not quite five minutes and seasoned with salt and freshly ground pepper.

Another luxury afforded by having the plants in the garden is that you can finally cook one of those dishes you've read about that ask for courgette blossoms. You can gather the male flowers from the plants without any qualms of curtailing the crop as these are the flowers that show no fruit development, or you can pick the very young fruit with the flowers still attached. The blossoms can be dipped in a batter and fried, to be served as part of an antipasto platter, they can be laid in a circular pattern on top of a frittata to serve for lunch. The blossom's journey from the bush to the oven should be reasonably quick as the blooms tend to wilt at the glimmer of the secateurs and the thought of what fate beholds them beyond the kitchen door.

With courgettes' propensity to produce fruit, the initial novelty will soon turn to complacency and that's the time to start playing around with different flavours and ways of cooking them. (It's the same with beans.) You could try letting them grow a little longer (which is not difficult) and taking to them with the potato peeler, producing long thin strips that you pop into boiling water for just a minute or two, drain, mix with a few drops of oil and serve like spaghetti, with a spoonful of fresh tomato sauce or pesto made with dark opal basil leaves on top. Of course, all the summer harvest can combine deliciously together in ratatouille, which can be served hot or cold, depending on the weather, and the sharper mix of caponata, which can be made in large quantities and kept in the fridge to bring out as you please. With summer dishes like these, the living can be very easy.

Other CUCURBITS lend a different charm to the garden. Although some gourds can be harvested for food, most are grown for ornament. They come in a diverse range of bewitching shapes. Thanks to their limited use in the commercial world, they haven't been genetically interfered with and as a result no two look the same. Seeds are available in assortments of either small or large fruits, as well as some specific gourds such as the prominent bright orange 'Turk's Turban', with its green and white striped cap, and the larger bottle-shaped fruits that can be made into birdhouses.

Seeds can be sown in spring once any danger of frost has passed. Gourds are sun-loving, sprawling plants that require a bit of space and are best diverted upwards over a trellis or over a stone wall where they can bask in the summer sun without the risk of their fruit rotting where they lie on the ground. They are fairly drought tolerant, although their fruit will be larger and more abundant if the plants are watered over long dry spells. There is no rhyme nor reason to the amount of fruit a plant will bear — some may produce two or three gourds, and others up to twenty.

Gourds are picked when they are fully ripe. The stem should be dry and the skin should not wrinkle nor show a mark when you have pressed it with your finger. The small gourds ripen throughout the summer but the larger ones need a long hot season and are harvested after the first frost. Leave a good stem on the fruit when you cut it. Wipe the fruit with a damp cloth; a few drops of disinfectant would help keep the bugs away. Prick a tiny hole in each end of the gourd and then dry in a cool, well ventilated spot for at least a month for the smaller ones and much longer for the showier fruits. They can be left hanging by their stems or stored on a wire rack and turned occasionally. Dried gourds will feel too light for their size and you'll hear the seeds rattling around when you shake them. Once they're properly dried, a coating of clear varnish will help preserve their brilliant colours.

PUMPKINS are a bit of a rarity in gardens these days, no doubt due to the amount of space they usurp as they grow. It's a shame, as to watch them reach their prodigious proportions in both vine and fruit is fascinating, if a little slow, for they require about six months of warm weather to mature. If you have a sunny 2–3 metres square that you want to cover up over summer, then that's the place for your pumpkins. You could also try interplanting something tall among the rambling vine. Beans or sweetcorn would fit in well; a group of bright sunflowers would also make for a cheerful corner in the potager.

There are smaller, bushier winter squashes that take less time to mature and are more suited to the modern garden and temperament. Butternuts and buttercups stand out as the best for storing and taste. They have the same requirements as the other cucurbits. They are ready to harvest as soon as their skin is firm. If they are to be stored for winter, it's better to wait until the leaves start to die off and the stems wither. All fruits should be gathered after the first hint of a frost. They should be stored in a warm, dry airy place — ideally on the wire rack you have for drying the artichokes and gourds. (An old bed base fitted over the rafters in a shed or the garage would be perfect.)

I find the best place to store the harvest is in the freezer. As peeling their skins can put your fingers at great risk and boiling the flesh has insipid watery results, the safest and most flavourful way to cook pumpkins is in the oven. Cut them into eighths, take their seeds out and place them skin side down in a roasting dish. Bake them in a moderately hot oven for 30–40 minutes or until cooked. Then scoop out the flesh into containers for the freezer — little pots of gold for many a delicious soup or meal over winter.

Butternut is better used fresh, rather than spending time in the freezer. It is the main ingredient for a very appetising sauce I make frequently in winter to eat with noodles or any other pasta I fancy. (See page 161 for recipe.)

LEEKS may seem humble but they're a magical plant. When leeks are harvested at their tender juvenile stage they have a far more refined flavour than either onions or spring onions and so they fit perfectly into any of the more subtle soups and sauces. They get on extremely well with herbs, other vegetables and the indispensable lemon, adding to rather than detracting from the overall taste. I always put them in my stock pot and often include a finely chopped handful into casseroles, pastas, risottos, pulses and Asian-inspired dishes.

Leeks are child's play to grow. Traditionally cultivated as a winter vegetable, the most prized plants were earthed in trenches or grown through drainpipes to emerge a pristine white for the table, the bigger the better. By growing your own you can have a year-round supply of the more succulent baby leeks which don't require the labour-intensive process of earthing and blanching. Nor do they need to be thinned quite as much, as we want to pick them pencil slim. Baby leeks are often called 'poorman's asparagus', and if you let them grow to the width of a finger or thumb, they make delicious eating, either braised in chicken stock or steamed, cooled and dressed with a vinaigrette. I make one with walnut oil that goes particularly well with their delicate taste.

The Kitchen Garden's Comeback

Leeks thrive in a sunny position and will need watering over the dry summer months. They are very cold-hardy. If you let the odd one develop into splendid-looking purple flowerheads, you will be guaranteed a succession of tender young things.

THE HERB GARDEN

Growing herbs is easy. The bottom line is that most of these plants require a lot of sun, although there are a few shady characters that will settle for less. Generally, plants with broad leaves or a dense canopy of leaves will tolerate some shade as the wider leaves are able to capture more sunlight when it's available. The less-demanding herbs include angelica, most mints, sorrel, lemon balm and parsley. Most of the others like it hot, so choosing a sunny situation for your aromatics will guarantee a constant stream of fresh and tasty contributions to the kitchen. If no such space exists, a good option is to plant herbs in containers that can be moved around to catch the sun.

Many of the culinary herbs we use can trace their origins back to the craggy hills around the Mediterranean, where they still prosper in surprisingly little soil. These herbs will feel quite at home in pots. Really good drainage will better resemble their parched birthplace. Put old broken bits of terracotta in the bottom of the container, making sure a flat bit won't cover the hole and defeat the whole purpose of the exercise. You could go a stage further by placing a cardboard tube over the central hole in the pot and filling the inside of the tube with sand. Put potting mix in the rest of the container and then remove the tube with one firm tug. The drainage thus assured, herbs may not grow quite as luxuriantly as they would in moist, richer soils but they will be much more aromatic.

Creating a permanent herb garden of reasonable size can be a most enjoyable project. The term 'herb' can be applied loosely to literally thousands of plants of which some part, leaf, stem, root, flower, berry, seed or even bark has proved beneficial to one's health, fragrance, beauty or food. For our purposes we'll focus on culinary herbs, as they are the most gratifying of plants to the gardener who cooks.

Many texts suggest planting your herbs as close to the kitchen as possible, for convenience. That's fine if it's the sunniest spot — otherwise it really isn't too arduous a task to take a little stroll down the garden path to gather your herbs. While you have the secateurs in your hand, you can always deadhead a flower or two along the way.

Herbs are not greedy plants, so there's generally no need to enrich the soil before planting. Forking it over will improve the drainage. If you are faced with a heavy clay soil you will have to open it up by digging in plenty of gravel and organic matter like compost and well-rotted manure. Try not to tread on the soil after it has been dug. The additional material will in effect raise the bed, which may then need edging with wooden boards, bricks or tiles. This will keep the soil in and as a bonus you'll have a neat-looking bed and lawn edge that are easier to manage.

Before you start digging, it pays to have a plan in your head, possibly even on paper. To avoid chaos check the eventual height and width your plants will reach. A herb garden is easily made in stages. Start off with the central portion of the big plan, and expand as the need or urge arises by adding extra borders. (Vita Sackville-West started off with just a dozen herbs and ended up with twenty beds in her garden at Sissinghurst.) This central point can be made to look stronger by height in the middle. Trees are risky as they will gradually shade more and more of the sun-loving herbs below. If you intend to go totally herbal, a standard of sweet bay, lavender or rosemary would be ideal. Keep that bay clipped, though — they can grow up to 10 metres high and wide and some species sucker and would need to be coppiced and controlled. A statue or a good-looking container could also provide a focal point, as would a specimen plant - perhaps a rose, standardised, weeping or clambering up an obelisk frame.

From this high point move down through the perennial herbs, from the tall umbels, angelica and fennel, to the medium-standing sages, rosemary, borage, dill, tarragon and on down to the lower-growing origanum, parsley, chervil, lemon balm and thymes. Smooth transition from plant to plant is better not interrupted by patches of bare soil. Plant out the perennials, allowing space for their ultimate width, and while they're making headway, cover the bare patches with annuals like basil, coriander and edible flowers, or a discreet layer of bark or gravel. All of these will keep the weeds away.

Layouts for herb gardens range from the formal to the unrestrained

The smoky bronze foliage of Foeniculum vulgare *'Purpurascens' makes a great companion to the bolder leaves of* Canna tropicanna, Rheum *(rhubarb) and the smaller spires of* Astilbe *'Fanal'.*

Following pages: Herb ricotta cake, pesto and chervil custards.

The Kitchen Garden's Comeback 107

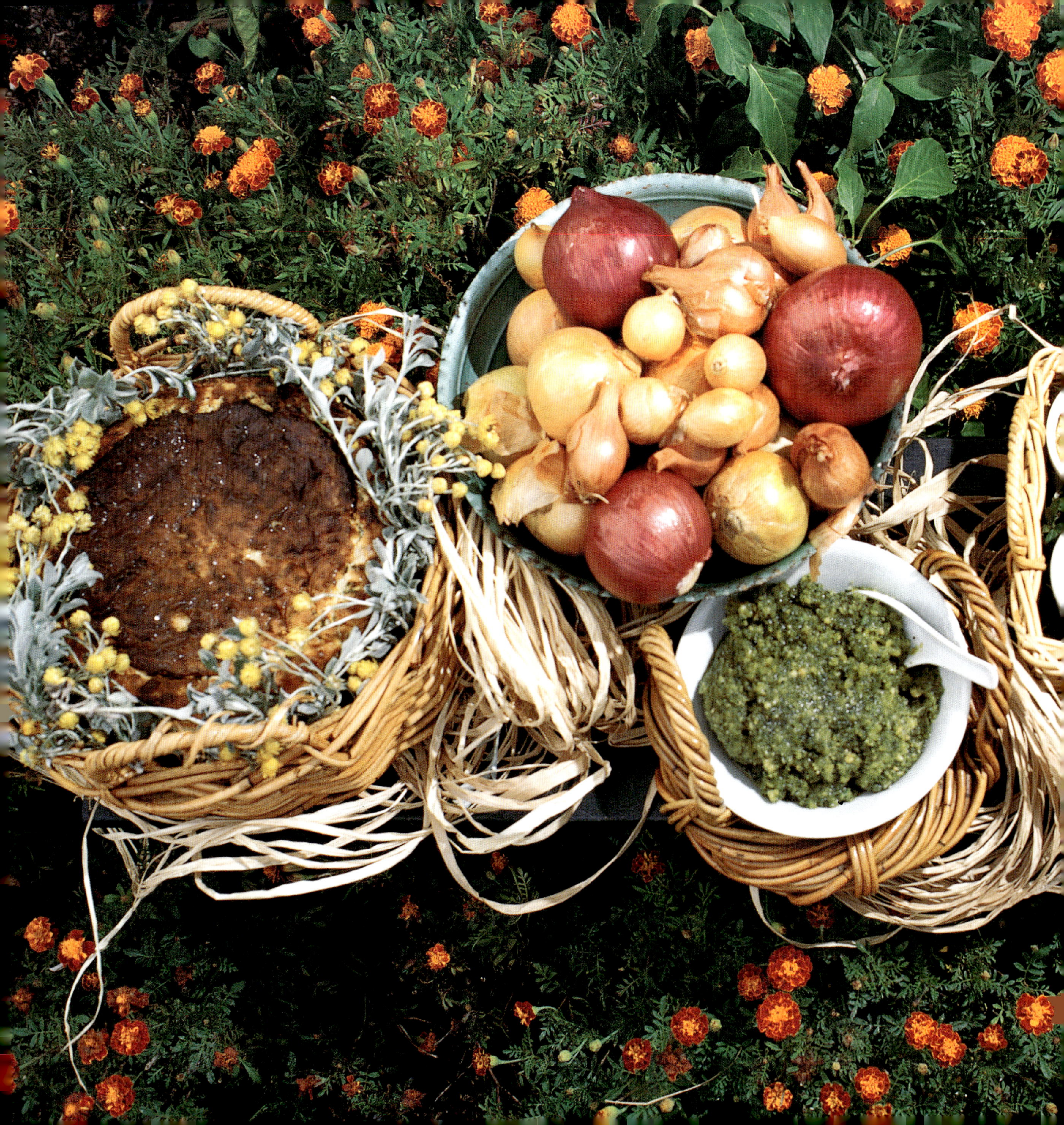

informal. If you fancy a formal design based on the parterre, keep in mind that patterns are best kept simple — diamonds and triangles, circles and half circles are all effective. Anything too complicated could result in a haze rather than a maze. Basic shapes (even a spoked wheel) are also successful in paved herb gardens where divisions are made with paths instead of hedges — very useful in wet weather. Some herbs make excellent edgers for these paths; a row of parsley, winter savory, chives (eye-catching in flower), nasturtium and little alpine strawberries will all mellow the brick or gravel underfoot. Each type of herb can be grown in its own compartment, particularly important if you plant mints, which will take over any unbounded bed. An advantage of these more structured gardens is that they look good from the moment they're planted, unlike informal groupings, which rely on plant growth for effect.

The uncontrived abandon of the latter is, funnily enough, hard to achieve. You have to be generous in order to look generous — it's only by planting a fair number of the same plant, producing great drifts of leaf and flower, that the impression of largesse is conveyed. Whatever the design, the same considerations of shape and colour used to plot a herbaceous border will help achieve a natural harmony within a herb garden. The outcome of such planning should give the gardener a desirable retreat, be it to find a bit of peace among muted greys, greens and blues in air infused with scents, or to be fittingly cheered up by an array of bright yellows, red and orange. Here you are allowed to sit back and soak in the atmosphere, because a bonus with a herb garden is that, once planted, it involves very little work. Herbs are the least demanding of plants — they hate being fussed over, needing very little in the way of extra food and water. Their own essential oils should keep a lot of the bugs away. If not, use an organic method to control them (quite often this means squashing the little blighters between your fingers or underfoot). Remember, these are plants you're going to eat.

Herbs require the occasional trim to encourage bushy growth and this, after all, is why you cultivate them. Pruning is plain common sense. Pick from the outside in, the largest leaves first. To encourage even bushier growth from herbs like thyme, mint, basil and winter savory, cut above a pair of leaves so they will branch out. When you snip chives, leave about 5 cm at the base. All the perennial herbs will benefit from a prune after they have flowered, when normally a plant will divert its energy towards producing seeds. Leave well alone if you want seeds,

The Kitchen Garden's Comeback

or the plant to self-seed. Most herbs will flower once a year. However, a second flourish, or at least a burst of tender young leaves, can often be encouraged by severe pruning after the first flowering. Angelica, lovage, chives and chervil will produce a better-flavoured regrowth when their stems are cut back by about two-thirds. There are exceptions. Thyme dislikes hard pruning and should only be trimmed lightly after flowering, and the more rampant mints and lemon balm should be cut back before they flower.

Probably the greatest pleasure you can draw from your own herb garden is inspiration. There is no better stimulus to deciding what to cook than wandering about your herbs, picking a sprig here and there. This is a magical time — more often than not in the late afternoon when the air is quite still — an amble where you can gather your thoughts along with the herbs. It's a time to savour as much as the fine meals it precedes.

After suffering from the most severe case of overuse ever encountered on a dinner plate, PARSLEY has laid low, put its feet up and allowed more assertive herbs to have their day. Not the least bit worried about its future, parsley is secure in the knowledge that it is still the most used and useful of all the herbs. Parsley has learnt to adapt to all styles of cooking and to get along famously with other herbs. Its mild sweet taste is enough on its own to flavour a vegetable purée or soup, but it's the way that this sweetness combines with other flavours that makes this herb such an asset in the kitchen. It provides a perfect medium to convey the tang of lemon peel and the pungency of garlic in cremolata mix. It is an ideal companion to the anise flavours of basil and fennel, or the fresh taste of mint. (The ricotta cake featured on page 161 blends all three flavours with whey cheese and would make a great luncheon dish, served with a salad of red leaves.)

Parsley comes in two types — the curly-leaved and the flat-leaved. The flat-leaved or Italian parsley is the one to grow. Although biennial, parsley is usually treated as an annual. Many plants will self-seed in time. Seeds are notoriously slow to germinate and would benefit from being soaked in boiling water overnight before sowing in spring. They can then be placed in a dark, warm place (the airing cupboard). Most people find it easier to buy seedlings which are very easy to transplant.

Parsley likes an open sunny position but will grow in light shade. It needs adequate watering over dry periods. Once the plants start to flower, the flavour of the leaves becomes unpleasantly strong to use. Meantime it adds fresh vibrant colour to both the garden and the plate over the summer months. Sprigs look good with other greens in a salad bowl and their taste is far superior to many an edible weed suggested for trendy salad mixes. It's just that its accommodating nature has led us to think of this jewel of a herb as uninteresting.

CHERVIL is parsley's shy cousin, who is quite happy to hide itself beneath the skirts of other herbs over the summer months and grow more confident and prominent for winter. For such a fragile-looking plant with soft feathery leaves and a delicate taste to match, this annual is surprisingly hardy. Seeds should be sown where they are to grow, as the roots do not take kindly to transplanting. Over the summer months, it needs a moist, shady position, otherwise the fine leaves will turn pink in the sun. If you let a couple of plants flower, they will self-seed for more picking the following year. In hot climates chervil grows best from the middle of autumn through to spring, and prefers full sun over winter. It is better to pick the lacy leaves just as you need them. They look good in the salad bowl and taste like a cross between a mild tarragon and sweet parsley. Chervil can take the place of parsley in many a dish, enhancing other flavours like garlic and lemon. Any of its subtle anise taste is lost when it is combined with stronger herbs. Used on its own, it can make a gentle difference to simple fish and creamy egg dishes. Chervil custards make an excellent lunch.

FRENCH TARRAGON never sets seed and can only be grown from root division in spring, when the new growth commences, or from cuttings taken over summer. It grows better in places with dry cold winters, tending to rot in the ground in mild wet areas where it is better kept in a pot so that you can make sure it doesn't get waterlogged. Clipping the plant over summer will encourage new growth, which is very handy as its fine leaves with their liquorice-anise flavour can do so much to sauces and dressings.

Tarragon has enjoyed a friendship with chicken for hundreds of years. For delicious grilled chicken, marinate the cuts in the fridge for a few hours, or overnight, in a mixture of ½ cup olive oil, the zest and juice of a lemon, 2–3 tablespoons of chopped tarragon, a crushed clove of garlic and a tablespoon of mustard. When cooking the drained chicken, baste with the leftover marinade. You could also serve the above chicken, or fish, or grilled lamb, with tarragon bread sauce.

Chervil custards

Chop a couple of **baby leeks**, or the white of a larger leek very finely **with two cloves of garlic** and sweat in a pan with a **tbsp each of butter and oil** for a few minutes. Break **6 eggs** into a bowl, add **salt and pepper** to taste, then the leek and garlic mixture. Stir in **500 ml chicken stock** and **1½ tbsp of chopped chervil**. Pour into 6 individual well-buttered ramekins and place these in a roasting dish that has enough water to reach over halfway up the ramekins. Cover and bring the water to the boil and cook gently for 15 minutes or until just set. Remove ramekins from the water bath and let them sit, covered for a further 5 minutes. Run a knife around the sides of the dishes and turn each out onto a small plate **of green leaves — rocket, corn salad** or whatever but try to include a few fresh **sprigs of chervil**.

Tarragon bread sauce

Take the crusts off **3 thick slices of white bread** and submerge in **½ cup of tarragon or white-wine vinegar**. Let stand for ½ an hour, then remove the bread and discard any vinegar that hasn't been absorbed. Peel **3–4 cloves of garlic**. Put in a processor with **1½ cups olive oil** and process until garlic is finely chopped. With the motor still running, add the bread and then a **good-sized bunch of tarragon**, trimmed and chopped. You may need to add a little more oil — the sauce should be thickly spoonable. Check the taste for **salt** and **pepper**. This sauce is good with chicken, fish and lamb, grilled or roasted.

Tarragon is the only herb worth your while infusing into a vinegar. (Most of the bottles of various herbs suspended in vinegar are used for decorative more than culinary purposes and most have well and truly passed their use-by date by the time they're opened. You find that real cooks have only a few bottles in their cupboards — usually a good red wine and white wine vinegar, a cider and a balsamic.) A tarragon vinegar will flavour dressings and the likes of the classical bearnaise sauce, or deglaze a roasting pan after you've cooked the chook over the winter months when there is no fresh substitute for its elegant flavour. It's simple to make. Open a full bottle of white wine vinegar and pour a little into a jug. Pop in a sprig or two of tarragon and top up with the reserved vinegar. Seal the bottle tightly and leave in a warm place for a couple of weeks to allow the flavour of the herb to steep through the vinegar. The bottle is then best stored in a cool dark place until it is required.

It is also worth freezing a few rolls of tarragon butter before the plant dies down over winter. Cream together 125 g softened butter with 2–3 tablespoons of chopped tarragon, a tablespoon of lemon juice and some salt and pepper. Chill for about half an hour to firm up and then roll into a log shape. Cover with tin foil and freeze. These logs are also extremely useful over the barbecuing months. Slice off rounds and slip them in the middle of your homemade hamburgers or underneath the skin of chicken breasts before you grill them. A couple of slices will make all the difference on top of a dish of steaming hot green beans or zucchini.

Basil is the other flavour worth saving, for this herb is the very essence of summer. It seems to soak up all the sun's goodness and pass it on to us in beautifully fragrant leaves. It's one of the season's pleasures to turn the hose on them on a hot day just to smell the perfume rising in the mist. They are actually one of the few plants that like being watered in the middle of the day. And you know the summer is over when just a few valiant leaves remain on the stems.

There are many basil varieties now available. Plant several and experiment with the different colours, sizes and tastes. Basil is an extremely tender annual that requires warm temperatures to germinate and grow, and the slightest hint of a cold snap or frost can set it back. In colder areas start off the seedlings inside in late spring and early summer and gradually harden them up by taking them outside for an airing over the hottest hours of the day, until warm days and nights are assured. They can then be planted in a sunny position in a reasonably rich soil to encourage their lush green leaves. More seeds can be sown directly into the ground at the same time for a later harvest.

As basil grows, pinch out the tips to make a bushier plant — the tips, of course, are for the kitchen. Add them to green-leafed salads, marinated eggplant or roasted capsicum, tomatoes, naturally, and — well, just about anything. Basil contains a volatile oil that evaporates quickly with heat, so the herb is best added to hot dishes towards the end of the cooking. Its leaves bruise easily and are better torn rather than chopped. Combine a handful of torn leaves with some finely chopped garlic, a little chilli, some cherry tomatoes and olive oil, and toss through drained pasta for a really quick summer meal. Serve with freshly grated parmesan.

The purple-leaved basils look good tossed through a dish of just-cooked green and yellow zucchini with a little more parmesan. The very large leaves of 'Genovese Giant' and 'Lettuce Leaf' can be used as wraps to hold a spicy meat mixture or a chicken mayonnaise. Cinnamon basil can be added to poached peaches or nectarines, the pastry base for a creamy tart and homemade cinnamon icecream.

Pesto could be called a culinary cliché, but you can't knock it. It's easy to make (see recipe on page 162) and has a string of uses, from coating spaghetti to accompanying grilled meats, fish and chicken, to livening up predictable vegetables. It's even wonderful on its own with toasted bread. You can freeze pesto for use in winter.

Pesto recipes are very adaptable. Other herbs like coriander and mint can take the place of basil, and almonds and less often walnuts can stand in for pinenuts. Many recipes keep the same pesto and leave out the cheese and are really just an amalgamation of herbs, nuts and oil, which is often better suited to a dish.

Basil can be chopped up and put into ice-cube trays, topped with water and frozen. The frozen cubes can then be packed in a plastic bag until they're required to add their aroma to casseroles and hearty winter soups. Unfortunately they won't be adding the rich green hues we associate with the herb, as the leaves turn brown, sometimes black, when frozen raw. Still, it's a handy way of storing the scented leaves when you're in a hurry. If you wish to preserve basil and keep it green, plunge the leaves into boiling water and immediately into icy-cold water. Squeeze out any moisture and purée the leaves with a little olive oil and a pinch of salt. Put small amounts in tiny containers or in plastic wrap and freeze.

THYME is often referred to as the 'poor man's herb' because once you have your fragrant-leaved plant, there is no extra outlay on your part. In fact any problems that arise in this perennial's cultivation are usually caused by over care — too much watering and too much food. Thyme is one of those sun-loving Mediterranean plants that will tolerate the dry poor soils of a gravel garden. There is a vast range of varieties — mainly because the herb hybridises so freely — and they can be divided into two categories, the bushier, clumping thymes and the ground-hugging, matting thymes. Both have their place in the ornamental garden and there are green, golden, grey and silver-foliaged plants to choose from. The clumping kind gives more to the kitchen.

The strength of the flavour varies greatly from plant to plant, so take the odd nibble before making a choice at the garden centre. There are also thymes that taste of orange and lemon and caraway. The common kitchen thyme, *Thymus vulgaris*, is the most widely available and one of the best. It will grow to 40 cm and is best kept clipped or it will become woody. Although thyme is a remarkably cold-hardy plant considering its warm-blooded ancestry, older, woody plants can be damaged by severe frosts and are best cut back by three-quarters each winter. Cuttings can be taken from the old wood before the weather turns cold. These should be put into moist soil in a partially shaded spot and left undisturbed for six months or so.

Over the summer months, thyme sprigs can be snipped and tossed onto the barbecue and added to the baste to perfume the food on the grill plate. Leaves can be frozen with water in ice cubes to add to a large jug of gazpacho for a summer's lunch or a prelude to a barbecue. Chicken portions can be wrapped with a sprig of thyme and a rasher of bacon and held together with a toothpick before being grilled or cooked in a little white wine.

During the colder months this reliable herb will anchor many a hearty dish. Its flavour goes particularly well with onions. Because this flavour is not dissipated with slow cooking, thyme is an invaluable addition to stocks, soups, casseroles and dependably delicious country terrines like the one on page 162. A sprig or two added to lentils or chickpeas during cooking will give the pulses a more interesting taste.

It doesn't lose this flavour with slow cooking and so is invaluable in casseroles and soups and, of course, it forms part of the magical bouquet garni in

Marigolds adorn a delicate sorrel soup, while nasturtiums liven up a country terrine under the gaze of a late artichoke bloom (Cynara scolymus).

Lemon grass adds its special tang to the Thai Prawn Salad. The grass loses much of its flavour once picked, and consequently is not widely available in shops — reason enough to grow your own.

stockpots. A sprig or two added to lentils and chickpeas during cooking gives these a more interesting taste.

CORIANDER also works well with pulses (see page 162 for a good black beans and tomatoes combo). Remember, however, that this is a herb no one is indifferent to and it would be considerate to serve the herb separately in a sharp tomato salsa or smooth green sauce if you are unsure of your guests' predilection towards coriander.

Two different types of plant have been developed — coriander for seeds and cilantro for leaves. The seeds taste completely different from the leaves, being more sweetly aromatic and without the smell that many find offensive (but doesn't seem that bad when it is likened to the aroma of dried orange peel). The seeds are harvested when they are fully ripe and have turned from green to grey-brown. They can be added to preserves, marinades, curry mixes, and even ground for baking. The leaves, stems and roots of cilantro are all used in Thai cooking, while other cuisines are content with the bright green leaves for colour and flavour.

An annual, coriander/cilantro can be sown at any time of the year in warm areas. There is also a hardy frost-resistant variety, 'Iman', which has been developed for winter sowing and growing in less kind climates. Seeds are best sown where you want them to grow as the plant dislikes being moved. It likes a lot of sun and reasonably good, well-drained soil. Leaves can be picked until the plant begins to flower. There is a very simple recipe for Thai Fish Cakes that uses both roots and leaves at the back of the book (page 163).

LEMON GRASS, like mint, is a herb for both cooking and cultivating. This grass is a most useful plant in the tropics where it is too hot for citrus. It will grow in New Zealand provided it has adequate protection from winter's cold. In many areas that may mean bringing the grass indoors for the worst months. In places with dry, mild winters it may be left in the garden with a mulch to protect the roots. Wet weather may cause the roots to become waterlogged and the plant will die. It will enjoy a warm sunny spot in the garden over summer and will require adequate watering in dry spells. Seeds are not available, so the only way to propagate lemon grass is by division of larger clumps.

What do you get for all this cosseting? Lemon grass produces a lemony oil without the citric acid — the fragrance without the zing — and its effect in Southeast Asian fare is subtle and exquisite. If you haven't lemon grass on hand,

Roasted garlic.

you can add lemon peel in its place but that is no real substitute. Nor is the woody, dried lemon grass on offer a patch on the fresh. The swollen bottom part of the leaf stem, just above the root, is the part used in cooking. It is a paler green-white colour and although it is far more tender than the rest of the stem, it is still quite tough and should be crushed before it is chopped. The crushing helps release the volatile oil of lemon.

Lemon grass can be added to stocks and soups, especially fish soups, and it is better removed before the dish is served, like bay leaves. Strands can be placed inside the cavity of a whole fish, and fine slivers sprinkled on smaller fillets before wrapping them in foil to cook. The grass can also flavour marinades for barbecued chicken, lamb and fish. Stems crushed at one end could be used as a little brush with which to baste the food. For sauces and dishes where the stem is not removed, it should either be chopped extremely finely or pounded to a pulp in a mortar with pestle. The flavour of lemon grass combines beautifully with the sour and again lemony taste of tamarind, another favourite in Asian cuisine. (The Thai Prawn Salad on page 162 combines these two flavours particularly well.)

Lemon grass can also lend its flavour to poached fruits. When peaches are at the height of their season, plunge them into boiling water, then peel and cut them in half, remove their stones and poach them in a sugar syrup to which you've added a few tender strands of lemon grass.

MINT should be grown in a pot to contain its vigorous, invasive habit. Plant it in an old bucket with drainage holes and then the bucket itself can be interred or concealed in the ground. Mint is happy in sun or partial shade in a moist, rich soil. In humid or very dry conditions it is prone to mint rust. There is a rust-free mint, *Mentha smithiana*, that is better in these situations, although it doesn't altogether live up to its name. Keeping the plants clipped helps with the rust problem, as it is mainly the older leaves that are affected. The smooth rather than hairy-leaved mints are best in the kitchen. Whole tender young leaves can be part of a green salad, and larger ones can be chopped to add their clean fresh taste to spicy beef or lamb composite salads. Mint is an important contributor to tabouleh, the fresh Lebanese Burghul Salad which makes a wonderful adjunct to barbecued lamb. (See recipe on page 163.) A mint and almond pesto makes a cool accompaniment to barbecued fish or lamb cutlets. Process ½ cup each of ground almonds, parsley and mint leaves and, if you like, ½ cup parmesan cheese. Gradually add

¼ cup of olive oil while the motor is running. This mixture can be diluted as needed with crème fraîche or cream.

Mint and watermelon make a really refreshing combination, either at the end of a meal with cubes of melon tossed with some chopped mint and fresh orange juice, or by adding to this some cubes of feta cheese and green salad leaves you have a quick lunch. More cubes of watermelon can be put in a blender with cubes of ice to make a cool pitcher of juice, decorated with sprigs of mint, to serve in the heat of the day. This may require thinning with water or you could dilute with bubbly for a sparkling outdoor brunch.

GARLIC, grown on your own patch, assures you of quality not always available on shop shelves, and thus a better flavour in your food. The bulbs are traditionally planted on the shortest day and lifted on the longest, but you should really let the condition of the soil determine the best time to set out the cloves. It should be neither cold nor sodden, rather friable and nicely moist. The cloves are best planted in autumn, two to three weeks before the first frosts, or later, in early spring. Garlic likes an open sunny situation, although it will grow in light shade but the bulbs will be smaller. Choose healthy firm bulbs and break into individual cloves. Set these 6–8 cm apart and plant the cloves pointed end up. Insert them to a depth twice their length. Try not to push the clove down too hard into the ground as the soil will compact below and inhibit root formation.

There are three different types of garlic. The large elephant garlic, *Allium ampeloprasm*, is deservedly popular as there is less peeling involved and it has a less pungent flavour. This will grow to over a metre, with flower stalks a metre higher again, making a dramatic show in the garden. The 'hardneck', or top-setting garlic, *A. sativum* var. *ophioscorodon*, will also produce flowers but on a coiled flower stem. The flowers don't open fully and the stems are better removed to redirect growth back into the bulb. The third kind of garlic, *A. sativum* var. *sativum*, is called 'softneck' and doesn't produce flowers. Its bulbs are smaller than the others.

Garlic needs a long growing time — from six to eight months. Autumn plantings can be harvested the following summer. The plants will let you know when they are ready by starting to wilt and turn brown. They should be watered until the foliage begins to brown, after which water should be withheld to let the plant dry out. Bulbs are best lifted after there has been a dry spell of about four to five days. Shake off any excess soil and leave them to dry on the ground if you can be assured of continuing fine weather. They can then be plaited with what's left of the leaves, peasant style, and hung in an airy place to dry and keep vampires at bay.

Roasting the bulbs is the best way to enjoy garlic in company. You get a great flavour — mild, with a sweet nutty taste — without the less sociable repercussions.

Drizzle some olive oil over the papery skin of the garlic bulbs, scatter a sprig or two of thyme among them and roast in a moderately hot oven for about 40–50 minutes. Covering the bulbs for the first 20 minutes will keep them nice and moist. They would also appreciate another drizzle of oil half way through roasting.

Cut the tip of the bulb and squeeze out the individual cloves. These can be puréed, topped with oil and kept in a jar in the fridge to add to whatever dish is crying out for the noble bulb.

SALAD HERBS

We may be forgiven for assuming that exotic salad mixes of the leaves of baby beets, mustards and wildflowers, placed 'just so' on designer plates in understated restaurants, are the latest thing. In fact, combining salads of unusual leaves is as old as the hills they hail from. In less enlightened times the collecting and eating of fresh young leaves was seen as an end to a long grey winter and a precursor to sunnier times. The plants themselves, some horribly bitter, were used to cleanse the body of impurities built up over a relatively inactive winter. The Romans consumed nettles while the French refined the spring rite into a creamy sorrel soup. A more contemporary version can be found on page 163. Salad greens became so prevalent in the 1600s that whole meadows found their way onto the table.

It's good to experiment, but in the quest to be different, you need to be aware that many wildflowers and weeds are seriously poisonous, while others just taste plain awful. With so many succulent, edible leaves readily available, it's probably no longer necessary to scour the countryside like a latter-day salad pioneer in search of something green for the plate. Growing your own salad greens couldn't be easier; many are far tastier if they're picked young, which is of course a bonus for the impatient, results-driven gardener. You could be harvesting your own tender young things around four weeks after sowing the seed, revelling in the sheer convenience of being able to snip a bunch as you need them. And there's no need to wait until spring to splurge and purge on the greens, as there are enough varieties to ensure something for the table all year round.

SALAD MIXES are what the French call *mesclun*, while in Italy they go by the musical name of *mitizcanza*. Both words are derived from the Latin, *miscare*, which means to mix or mingle and that is exactly what a good blend of salad herbs should do. Besides the various colours of the leaves — luxuriant dark greens, rich bronzes and full-bodied burgundies — today's mixes contain an impressive selection of leaf shapes. Some are smoothly rounded or shaped like tongues, others frilly, feathery or fashioned like oak leaves. Then you get to the peppery, nutty flavours; even the blander ones are useful as a counterbalance to the sharp tastes. Whatever you choose to grow, pick them when they're young. As they age, the leaves become tougher and decidedly bitter.

Some of the Asian mustards available in the salad seed mix are bitter from the word go, and they grow so quickly it's hard to keep pace before they reach their salad use-by date. Some of this bitterness can be curtailed by sweetening the soil before you sow your salad mixes. Acid soils are common in this country, especially in areas with a high rainfall, but they can be neutralised with a dressing of lime. Check your soil's pH level, if you can, before applying lime, and follow the directions, because too much may inactivate other important nutrients. Wait at least three weeks after dressing the soil with lime before applying any fertiliser.

Another way to help reduce bitterness is to give the plants some shade and adequate moisture over the summer months. Winter salad greens could use some shelter from cold frosts.

Because we want the greens at their baby stage, sow a small area at a time. Dig, level and thoroughly water this patch, then sow the seeds thinly, cover with just a centimetre of sifted soil and press it down with a board. If the topsoil is dry, it can be gently dampened down, and from there on keep the ground moist but not wet. Some sow seeds by the row, only sowing what is required for a week or a fortnight's harvesting. This is by far the best method and you soon get into the rhythm of regular sowing and harvesting.

The sugar content in lettuces is at its highest early in the morning, so that's

Smart dressing

The ratio of **6 tsp of olive oil** to **1 tsp of vinegar** is pretty much spot-on for dressing today's greens. The old icebergs used to be clothed in vinaigrettes made with one part vinegar to three parts oil and whatever fresh herbs were available, but now that we are growing a selection of greens, it would be a shame to mask their individual tastes with a heavy dressing. Cooks are also spoilt with a wide selection of oils so good that it would be a sacrilege to adulterate them with sharp vinegars and strong herbs. Really good quality oils are best used on their own — better still, left on the table for people to dress their own greens. That way there is no risk of the tender leaves turning limp and lifeless. Young shoots are very fragile and should neither be dressed too heavily nor tossed too energetically. If the greens have reached their teenage stage, they may need a little sweetening to offset the bitterness. A dressing made with raspberry vinegar and a little redcurrant jelly is a useful foil to the sharp russet radicchio leaves over winter.

when they should be picked. Either snip individual leaves or cut back the whole plant. If you cut the plant back to 2 cm it may well come again. The second wave of leaves is never as sweet as the first harvest, and for that reason many gardening cooks prefer to lift the whole plant after its first flush and replace it with more seed. This makes for quite intensive cultivation in perhaps the only square metre patch, so it is a good idea to repay the soil for all its hard work with regular feeds of liquid fertiliser.

Choices of plants abound and no decent salad would be seen dead these days without at least three or four different leaves. Some salad herbs stand up to the heat better than others. The loose-leafed 'Red and Green Salad Bowl' lettuces don't mind hot weather and provide good bulk for salads. 'Royal Oak Leaf' is an improvement on the ordinary oak-leaf and won't turn sour in the heat. Nor will 'Green Ice' with its crisp, glossy green leaves. 'Lovina' adds another dimension with its bronzed red ruffled leaves. The green miniature cos lettuces 'Little Gem' and 'Diamond Gem' make perfect summer eating. The deep-red leaved cos, 'Rouge d'Hiver' and 'Rosalita', prefer lower temperatures. There's a good range of greens at their salad best during the in-between times when the weather is neither too hot nor too cold. Lettuces for sowing in spring, early summer and early autumn include 'Black Seeded Simpson' with frilly light-green leaves, the dark green 'Loma', and the rosy-coloured butterhead, 'Sangria'. Another butterhead, 'Merveille des Quatre Saisons', has dark reddish-brown outer leaves and a bright-green centre and, despite its name, is better in the between seasons as it will bolt in hot weather.

Of all the Asian brassicas, mizuna is the most useful in a salad. A good doer in most climates, mizuna retains its fresh mild taste over summer as long as it is kept watered and will even survive frosts in winter. Very generous with its bright green feathery leaves, it's a familiar mainstay of commercial salad mixes. A close relation, mibuna, has a slightly stronger flavour and is less tolerant of temperature extremes. Shapely plants, they form an attractive clump that lends itself well to life in a container, always a factor for those with limited garden space. To harvest, simply snip leaves as required from the outside in.

Leaves for less clement days include miner's lettuce (winter purslane) and corn salad (lamb's lettuce or mache). Both are small, green and have a mild taste that give sweet relief to the other more bitter 'greens' available in winter.

ENDIVE cultivation has been a bitterly disappointing experience for some

Radicchio *'Guilio'*.

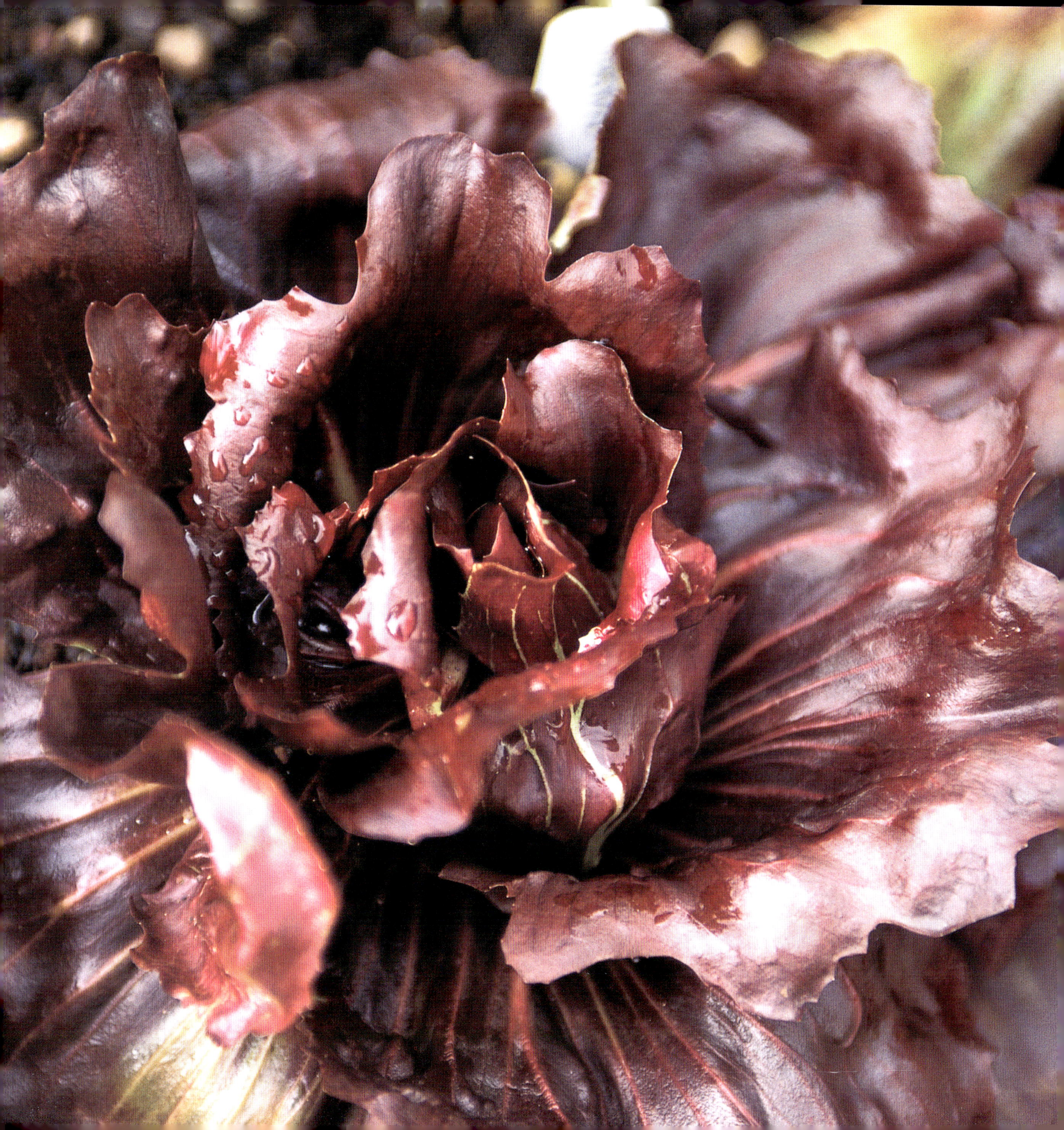

gardeners, but it's worth persevering with. The leaves look fantastic, elegantly long and ruffled, dark green on the outside and yellowy white in the centre. For all its frilliness, endive can stand up to whatever weather summer or winter decides to unleash (although some have been known to turn to mush in a particularly rainy winter). The leaves can be very bitter and are supposed to come right with blanching. Just space the plants fairly close together in the garden and hold them closed tight with a piece of string so that the inner leaves never see the light of day. Regular watering over summer is also meant to ease the bitterness. Many gardeners may be encouraged to try them again, now that there are self-blanching varieties available. 'Toujours Blanche' and 'Saint Laurent' sound promising.

There is some confusion with the names of these more bitter salad plants. The frilly-leafed plant we call endive is referred to as chicory by the French and, just to be difficult, they call the forced chicories, like witloof, endives. Witloof is cultivated under a cloak of total darkness and, to my mind, is easier procured from the shops, where they are displayed, wrapped in blue-coloured paper in case bitterness creeps in even at this late stage. The white leaves make wonderful 'boats' to hold tasty winter salad mixes.

RADICCHIOS are also part of the chicory family. These days the term 'radicchio' seems to cover both the red and green-leafed chicories that come into their own over winter. They form beautiful rosettes of leaves, some flushed deep red, others a cool green, or flushed and freckled, so they make quite a picture both in the garden and on the table. These perennials send down long taproots to secure themselves a place in the garden for years. The red-tinged leaves lose much of their bitterness over the colder months. The inner leaves are more palatable than the outer ones, which, if they look far too pretty to discard, can be used as a decoration to line platters or bowls. The green-leafed chicories retain their bitter taste and are best used very, very young. The hearts of 'Red Verona' and 'Treviso Early' are delicious grilled. Cut the hearts in half or quarters and fry in a little butter or oil for a couple of minutes. Place in an oven dish, sprinkle with grated parmesan or crumbled blue cheese and grill.

SPINACH offers salad makers crisp bright-green leaves which remain attractive after preparation. (To watch whole bunches wilt to perhaps a cupful when cooked is disappointing, to say the least.) Spinach prefers the cooler season with its shorter days, as the plant tends to bolt when the days are long. The seeds germinate poorly in warm soil and those destined for autumn or winter tables would benefit from a week's sojourn in the fridge before going into the ground. The best for salads are the smooth leaved rather than the crinkly, savoy-leaved varieties. 'Cascade' and 'Samson' are good. You can pick the leaves as you want them; try not to strip a plant in one session. Whole young leaves sit well in a bowl and will stand up to quite strong dressings or hot additions such as chicken livers or mushrooms, sautéed in a little butter or oil and chopped tarragon and finished with a good squeeze of lemon juice. Rashers of bacon, grilled and chopped, also go well with the leaves.

ROCKET is best grown in spring and autumn, as it tends to bolt and go to seed in high summer. Its leaves have a nutty flavour that blends nicely with more delicate lettuces. As the leaves age they develop a peppery taste. These two flavours make them a useful leaf to pop between the sheets of a cheese or roast-beef sandwich. Rocket can also be added with other herbs, or used alone in a pesto sauce. A handful can be thrown into the pot of pasta towards the end of its cooking, the lot then drained and tossed in a little olive oil and served topped with shavings of parmesan cheese. Cook a steak to your liking and serve it on a bed of rocket leaves tossed with a dressing of a spoonful each of good olive oil and red-wine vinegar mixed with a little lemon juice.

SALAD BURNET, with its graceful stems of lacy leaves and generally elegant appearance, puts a nice finishing touch on many dishes. A single stem perfects a bowl of vichyssoise and adds a judicious measure of colour to a pale chicken or fish dish, without stealing the show. A few stems dress up a plate of sandwiches with a minimum of fuss. The leaves have a cucumber taste that makes them a contender for sandwich fillings and, of course, salads. The flavour is more pronounced in younger leaves and is at its best in late spring before the free-seeding plant flowers.

Rocket is a wonderful complement to lettuce.

BLOOMS TO CONSUME

A few flowers scattered through food can transform the everyday into the blooming wonderful. However, as with most embellishments, just a little is enough. Less is best.

Frosting flowers

Beat an egg white until it is just beginning to go frothy. With a paintbrush, gently paint this egg over the completely dry petals of your selected flowers.

Dust caster sugar over the flower and place it on a rack to dry. This may take up to a couple of days, depending on the humidity. To speed up the process you can place the sugared flowers in the oven at a very low temperature with the door ajar for a few hours. Store the dried flowers in airtight jars. Flowers that crystallise well are rose petals, primroses, polyanthus, violas, japonica and, of course, violets.

While many flowers are edible, some taste a whole lot better than others, and because some are deadly poisonous, it's safer and more palatable to play around with only the well-known edible ones. First, correctly identify the flower, then smell it to get an indication of its taste — and eat only flowers that you are absolutely sure have not been sprayed. Always rinse them thoroughly, but gently, to get rid of any insects.

The flowers of herbs often have a milder version of the same flavour as the leaves. The little blooms of thyme, rosemary, sage, oreganum and dill will all give a pretty touch to soups, sauces and pastas. A scattering of pink chive flowers looks great on an omelette or on top of salad greens. Larger starry blue borage flowers have a great impact on a salad; just pinch out the hairy centre before adding them.

More striking still are the bright oranges, reds and yellows of nasturtium flowers. These taste slightly peppery, like watercress. The lily-pad-like leaves are also edible and have a stronger peppery taste. Nasturtiums are so easy to grow they have a hard time being taken seriously. They will flower continuously from spring through to autumn in the poorest of soils and thrive in dry conditions. There are also pretty trailing varieties that are excellent in hanging baskets. Although annuals, nasturtiums self-seed freely. There are single, semi-double and double varieties to choose from. I think the single blooms look best in the salads — the others are too frilly for food. 'Empress of India' is a dwarf non-trailing variety with deep velvety orange-red flowers and red flushed leaves which would add a certain drama to the salad plate.

An even more cheerful colour comes from the bright orange blooms of the old-fashioned marigold (*Calendula officinalis*). The flowers were known as 'poor man's saffron', having a vaguely similar musty, peppery taste (to saffron, not to poor men) and because the petals bestow the same glowing colour to food as the valuable crocus stamens of saffron, which cost more per ounce than gold. Calendulas are still used today as a natural colouring for butter and margarine. The petals are just the thing to strew over a dish of curry, which might otherwise look deadly dull and unappealing. The plant will be more than generous with its blooms for years in a well-drained soil, in sun or light shade.

Violas taste like sweet baby lettuce and look quite at home in a bowl of salad greens. The largest of the viola family are referred to as pansies; violas are smaller and johnny-jump-ups or heartsease, *Viola tricolor*, are smaller again. Most

The art of tea

There should be at least one occasion each summer that calls for afternoon tea on the lawn. Such events serve as a marvellous excuse to bring out the finery: the embroidered tablecloths and those matching cups, saucers and side plates that have been gathering dust in the back of a cupboard ever since they were left to you by a kind great-aunt. It is also time to flick through the same great-aunt's recipe books to find nostalgic fare that can be prettied up with a sprinkling of fresh flowers from the garden. For recipes see page 164.

self-sow with the greatest of ease. The diminutive heartsease are especially useful in the kitchen as they grow in such abundance in moderate temperatures that you can use them just as exuberantly in green and fruit salads without the slightest pang of guilt for denuding the garden. Violas with subtle shadings give a delicate touch to desserts and cakes, either fresh or frosted. Frosting flowers is a simple process, but it requires a little patience. Cakes, biscuits and creams can be transformed into fragrant delights by using flower-scented sugars. These are made by layering fresh dry blooms and ordinary sugar in a jar and allowing the fragrance to diffuse before removing the spent blooms.

Of all the edible flowers, violets are a stand-out favourite. They're such a glorious blue and their scent is to die for, but their best attribute is probably their timing, for they arrive hard on the heels of the bleakest weather. They are easy to grow from seed and will self-sow readily. One of the most fragrant is the original, *Viola odorata*. Growing well in the shade, violets will produce more flowers if allowed a little sun and where they are not overcrowded, so it helps to divide and replant them every other autumn. They like a slightly acid soil with plenty of compost and a good feed of blood and bone twice a year. There is no better adornment than a solitary bloom sitting on top of a little pot of lemon or chocolate cream. What's more, it will leave a lovely taste in your mouth.

The Kitchen Garden's Comeback

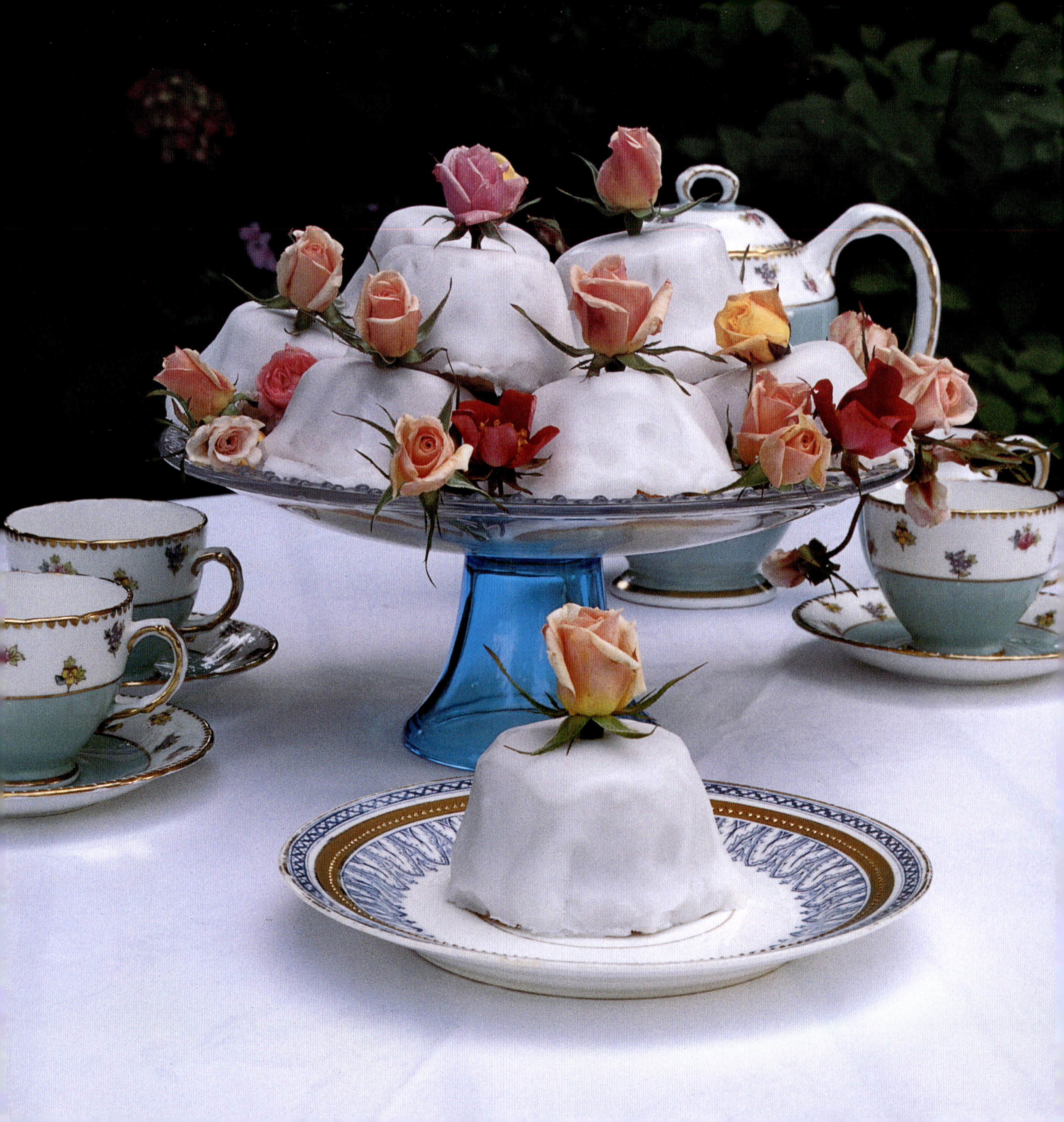

Romancing the Rose

Maggie: How is it possible to select a favourite flower from the millions of outstanding candidates? But having said that, for all-round performance what's not to like about the rose? While I'm happy to wander among a bed of fragrant rose blossoms or to talk with the likes of Sam McGredy or David Austin about their life-long work, Mary, with her ever adventurous palette, has an all-consuming interest in the fragrant flowers.

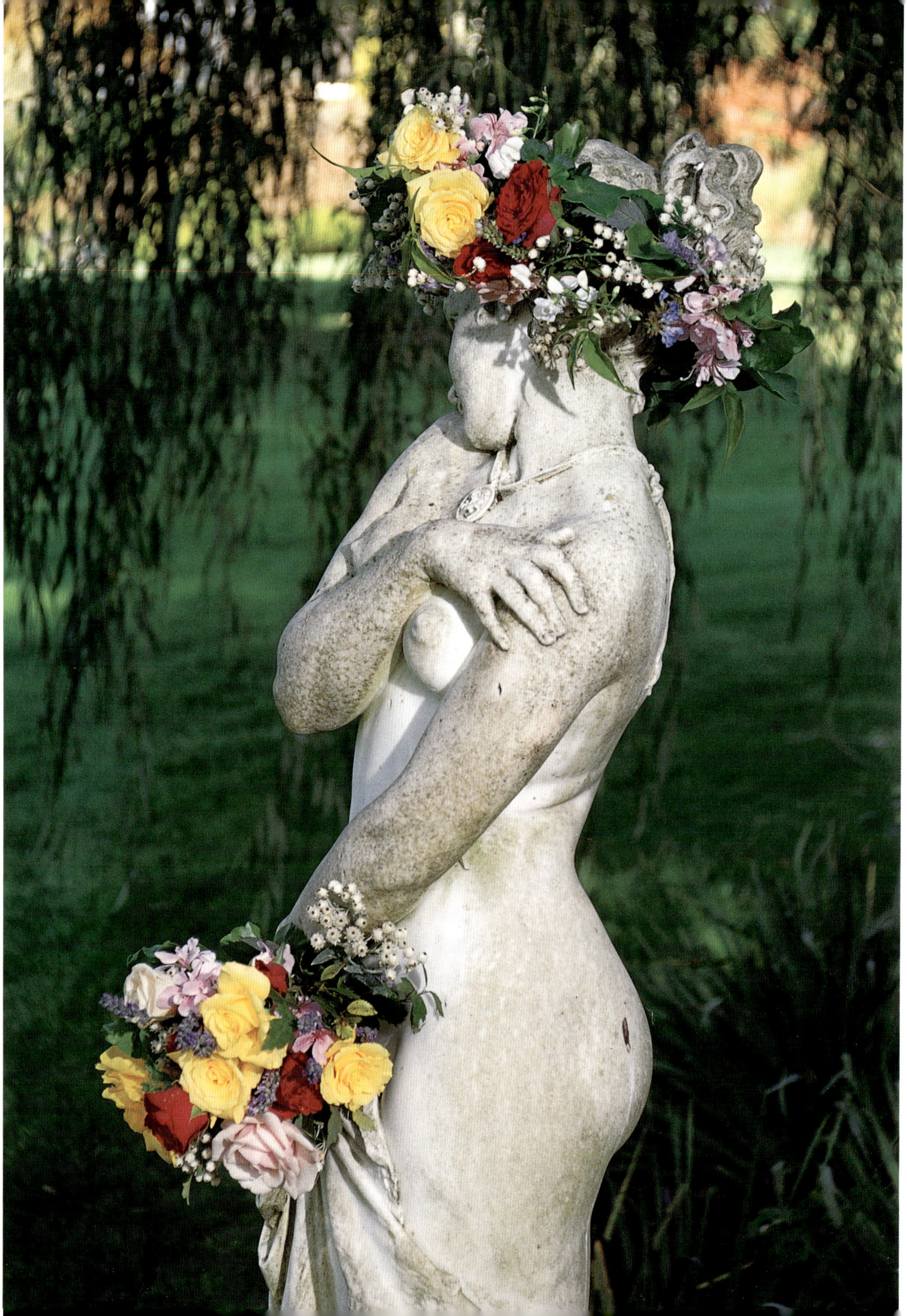

THE EDIBLE ROSE

The rose was called the 'queen of flowers' by the Greek poet Sappho and subsequent poets, artists and lovers have been drawn to them. This ancient flower seems to have been especially designed to captivate our senses. Blooms of all shapes and sizes are brushed from a palette of princely crimsons, blood reds, lolly pinks, sunny yellows, delicate white and creams — some touched with just that hint of coffee, beige or green.

Selecting a rose can be like choosing a shade of paint without the test pots, running the risk of discovering that, as the great Gertrude Jekyll put it in *Home and Garden*, 'only a few of these will be in friendly accordance and a good number will be in deadly disaccord'. Catalogues with good photographs help, but I recommend biding your time until the plants are flowering before making your final choice.

The trick is to be generous with roses. They look all the better in a crowd (although the single stem may still hold its place on the breakfast tray, depending, of course, on who put it there). The great joy to the gardener is the reassuring knowledge that the more you pick, the more your rose will bloom, as it only flowers on new growth. (Apart from once-flowerers, that is, but more about them later.) It's a licence to be extravagant.

It can also lead to the kitchen where you can use the rose's colour and perfume in all sorts of ways, right down to the food and drinks. A cake iced very plainly will become gorgeous when studded with little buds of 'Cécile Brünner'. Pitchers of home-made lemonade will be transformed by the addition of a few colourful petals. Ice cubes can be jewelled with small bright pink or red petals. (Include the blue of borage flowers to really set them off.) You could make your own wine cooler by freezing long-stemmed buds in a cylindrical shape. It will look like a vase shrouded in mist, cooling both the eye and the wine.

Bowls of cherries, strawberries, raspberries and plums will look all the more sumptuous with a scattering of red rose petals such as 'Dublin Bay' or 'Waikato'. Ramekins of strawberry cream can be served on a bed of 'Strawberry Ice' petals. (There's also a rose called 'Raspberry Ice'.) Decorating with roses needn't be fiddly. The romance of summer can be captured simply by camouflaging an old garden table with a billowing cloth that falls to the ground and strewing a handful

Opposite: A statue of Aphrodite by Donato Barcaglia, Milan, 1879.

Previous spread: The base for these delicate rose cakes is the Victoria Sandwich recipe on page 164.

Rose vinegar

Roses also give their own tang to this special vinegar. (When making floral vinegars use a good white wine vinegar as others could kill the subtle variations.)

Place **a handful of rose petals** and **½ cup of raspberries** in a bowl and crush ever so slightly. Pour over **4 cups white wine vinegar** and stir well. Ladle into a suitable jar and seal. Leave the jar in a warm, sunny place for a week or two. Using a very fine sieve, or muslin, strain the mixture into bottles and seal. Store on a cool, dark shelf to preserve the flavour. A spoonful or two of this vinegar can be added to homemade mayonnaise to make a particularly good accompaniment for chicken. It will also give fruit salad a certain piquancy.

Crystallised petals

As with all edible flowers, rose petals can be crystallised by the method described on page 126. Once dry, these sugar-coated petals will last a couple of days. They will keep for up to two months if they are brushed with a mixture of **1 tsp gum arabic** (from the chemist shop) dissolved in **25 ml vodka**, then coated with **sugar** and left to dry. They can be stored in an airtight container. The petals are crunchy and soft and sugary at the same time. Frosted rose petals are used to garnish cakes and other sweet treats. Fresh petals would serve as well if not better. They'd certainly be more colourful.

---

of petals over the top. But, be warned, if you take your cooking seriously, you may be upstaged. I remember once serving delicious zucchini fritters on a large platter covered with pink and red rose petals. They drew more praise than the food itself.

The rose can also impart its distinct colour and perfume into food. Fragrance becomes flavour in all manner of predominantly sweet dishes. (Although rosewater is used in some savoury Middle Eastern cooking.) First of all, it is important to smell the bloom. The headier the perfume, the stronger the taste. It may help to wander around the garden taking little nibbles to become familiar with varietal tastes, though it would probably pay to do this when the neighbours aren't looking. For obvious reasons, eat only flowers that have not been sprayed. This also rules out dining on a bunch from the florist. As a loose rule, some older varieties tend to have more flavour than newer hybrids. Rugosas and damasks are particularly good. Deep reds, then strong pinks, are the better colours to choose.

Like flowers for the vase, the blooms should be picked early in the morning before the sun's rays have touched them. Always rinse the flowers thoroughly, but gently, in cold water to get rid of any insects. Dry them carefully, then trim off the white parts at the base of the petals as these tend to have a bitter taste. You can now preserve the delectable rose flavour in the form of rose water, jam, sugar or vinegar. You could even make your own attar of roses, which is actually the minuscule oil secretion from the flower and worth more than gold to the perfume industry. The best, incidentally, comes from Turkey.

Some flowers with distinctive scents transfer their perfume to sugar with the greatest of ease. These include lavender, violets, various geranium leaves and, of course, roses. To make rose sugar, arrange dry petals between layers of ordinary sugar in a jar. Put the lid on and leave in a sunny spot for a week or two. Remove the petals and use the sugar to flavour cakes or delicate cream fillings for fruit flans. This sugar makes wonderful meringues — you could even add a wisp of food colouring to give them a pink blush. Whipped cream sweetened with this special sugar will set off a dish of summer berries.

Rose petal sorbet is a light refreshing way to round off a lovely summer's evening (see page 133 for this recipe).

A table set out in a shady part of the veranda with tall glasses and a jug of rose-petal punch is a perfect invitation for late-afternoon drinks. Your elixir should be started a few hours beforehand by putting a good handful of strongly scented petals into a bowl. Sprinkle a tablespoon of sugar over the petals (you could use your flavoured sugar here), then add the juice of a lemon and a bottle of sparkling mineral water, and chill. Later, when you are ready, strain the liquid into a large serving jug and pour in a bottle of cool white wine.

If you have left your roses untrimmed until autumn, you will have a stunning display of hips (or heps) to revive interest in the now-depleted garden. These can be used to great effect in glowing arrangements with leaves, grasses, seedheads, berries and the late blooms of dahlias, daisies, zinnias, marigolds and roses. Vibrant yellow and reds will dance with golds, greens and browns to warm up the home just as the days are getting colder.

Rugosas provide the best hips. They are large and round and look like cherries. They're more tomato in colour than orange. Hips contain more vitamin C than oranges and lemons. In many old cookbooks you will find recipes for rosehip cordials, chutneys and jams. Such uses for the shiny fruits enjoyed quite a revival in Europe during World War II when shipments of citrus weren't top priority. These concoctions tend to be a bit cloying — reminiscent of sweet medicine. There is one, though, for rosehip jelly, which can easily find a place on our shelves.

Rosehip jelly

Gather a bundle of rosehips. Wash them well and rub them over to remove the spines. Put the hips in a pot, just cover with water and boil, with the lid on, until they're very soft. This will take about an hour. Strain through a fine sieve or muslin, preferably overnight. The next day, measure the liquid and return to the pot, adding 1 cup of sugar to each cup of liquid. Stir to dissolve the sugar, then bring the mixture to the boil. Settle the syrup to a simmer, with the lid off, until setting point has been reached (i.e. when a drop tested forms a few wrinkles on a cold saucer), then put into sterilised jars and seal. Hips don't seem to contain as much natural pectin as, say, crabapples, so you may wish to add some commercial pectin, following the maker's instructions.

This jelly will liven up the morning croissant, make a rich glaze over fruit tarts and is surprisingly good with cold meats.

Rose petal sorbet

Make a sugar syrup by dissolving **1 cup sugar** in **1 cup water** over a medium heat. Bring this to the boil and simmer for 5 minutes. Let cool. In a blender put clean (unsprayed) **petals of 4 roses** and **1 cup white wine**, and process for a few seconds.

Add juice of **1 large lemon** and **sugar syrup** and process a few seconds more.

Pour mixture into a shallow container and freeze until mushy. Take out and beat well, then return to the freezer until needed. Serve spoonfuls in delicate long-stemmed glasses with some fresh rose petals scattered round each base. Serves 6.

WAR OF THE ROSES

I know you're not supposed to have favourites, but how could you not count rose breeder Sam McGredy as one of the great characters of the gardening world?

A fourth generation rose breeder, Dr Sam McGredy OBN, CBE has won so many honours it would take pages to list them all. His enduring legacy and greatest triumphs are the thousands of outstanding roses he's bred. Roses that are household names worldwide: 'Dublin Bay', 'Bantry Bay', 'Aotearoa', 'Sexy Rexy', 'Olympiad' . . .

Born and bred in Portadown, Sam McGredy came to live in New Zealand in 1972 to escape the sectarian violence in Northern Ireland. He was moved to tears when he first saw a haka, and, as an ardent rugby follower and appreciator of decent wines, he embraced the Kiwi way of life like a zealot. He made an immediate impact on New Zealand horticulture by convincing the government to introduce patents on plants, enabling breeders to charge a royalty on their hybrids and finally make a decent living.

Sam bred the only flower my father ever grew. When I was fortunate enough to have a McGredy rose named after me, Dad went out and colonised a corner of Mum's garden with his three bushes. He felt it was a great honour for our family.

It is, of course, a singular honour, but having a rose named after you has its moments. My garden show colleagues had a lot of mileage from one grower's description of the ideal growing conditions for the 'Maggie Barry' rose: 'A poor performer in a cold bed; happiest when laid up against a warm wall . . .'

I've observed with some pride my namesake rose flowering magnificently in gardens I've filmed all over New Zealand, and although she has better than average disease resistance and big thorns, what can you say when she's struck down by bugs or ravaged by possums? The growing habits and virtues of specific McGredy roses can be found in many other books, suffice it to say, no garden should be without at least one.

It may surprise some to learn that Sam McGredy doesn't list gardening as his favourite pastime; he says he'd rather shop till he drops. When it comes to 'retail therapy', Sam's not the sort of man to wait in the car. He shops for his

Maggie with (top) Sam McGredy, New Zealand's own rose breeder; and (above) David Austin, admiring one of his hundred or so hybrids.

whole family, spending entire days moving purposefully from shop to shop before buying up large. He has earned his place and deserves due recognition as an international authority on great malls of the world.

A rare man indeed. As is David Austin, the breeder of 'new old roses'.

For those who think a rose is a rose is a rose: be warned, you could be entering dangerous territory. In some circles it's politically correct to grow only the 'old-fashioned' roses, and admitting to liking a rose bred after, say, the 1930s, is to risk the odium of one's peers. Devotees of the 'modern' scoff at the perceived sentimentality, dismissing the old bloomers as riddled with disease and of inferior staying power. The War of the Roses rages on and on, but for those inclined to compromise, the 'English Rose' range has narrowed the great divide.

The 'English Rose' series that David Austin began in the 1960s when he bred 'Constance Spry' now has around 100 roses, all of which possess the characteristic old-fashioned look with the vigour and repeat-flowering ability of the modern roses — the good looks and perfume without the bad habits.

Not a colourful character in the dynastic Sam McGredy tradition, David Austin is a quietly spoken Shropshire farmer who only became a rose breeder through a twist of fate. During World War II, the family farm was requisitioned for an airfield and by the time the Air Force was finished there was so little workable land it was no longer an economic farming unit. The change in circumstances gave the young David the opportunity to develop what had only been a hobby into a commercial rose-breeding business.

Like many breeders, David Austin is often approached by organisations or individuals who request he names a rose after them. So we have 'Abraham Darby', one of the founders of the Industrial Revolution, named on behalf of the Ironbridge Museum Trust, and 'Ambrose Rose', named at the request of the BBC for the ever-popular radio soap 'The Archers'. Even a couple of dress designers have been immortalised: David and Elizabeth Emmanuel will be remembered not only for Princess Diana's wedding dress but also for their voluptuous pink rose.

According to David Austin, 'Graham Thomas' is one of the most sought after of all the English Roses. Named after rosarian and mainstay of Britain's National Trust gardens, Graham Stuart Thomas, the fragrant yellow blooms produce throughout the summer. Having 'Iceberg' as a parent probably accounts for its very vigorous and free-flowering habit, and if you want to keep 'G.T.' in a bush shape, you'll need to prune back the long climbing shoots ruthlessly. The Austin roses seem to thrive Down Under; when he visited New Zealand in 1994, David Austin said he'd never seen his roses grow as large as they do here. The good performance probably has a lot to do with our mild climate, but let's not forget the skill factor: we Kiwi gardeners are obviously doing something right.

ROSES IN WINTER

In the midst of the winter gloom there is a hardy breed called hellebores that is both willing and able to produce the most delightful flowers just when we need them most. Their leaves are elegant, but understated, and their delicate, saucer-shaped flowers don't shout at you. Rather, they whisper in soft pastels — from milky white to pale green, to peach and every shade of pink to burgundy.

They give life to flower and shrub borders that lack lustre in the middle of the year. But in the first place they are woodlanders and are at their best in drifts underneath trees. Although a hellebore may be grown as a single specimen, they prefer to be in groups as a groundcover, growing to only about 60 cm.

Despite their genteel appearance, hellebores are tough — and the good news for those in southern climes is that they are totally frost proof. You may go out after a particularly cold night to find them collapsed to the ground, but they will be standing straight and proud by midday.

Hellebores are easy to grow. The less they are disturbed, the more they will bloom, so go easy with the hoe. They tolerate most soil, preferring it moist and neither sweet nor sour. They like shade in summer and some sun in winter. Their ideal resting-place is underneath deciduous trees — when the leaves fall they provide a covering of mulch for the plants.

The only other attention is tidying up their foliage at flowering time. Cut the dead leaves back to soil level. This allows a better view of the emerging flowers. Leave some flowers until they fade and set seeds, remembering self-sown seedlings provide some very interesting variations in colour. Hellebores in garden borders are best divided every four to five years. In the woodland setting you can leave them undisturbed. Left to their own devices, they will volunteer plenty of good seedlings.

Ilnacullin

One of the many virtues of the pastime of gardening is that even though the excitement happens in our own backyards, it is a very international and outward-looking pursuit. Italian, Spanish, French and English design styles all unashamedly 'borrow' from each other. Often the European complements and accommodates the oriental and, of course, there's plenty of 'cross pollination' and antipodean influence when it comes to the planting.

Since the garden show began on television in 1992, we've deliberately featured a broad range of gardening styles and personalities. In addition to the hundreds of excellent New Zealand gardens, we've filmed properties in Australia, the Pacific Islands, England and Ireland. One of the most eclectic of the European gardens we visited was Ilnacullin, owned by an Englishman, located in Ireland, designed in the Italian style and relying predominantly on Southern Hemisphere plants.

The island garden of Ilnacullin is located in the sheltered harbour of Glengariff, Bantry Bay, in County Cork, southwest Ireland. The warming influence of the Gulf Stream makes for an almost subtropical climate, troubled by only a few light winter frosts and blessed with a high annual rainfall of around 1855 mm. These mild, moist conditions are ideal for growing an extensive range of New Zealand plants and Ilnacullin is justly famous for its rich diversity of perennials and shrubs.

But it wasn't always the case. When businessman Annan Bryce bought the 15-hectare island from the War Office around the turn of the century, Illnacullin, the island of Holly, was an inhospitable rocky outcrop. Its only building was a solitary Martello tower, the first of many fortified observation points built around the coast, a legacy of the English paranoia over a Napoleonic invasion of Ireland.

Annan Bryce was an enthusiastic plantsman and he commissioned one of the great British architects of the day, Herold Peto, to design a garden intended to be the exotic setting for a grand mansion. Sadly, Bryce lost his fortune in the Russian Revolution, so the house was never built, but the garden has endured as a Peto masterpiece and is now considered one of Ireland's finest public gardens.

Making a garden on Ilnacullin was never going to be easy. For a start, there was no soil on the island, so thousands of tonnes of it, plus all the English stone used, had to be shipped in. Today, the gardeners waste nothing and try to be as self-sufficient as possible, recycling weeds and plants and plenty of seaweed into a rich compost.

Harold Peto was a disciple of the Italian design style and Ilnacullin shows the effects of his love affair with things Italian. At the heart of the garden are two buildings: the casita (teahouse), and the temple made from Carrara and Connemara marble. They're complemented by lush Southern Hemisphere mainstays like manuka, hebe, clematis, eucalyptus and cabbage trees. The oriental influence blends in, too, with a collection of rare bonsai conifers, some thought to be 300 years old. Used as features, they're set in paved frames around the sunken pond.

Ilnacullin is open to the public for eight months of the year and some 86,000 visitors, many equipped with picnic baskets, take the ten-minute boat ride to enjoy a day out in this intimate Irish garden.

The white form (this page) and pink form (opposite) of Helleborus orientalis.

There are three main species of hellebores available. The first to flower is *H. niger*, the winter rose (known as the Christmas rose in the Northern Hemisphere). It has dark leaves and white flowers that flush pink as they age. There is a New Zealand-raised cultivar, 'White Magic', which is a strong, sturdy plant and which does better in warm climates, where it seems to be more vigorous than *H. niger*.

Next to flower is *H. lividus* subsp. *corsicus* (now known as *H. argutifolius*). This is a slightly taller, more shrubby plant. Its pale green, bell-shaped flowers appear early in winter and will last until spring. True to its Mediterranean origins, it likes a little more sun than other hellebores. It doesn't bloom until its second year, but this is well worth waiting for. There's now a taller hybrid, *H.* x *sternii*, which has silvered leaves, beetroot-red stems and copious, quite large flowers, pale green and wine backed.

H. orientalis, the Lenten rose, is perhaps the most well-known hellebore.

This is the one that comes in all the shades of pink. The flowers are often tinged with green or speckled with purple inside. *H. orientalis* will tolerate quite deep shade. It flowers from early spring. In time it will form large clumps, making a good groundcover and keeping down the weeds as it goes. It hybridises very freely, so be prepared for new varieties popping up each year. It was once thought it could cure insanity — but don't go rushing into the woods, as all parts of the hellebore are poisonous.

Many gardeners will brave the elements during winter to satisfy the urge to pick something from the garden to bring inside. Hellebores are notoriously tricky as cut flowers. You can pick the heads quite young and float them in a shallow dish of water. For longer-stemmed displays, wait for the petals to age and turn papery. Prick the stems in several places to release any trapped air, and put them in water as soon as possible after pricking.

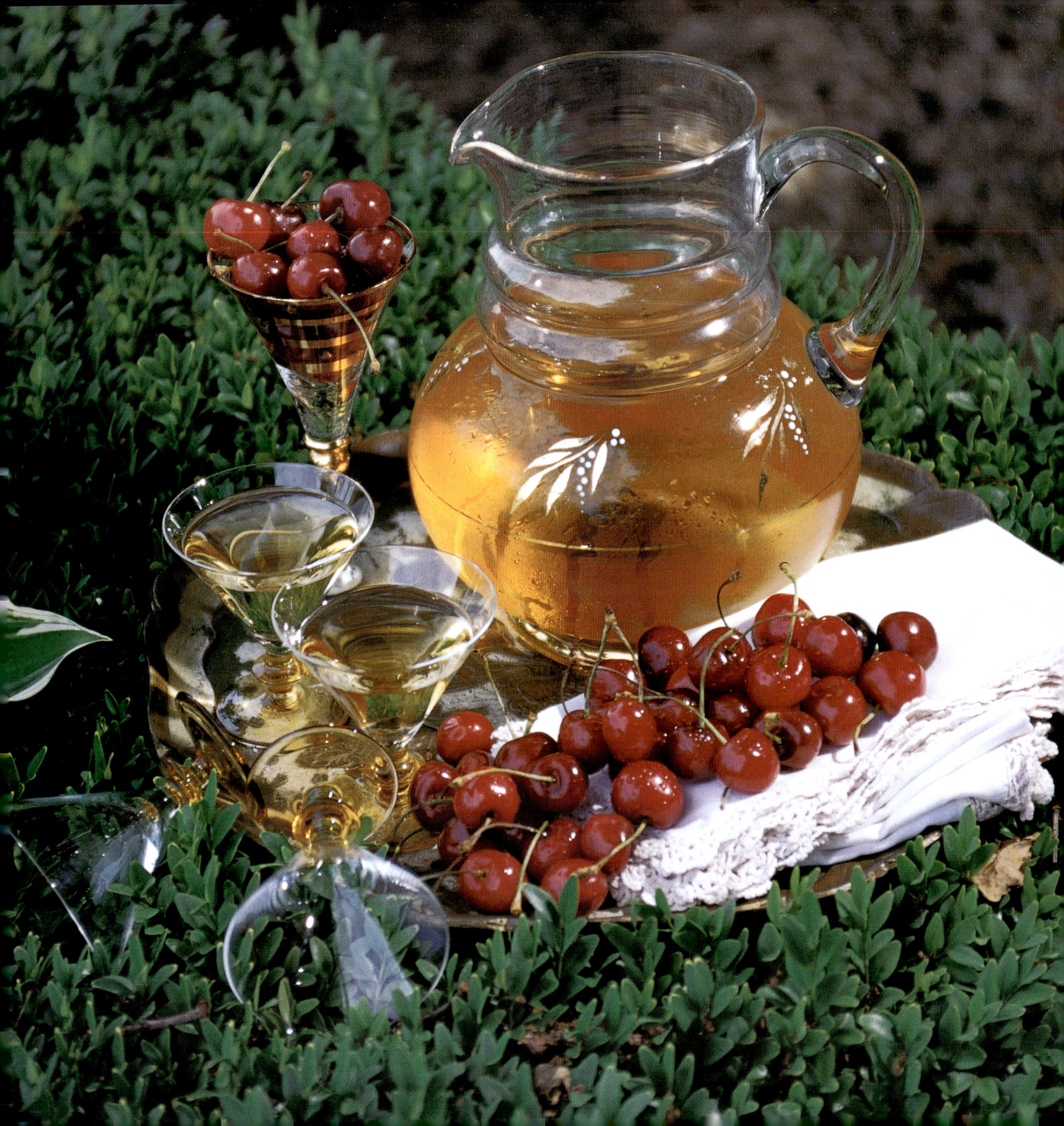

Pleasure Grounds

Mary: Once your garden has those special features that set it apart from the rest and make it your own, then it's time to sit back and enjoy sharing it with your friends. Both Maggie and I share a vision of a relaxing meal in a garden setting at the end of a long day tending our plants. I've brought together a few ideas for New Zealand entertaining to enhance the evening, inspired by Maggie's account of her trip to Vaux-le-Vicomte and her unswerving devotion to gardens by moonlight.

MOONLIGHTING

More than 2000 years ago Persian gardeners were aware of the value of the courtyard. They built cool havens to give respite from the incessant sun and these extensions of the house were pleasurable oases filled with the most glorious perfumes. The Persians called these fragrant retreats 'pairidaeza', the origin of a word at the top of many gardeners' wish list: 'paradise'.

By the time many of us get out into the garden, the plants that have been bathing in the sun all day are but a blur and any subtle or dramatic colour combinations are completely lost to the darkness. As one sense fades with the light, it's replaced with a heightened awareness of fragrance and, as the Persians discovered, there are hundreds of plants that excel in the evening.

NIGHT-SCENTED STOCK'S (*Matthiola longipetala* subsp. *bicornus*) pinkish flowers are nothing much to look at, but at night their scent is sweet and strong. Growing 50 cm high in a sunny, moist but well-drained location, it's a shortlived perennial, most often treated as an annual. Sow the seeds where you want them to grow and if that's in a container, make it a large one so the effect of its night scent is all the more spectacular. From the same family is the old-fashioned border plant sweet rocket (*Hesperis matrionalis*), which has clusters of white or pale purple flowers from mid-spring to midsummer. Its blooms are particularly fragrant on humid nights.

The COMMON EVENING PRIMROSE (*Oenothera biennis*) has an uncommonly good lemon scent well suited to its yellow flowers, which open on summer evenings. Quickly attaining a metre in height, it's drought tolerant, thriving in a warm sunny spot. The fragrant yellow flowers of *O. odorata* turn red with age, possibly to match the reddish flush of their stems. *O. speciosa* grows into clumps about 50 cm high and requires full sun and average soil. The pink-tinted white flowers appear in their masses over an extraordinarily long period, from late October until April. 'Prima Donna' is a shorter version with a sprawling habit; it will quite happily spread over a sunny bank. This is another perennial with a short but very sweet life, seeding freely and producing many offsets which can be lifted and replanted over winter.

TOBACCO PLANTS (*Nicotiana* spp.) used to shyly wait until dark before opening their flowers and releasing their scent into the night air. More recent strains

The light colours and distinctive shapes of Verbascum *(below) and* Nicotiana *(opposite) make them ideal candidates for the moonlight garden.*

remain open all day but often, sadly, at the expense of their fragrance. The sweetest scents come from the palest forms — the creamy whites and the comely greeny whites. Excellent in light shade, they'll also cope with full sun in a moist but well-drained soil, flowering from early summer until the first frosts. Again, these are often treated as an annual but if they are cut back for winter they can shoot away again in spring. The stately *N. sylvestris* rises to an imposing 1.5 metres in even the shadiest sites. Its lush green foliage and long trumpet flowers put on a great show during the day and the flowers give off a gentle fragrance by night.

DAPHNES will enliven the cold winter air for anyone mad enough to join them and of course their fragrant blooms are always welcome inside. *Daphne odora* will start flowering early in winter. 'Rubra' forms a spreading shrub, its flowers flushed red on the outside, and its long stems make for good picking for the vase. 'Leucanthe' has a more upright habit with pink and white blooms and, unsurprisingly, 'Alba' has white flowers. *D. bholua* is also an upright plant with pale flowers that arrive in the middle of winter and stay for months. There is also deciduous *D. mezereum* that puts on a good show of bright red berries once its very fragrant lilac, pink or white blooms are spent. Beware the berries, which bring cheer but are poisonous.

Cherry pie

Warmer parts of the country can enjoy the delicious almondy smells of heliotrope, (*Heliotropium arborescens*) or cherry pie. Its odd nickname recalls earlier times when cherries were preserved in an almond-flavoured brandy. This evergreen bears its fragrant purple-lavender flowers from late spring to autumn. The paler flowers have a stronger scent. In less clement climes it can be treated as an annual and would make a splendid carpet for less redolent standards, so you can still enjoy its heady perfume by an open door on a summer's night. Hard pruning after flowering will keep it shapely.

NIGHT-SCENTED JESSAMINE (*Cestrum nocturnum*), sometimes called queen of the night or, more correctly, lady of the night, is hard to improve on for its nocturnal charms. (Apparently there are other queens that come out after dark, including the climbing cacti *Selenicereus grandiflorus* and *Hylocereus* spp.) Come late summer and autumn, the air is filled with a very heady scent from her pale-green flowers, which are followed by green berries that turn a lustrous white in winter. Unchecked, in a frost-free environment she'll grow rather waywardly into a bush 3 metres high and wide. Her sister, *C. parqui*, will bloom on and off throughout the year in a mild climate. The fragrant clusters of yellow-green flowers give way to small black berries that seed so freely they can become a bit of a worry. The perfume of both species is so commanding that many books suggest they are planted far from the house and away from open windows, in case sleep is disturbed by the dreamy night scent. Some people just don't know when they're well off.

These minor concerns aside, the ideal location for your fragrant night garden is close to the living area or in pots that can be placed strategically where you and yours plan to while away the evening.

Although colour usually takes a back seat at night, some shades shine, transforming an otherwise creepy and menacing shrubbery. The silver-leaved *Senecio* (*S. cineraria*) are reminiscent, on a moonlit night, of chunks of coral and any plant with white flowers acquires a luminosity unnoticed in the clamour of daytime's colour. To outline a BBQ area or guide a passage through the darkness, plant an edging of the silvery scented *Santolina chamaecyparissus* or the irresistibly tactile lambs' ears (*Stachys byzantina* 'Silver Carpet'). Some of the variegated ivies have shiny silver markings that catch the moonlight. *Hedera helix* 'Silver Queen' (syn. 'Tricolors') has grey-green leaves with cream edges tinged with pink in winter; 'Glacier' has similar colouring, as has the larger *H. canariensis* 'Gloire de Marengo', which looks as if it's been hand painted.

Gold markings don't lose all of their radiance when the sun goes down. *Hedera helix* 'Goldheart' is probably the best of the gold-tinted ivies. The golden heliotrope, *Heliotropium arborescens* 'Aurea', warms and perfumes the air at the same time. *Helichrysum petiolare* 'Silver' and 'Limelight' both live up to their names and positively glow in the dark.

White flowers stand out most against a dark backdrop. The detail of an

Gaura lindheimeri 'Whirling Butterflies'

individual plant can be completely lost at night, so for a dazzling display, group them en masse. Balls of white roses and the ghostly spires of delphiniums seem suspended in the sky, while scatterings of starry daisies and alyssum create another galaxy closer to the ground. *Gaura lindheimeri* forms a good-sized clump, a metre high and wide, with rather inconspicuous flowers from spring until autumn. The buds are pink and open to small white blooms. At night its stems disappear into the darkness, leaving the dainty little flowers hovering in the balmy air. One cultivar called 'Whirling Butterflies' best describes their effect. From butterflies to ducks' heads, *Lysimachia clethroides* grows to about the same size as gaura and over summer the spikes of starry white buds nod gracefully, reminiscent of ducks' heads, complete with curved beak. The spikes straighten up as the flowers open. In the meantime the plant gives a whimsical touch to the moonlit garden.

ANGEL'S TRUMPETS are perhaps the most dramatic of the after-dark flowers. *Brugmansia* (once known as Datura) is the taller species and their giant trumpets hang downwards like lanterns in sumptuous milky shades of apricot, pale pink, yellow and a very creamy white. *B. sanguinea* has the ruddier tones of a ripe peach and often very large flowers indeed, some between 30 and 40 cm long. Hanging heavy with fragrance, they are a breathtaking sight by moonlight. Be aware some species will grow into large woody shrubs or even small trees, although a savage annual pruning will keep them compact and looking good. When young they can be coaxed into forming a single trunk, which can look very effective in a container. Brugmansias prefer a sheltered partially shaded position with a rich, well-drained soil. They are marginally cold-hardy and in places that experience heavy winter frosts the plant is best cut down to the ground and covered with a protective mulch over winter.

IPOMOEA. If you're ever at a loose end you could always watch moonflowers unfurl in front of your eyes in the best after-dark floorshow tradition. The nocturnal voyeur won't be disappointed by the climbing moonflower, *Ipomoea alba*. In the space of one or two minutes each summer evening the buds uncurl in a spiralling action to reveal glowing blooms of the purest white. Each one only lasts 24 hours but the masses of flowers ensure the performance is repeated night after night. This frost-tender perennial has a tendency to sprawl up and away from its audience, so it's often grown in a container where its rambling

Pleasure Grounds

Brugmansia, *also known as Angel's trumpets.*

habit can be held in check and its performance not wasted on the stars. If knocked back by cold weather the moonflower may come away in spring as long as the roots are not frozen or waterlogged, but in very cold areas it's best treated as an annual.

A curtain-raiser could be arranged with the marvel of Peru or the 4 o'clock flower *Mirabilis jalapa*, which opens late afternoon and doesn't close 'till early next morning. The plant grows to about 60 cm high, with the same spread, and thrives like a weed in our climate. The perfume from its small trumpet flowers of red, pink, white or yellow will fill the later afternoon air but is at its heady best after dark. Another plant not averse to turning the odd trick at night is the burning bush (*Dictamnus albus*). This frost-hardy perennial bears spikes of starry white flowers early in the summer. These flowerheads and its glossy light-green leaves are covered in a volatile lemon-scented oil which can apparently be ignited on a warm still night. It's said the plant is briefly engulfed in flames and then continues to

Gardenias

The perfume of gardenia is arguably the best of all floral scents. The shrubby plant can also be trained as a great-looking standard with dark, glossy, evergreen leaves and, quite often, hundreds of lustrous white blooms that turn pale yellow as they age. Sometimes the leaves turn yellow as well, but this problem can usually be overcome with a dose of Epsom salts. These precious plants need cosseting — not that they have to be wrapped in cotton wool, but they are tender and need care. They like a warm spot away from the wind and they'll need protection from frost over winter. Gardenias will grow in full sun or light shade. Their soil should be rich, moist, free-draining and slightly acidic. Their fibrous rooting system stays close to the surface and is best protected with an insulating mulch. They also require frequent watering over dry spells, and some light hosing will raise the humidity level to their liking. For all this they will reward you with gorgeous fragrant blooms from late spring, through summer and occasionally into autumn. One of the best in a container is *Gardenia augusta* 'Professor Pucci'. The highly perfumed double cream flowers are a feature throughout summer, but make sure the Professor never runs short of a drink and give him some shade from midday sun.

burn like incense, but miraculously, no harm comes to it. Immolation aside, the plant is slow growing and difficult to propagate, but once established it will live for an extremely long time if left undisturbed in a sunny spot with well-drained soil.

Shape should not be overlooked in a moonlight garden: the more obvious the shape, the better. Palm fronds make an exotic silhouette against a starry sky and the dramatic leaves of agaves, arching flaxes, and spires of delphiniums, verbascum and kniphofia will stand out and cast shadows in the moonlight. The bold leaves of hostas will make their presence felt, especially the varieties with white or silver margins. A shapely specimen tree could be discreetly artificially lit to illuminate its shape or decked out with Christmas-tree or fairy lights for a more frivolous atmosphere. Or you could really get carried away and paint the trunk white and string up good old multi-coloured light bulbs for the Greek taverna effect.

As Australian designer Edna Walling advised: never overlook bark. Many of the birches have dazzling silvery-white trunks. Some, like the paper birch, have bark that peels off into long thin curls. The popular silver birch (*Betula pendula*) also has shimmering leaves that catch the light by day and night. Or if you want a home among the gum trees, consider the eucalypts. We're talking tactile here; some have smooth and shiny trunks, others are mottled and seem to gleam at night. Australia's most famous driveway, at Cruden Farm outside Melbourne, was planted by Dame Elizabeth Murdoch some 70 years ago. The avenue of lemon-scented gums is now a magnificent and stately entrance, alternately glowing in the sun and shining in the rain. The sharp lemon scent is especially strong in the early evening. These trees were a practical as well as an inspired choice — at night the car lights pick up the brilliantly white trunks to guide them on their way.

Candles can add as much to the mood of a moonlight garden as the plants themselves. The downside is the inevitable insect invasion. Candles that repel bugs are effective, but beware the night when the scent of citronella overpowers all others (though perhaps that's just all part of the outdoor package). Floating candles on a pond or swimming pool clearly illuminate a potentially hazardous sheet of water.

As long as it isn't coming down from the heavens, the sound of water will accentuate the night-time garden experience. The Persians regarded water as an

The silvery slender lines of the titoki trunk and stone seat make an effective duo in the night light.

essential element in their paradise gardens, all the more precious in their arid surroundings. In ancient Japanese gardens, pools were used to reflect the moon. The sound of water gently gushing out of a lion's head or trickling into a pool can mask any intrusive noises of a more hectic world beyond the garden gate. The next best sound is the rustle of bamboo or smaller grasses or, if all else is absent, there's always the cicadas.

One of the main joys of entertaining in the garden at night is that darkness will conceal any imperfections. You need only illuminate what you want to be seen. Tables can be set simply yet romantically: a pale cloth hanging all the way to the ground will cover up any of the table's shortcomings and strands of ivy twisted around candlesticks will link the table to the garden. Simple food will leave the table uncluttered and the cook unflustered. A single dish with a green salad is often enough, and to avoid any anxious moments, it's best to stick to the tried and true. I have two fail-safe dishes that I fall back on with great regularity. The first is so easy that I'm embarrassed to reveal it. It's a simple Thai Chicken Curry. My other trusty standby is a Leek Risotto. Once you have had a couple of attempts at risotto, you can almost make it blindfolded — or at the very least, you can cook it in front of your friends, stirring as you entertain. The trick is to have everything chopped and the stock simmering gently on the stove before you start cooking (See recipes on pages 164-65.)

What is more satisfying on a sultry summer's night than a big mixed salad. Fresh leaves from the garden make a soft bed on a platter for little cherry tomatoes, some glistening olives, steamed asparagus, maybe some sliced marinated artichokes and topped with slices of grilled fillets of beef or lamb that are still pink in the middle. A dressing with sesame oil and roasted sesame seeds would perfume the greens. (Sesame oil can be quite overpowering in a dish, so it is better diluted with a good vegetable or olive oil — 4 tablespoons to 1 tablespoon of sesame oil is a palatable ratio.) Alternatively, the fillets could be marinated in a spicy Thai paste and cooked quickly in a wok or on the barbecue and placed on a bed of cool lettuce, snow peas, bean shoots and cellophane noodles.

Or the wonderful fragrances of lemon grass and tamarind could filter through a salad of fresh greens and prawns. If a fish dish seems appropriate, grilled tuna, salmon or hapuka steaks could be added to a salad of steamed beans and potatoes, garnished with anchovies and olives for a fresh version of the Niçoise classic.

Sweet nothings: Chocolate treats complete the evening with Renées Little Pots of Chocolate, Florentines and chocolate leaves.

Following Page: One course meals: Beef Salad, Vitello Tonnato and Niçoise Salad.

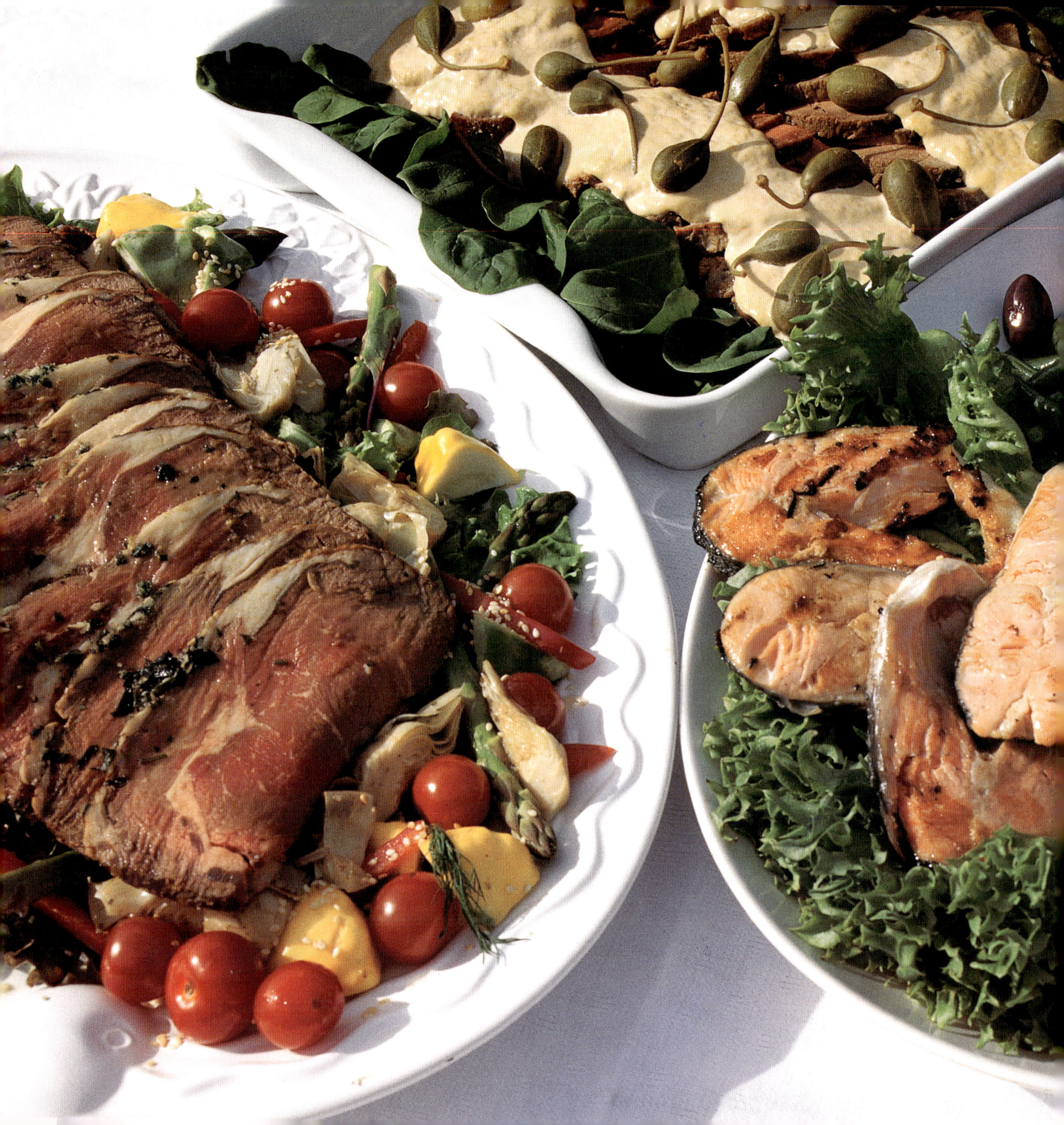

At this meal by moonlight, to my mind nothing would look more splendid than a neatly arranged platter of the aristocratic Vitello Tonnato. This is one of those sneaky dishes that appears more complicated than it actually is. (See recipe page 165.)

These suggestions are for one-course meals. Most can be arranged decoratively on a big dish and left to be served at room temperature. With one of these dishes ready and something sweet in the fridge, the cook can sit back and smell the roses. (Things start to go wrong, more often than not, when too many choices are being offered by the home caterer. It's the hardest call for a generous cook to say 'when'. I try to turn the tables and instead of apologising for the lack of choice, say, 'Here it is. I hope you enjoy it.' And of course they do.)

And the sweet nothings in the fridge? A soft pink cream of the best fruit summer has to offer — strawberries. (See page 166 for recipe.) As an alternative, you couldn't go wrong with bringing out our friend Renee's little pots of chocolate. (See page 165.) I put this rich mousse into small demi-tasses, with a couple of chocolate leaves on each sauce. Any firm leaves with a smooth surface can be used. Camellia leaves are best, with lemon leaves a close second. They should be clean, free of any pests and diseases and thoroughly dry. Melt squares of dark chocolate and spread over the top side of the leaf, leaving no gaps. When the chocolate has completely set, gently peel back the leaf from the chocolate, working from the base to the tip. Work quickly as the heat from your hands can soon melt the chocolate. The leaves can be stored between layers of greaseproof paper in an airtight container in the fridge. You could try coating peppermint or spearmint leaves with chocolate and serving them, leaf and all, as authentic after-dinner mints.

The last great perfume to complete a moonlit dinner would be the smell of decent coffee. Coffee's magic is accentuated if you grind the beans yourself. It's said to vie with the smell of grilled bacon as the best aroma to filter from a kitchen. I like to put a plate of Florentines out with the coffee. They can be made in advance as they store well without their chocolate coating — which is easily applied earlier in the day. See page 166 for the recipe.

This could be the time for the sound of Maria Callas to take over from the cicada chorus and as her glorious voice soars with joy and exaltation, you can settle back, relax and contemplate the drama of the universe from your own fragrant paradise.

Pleasure Grounds

BARBECUES

As temperatures rise, tempers usually follow so, as the old adage suggests, it's time to get out of the kitchen. This is when the garden setting really comes into its own. Balmy herbs can be planted close at hand to distract the mossies and stimulate appetites. Basil, hyssop, nasturtiums and garlic will all do their best to repel insects. Some can then be gathered to imbue whatever's cooking with their special flavours. A lively scene can ensue very quickly — music playing, dinner sizzling, family and friends proffering advice on how best to cook the racks of lamb, with one hand on a glass and one eye on the cricket.

The table can be just as animated. These are the nights for bright colours. They call for linen cloths in forest green or tomato red or the deep blue of a Grecian sea; lime-green with a mango-orange or saffron-yellow for more than a

Skewers of minced lamb, meatballs wrapped in lemon leaves and baby squid.

hint of the tropics. Napkins can be boldly checked or striped. Chunky Mexican glasses and vivid ceramic platters that have made their way from little Portuguese and Italian villages can sing out contrasts or strike a harmonious chord in the cheerful setting.

A grill plate bedecked with vegetables is also a glorious sight. The princely purples of the aubergine nestle cosily beside long narrow strips of zucchini and the bright yellow and reds of capsicum. A head of garlic pops up among them, hinting of the generous flavours to come. Juicy ripe tomatoes glisten when stroked with a fragrant oil. As we can read from any restaurant menu or food magazine, absolutely anything can be chargrilled — sometimes there's more char than grill. Some vegetables need a little more coaxing over the hot coals than others. Both potatoes and kumara do better if they're smeared with oil, salt and freshly ground pepper and wrapped in tinfoil. Add some rosemary or a couple of mint leaves to the potatoes and a sprinkling of cinnamon to the kumara. Daikons, those extraordinarily long Japanese radishes, cut into similar sized rounds, can also be brushed with oil and wrapped in foil. These vegetables will take a good 45 minutes grilled over a medium heat. For the baste, use an olive oil and lace it with a few sprigs of thyme, tarragon, some black peppercorns, a couple of bay leaves, some peel from a lemon and a little garlic. This can be warmed over a gentle heat to release the herbs' own aromatic oils.

It wasn't that long ago that the smell of rosemary through the house meant there was a roast in the oven. We have since fallen under its spell and it is by far the best herb to have close at hand by the barbie. I have seen a friend lay an entire bush over the rack of a gas barbecue, place a leg of lamb on top and cover it with a deep lid from an old enamel roasting dish. He then turned the heat down very low and left it alone for nearly an hour and a half, replenishing the aromatic bed with yet another armful of fresh rosemary halfway through. It was the most decadently delectable roast I have ever tasted. The same friend makes another much quicker dish with rosemary using baby squid. He cleans the tubes and marinates them in olive oil and chopped rosemary for a couple of hours. He then seasons them with rock salt and cooks them on a hot plate on the barbecue for just three minutes, turning as they cook. These are sliced and set on a bed of rocket leaves with lemon juice and a little of the oil drizzled over them. Very simple and delicious.

Meatballs in lemon leaves

In a mixing bowl combing **500 g minced veal**, **1 lightly beaten egg**, **1½ cups breadcrumbs**, **1½ cups grated parmesan cheese**, **½ cup finely chopped parsley** and **basil**, **salt** and **pepper** to taste. Form this mixture into little balls, (about 20) then coat them in olive oil by rolling. Wrap around each a young **lemon leaf** and secure with a toothpick. Grill the balls over a medium heat, turning until the meat is cooked on all sides. The lemon leaves will probably burn, but are removed for eating after passing on their own aromatic oil to the balls.

Lamb kebabs

Process to a smooth paste **500 g minced lamb**, **½ an onion, finely chopped**, **2 cloves crushed garlic** and **½ tsp each** of **cinnamon**, **garam marsala** and **cumin**. Add **salt** and **pepper** to taste. Soak long bamboo skewers in water or **lemon juice** for at least 10 minutes. Using your hands (it may pay to oil them as the process can be messy), mould large spoonfuls of the paste around the skewers to make a sausage shape. Pop these in the fridge for a couple of hours to allow the flavours to develop. Brush with **oil** and grill over a medium heat for 10–15 minutes, turning from time to time. Makes approximately 10 kebabs.

Some of the sturdier sprigs of rosemary can be stripped of most of their little needle-like leaves, leaving a good tuft at one end, and used as skewers. They need to be soaked in water for at least five minutes before threading meat or vegetables through them. A bushy sprig will also serve as a convenient brush to baste food with — releasing its fragrance into the oil, and it doesn't matter if its ends suffer the inevitable singeing. And as for that nostalgic smell of rosemary through the house — it's still around as cooks discover the herb's aptitude to dispel less pleasant smells from the air. A sprig in the oven or on top of an element will cover up any burnt experiments.

Sweetcorn grills beautifully. Soak the unhusked corn in a bucket of water for at least 15 minutes, then peel back the husks leaving them still attached at the base, and remove the silk. Spread butter over the kernels and stick a couple of sage leaves to the butter. Alternatively, you could spice up the butter with a pinch or two of cumin and some finely chopped spring onions. Replace the husks and wrap in tinfoil. These will take about 30 minutes to cook. I think corn on the cob is best served on its own in a large bowl or basket accompanied with more butter, a pepper grinder and copious napkins. Its sweetness and size tends to take over a plate, making more than a meal of it.

Other vegetables can be brushed with fragrant oil and grilled until cooked but still holding their shape, roughly about 15 minutes. The balmy oil will save the vegetables from drying out on top of the coals.

Apart from ever-popular patties, there are many mince recipes you can cook on the barbecue. Tiny meatballs of veal wrapped in lemon leaves take no time to grill on the plate and make tasty morsels to nibble with drinks, while the main course is cooking. A spicy lamb mixture that's wrapped around skewers to form an upmarket hot-dog always goes over well. They can be served with a bowl of plain yoghurt mixed with lemon juice, chopped parsley, mint and coriander, with perhaps a whisper of garlic. Similarly concocted kebabs of minced beef with cinnamon, nutmeg and a dash of ground cloves would go nicely with a fruity sauce.

'Salsa' is simply the Spanish word for sauce. As salsas are traditionally made with fresh ingredients — there's no cooking involved — they make a tasty complement to the charred part of the grilling. The original salsa combines finely chopped tomato (skinned and deseeded) with chilli, garlic, a little onion and finely chopped herbs, all moistened with a little oil and lemon juice. However, there's many a cool combination to be found in seasonal fruits and herbs. Melon, cucumber, mangoes and pawpaw can all replace the humble tomato for more exotic mergers with mint, coriander, lemon grass and some of the scented basils. Roasted kernels of corn and chilli make a fiery marriage for those who like it hot. Peaches make a soothing salsa to go alongside grilled meats, especially chicken (see recipe page 166).

The most versatile of all is a salsa verde, a green sauce. This is made by blending a bunch each of parsley and basil, and possibly a little mint, with a couple of cloves of garlic, 2 tablespoons of rinsed capers and 4 anchovy fillets. When this assortment is roughly blended you gradually add about ¾ cup of olive oil, with the processor running as if you were making mayonnaise. To this you mix in either the juice of a lemon or a couple of tablespoons of red-wine vinegar. This sauce makes a great companion to any meat.

The finished squid with melon, mint, peach and coriander salsas.

Relishes, briefly cooked seasonal fruit and vegetables, frequently spiced, and meant to be eaten fresh, add a bit of zing to many traditional barbecue dishes. Like salsas, relishes are open to all sorts of suggestions for combinations. Apples, pears, feijoas and tamarillos can all hold their own here. The quickly prepared apple and boysenberry relish on page 166 is delicious with pork sausages.

The most popular relish has relinquished its lovely name, preferring to be called a marmalade. Onion marmalade is the result of copious slices of onion being cooked with sugar over a gentle heat until they caramelise. There are several variations on the marmalade, some using half a bottle of red wine; others have a splash or two of marsala added to the mixture. The recipe on this page is for a basic mix that has worked like a dream for me.

Whether at home or at the bach, there's great satisfaction in barbecuing the catch of the day. Barbecuing fish is a joy with those wire cradles that you simply turn over half way through. A one kg fish won't need cooking for more than 15 minutes all up — it is better to veer on the undercooked side rather than overdoing it. Fill the cavity with lemon wedges or some strands of lemon grass along with a few sprigs of thyme if you have any. There is no need to scale the fish if you wrap it in vine leaves before nestling it into the cradle. When the fish is cooked its skin should peel away with the leaves. Alternatively you could scale the fish and rub the skin with a little red curry paste before cooking.

Grapevine leaves can be wrapped around individual fillets of fish. The leaves should be blanched first to make them more malleable, then maybe add tarragon butter, wrap the fish in a vine leaf, secure with a toothpick and cook the parcel on an oiled grill. Banana leaves also make great wrappers. Again, the leaves should be scalded to make them pliant. Prepare the fish fillets as above, wrap each in a leaf secured by a toothpick and grill for 5–8 minutes or until just cooked. The meatier flesh of tuna, kingfish, hapuka and even kahawai are made for barbecues, as these don't dry out or break up like some of the more delicate catches of the day — although any fish is grillable with a little care. Fish that has been marinated in a fragrant oil is less likely to dry out.

Mussels and pipis cook well on the barbecue but I am loath to throw them on the grill and waste that tasty essence that comes from steaming the shellfish — especially mussels — open in a little white wine. To me it is nectar straight from heaven. Scrub the shells thoroughly and throw away any broken or open ones.

Onion marmalade

Melt **200 g butter** in a heavy-based pan. Peel and slice **10 Spanish red onions** (or ordinary brown ones, but the red variety is sweeter) and cook in the butter over a low heat, taking care not to brown them. Add **1 cup brown sugar, ⅔ cup balsamic vinegar** and a **few sprigs of fresh thyme**. Season with **salt** and **pepper**, then continue to cook the onions over a gentle heat for about 40 minutes. The mixture should be thick and syrupy. This can be stored in a jar in the fridge for up to a week.

Château Vaux-le-Vicomte

Even for a country as accustomed to grand, tragic epics as France, the story of Château Vaux-le-Vicomte stands out. Renowned for its extravagance, the court of Louis XIV was led and encouraged in its excess by the Sun King himself. But as one of his courtiers, Nicolas Fouquet, discovered the hard way, it was unwise to try and indulge in a lifestyle deemed to rival that of your monarch.

In 1641 the elegant Fouquet commissioned the young André le Nôtre to design a garden to compete with the great estates of Italy and Spain: it was to be the grandest garden ever seen in France. At the time, Le Nôtre was up and coming; he'd worked with his father on the Tuileries gardens in Paris and was later to design Versailles for the Sun King, but it was at Vaux where he first defined the garden style for which France would become known.

The site measures 1.5 kilometres from the grand iron entrance gates to the colossal statue of Hercules, but the intricate charms of this vast garden are not all visible at first glance. The ornamental parterres, based on the elaborate patterns of Eastern rugs, are punctuated by formal, clipped topiary. The statuary, on a predominantly mythological theme, link the many ponds, which are flanked by stately avenues of chestnuts leading to a huge concealed canal.

On 17 August 1661, Nicolas Fouquet gave the party to end all parties, the first and last occasion on which his garden was allowed to be the pleasure garden it was designed to be. The event was considered incomparable, and Molière wrote a new comedy especially for the night. Guests were refreshed by scantily clad nymphs, serving the finest food and wine, and enchanted by the extravagant theatricals, water displays and fireworks.

But the triumph of the occasion was soon to be eclipsed by the dark rage of the Sun King: it didn't pay to outshine the young Louis XIV for even a single night. A couple of weeks after the grand fête, Fouquet was arrested by d'Artagnan and accused of theft and misuse of his position as financial secretary of France. Following a three-year trial, he was imprisoned in a dungeon where he was closely guarded until his death seventeen years later. It is said his fate inspired Alexander Dumas to write his novel *The Man in the Iron Mask*.

Over the centuries, the estate deteriorated along with the fortunes of its owners, until it was finally restored and opened to the public in 1919. For me, Vaux-le-Vicomte has it all, and I rate it as one of the most outstanding gardens I've visited. The scale is awesome, but the strength of the design allows all the grandeur and formality without sacrificing its style and personality. After four visits I'm still captivated. To better appreciate a large estate like Vaux, I'd recommend fortifying yourself with a substantial lunch and, wearing comfortable shoes, devote at least three hours to experience this masterpiece of seventeenth-century gardens.

Place in a large saucepan with a few centimetres of white wine or wine and water, a couple of slices of lemon, some chopped spring onions, a couple of cloves of garlic and a little salt and pepper. Put a lid on the pot, bring it to the boil and steam the mussels open. Take out the mussels as they open and discard any stubborn ones that refuse to show what they're made of. Reserve the juice at the bottom of the pot, for this is the ultimate blend of wine and mussel juice. It can be augmented with cream and lemon juice and a fresh handful of finely chopped spring onions and poured over the opened mussels meunière-style to be mopped up with crusty French bread. Or a can of peeled tomatoes can be added to the essence along with some chopped basil and parsley and garlic and served with more bread. Not long ago I stumbled upon yet another way with the nectar. I reduced the cooking juices to a mere ⅓ cup, put this concentrate in a blender with a little more garlic and some chopped parsley and slowly drizzled olive oil into the mix as the motor was running, just as you would making mayonnaise. The emulsion thickened to just the right consistency to pour over a salad of fresh greens and the shellfish and tasted wonderful.

Where there's smoke . . .

It used to be the scourge of a barbecue, getting in your eyes and following you around no matter where you positioned yourself. But smoke can be redirected into the food with some wonderfully flavourful results. The food takes on the distinctive flavour of whatever you use to smoke it with. The same methods are used by many fishermen with their metal smoke-boxes, except that our heat source comes from the barbecue, not a kerosene burner. You can smoke food using both charcoal and gas burners. The best results come from the kettle barbecues with their rounded lids. You need a lid to contain the smoke, but you can improvise with the lid of an old enamel roasting dish, an inverted wok or even tinfoil fashioned into a tent with wire coathangers. As with fish smokers, most of the smoke comes from woodchips or sawdust. These could be soaked in water for a couple of hours before using. Recently cut wood is moist with sap, so won't require soaking.

The choice of woods is important. Never use any wood unknown to you — it could be poisonous, as could treated timbers and orchard woods that have been sprayed. Avoid soft resinous woods like gums and conifers as their flavours can be too strong and unpleasant. Hardwoods are better, especially wood from

Fruit tree prunings impart superb flavours to hot smoked food.

fruit and nut trees. Apple, crabapple, walnut and almond will all extend their unique flavours. Cherry is somewhat bitter. Fishermen will tell you how aromatic manuka is in the smoker. Oak will give a mellow flavour.

The Americans are old hands at smoking, having discovered long ago the sweetness of maple and the heartiness of hickory. Commercial packets of these wood chips are available here, as are bottles of 'liquid smoke' which will give you the flavours of hickory and mesquite without the need for wood. Jack Daniels even market the charcoal used to filter their brew. Besides using wood, you can get a really aromatic smoke with grapevine prunings, nut shells and, of course, herbs. Various blends of tea leaves and spices can also be added to the fire.

For a quick smoke you can simply toss the wood shavings over the hot coals or the lava rocks sitting below the grill on your gas barbecue. Their impact on the food will be fleeting. For a more enjoyable smoke, you can put your aromatics in a smoke-box. These are handsome little black cast-iron boxes with holes to vent the smoke. Or you can roll your own, wrapping the shavings and herbs in a log of a double thickness of tinfoil, leaving each end open for the smoke to escape.

Food for smoking can be marinated or rubbed with an aromatic oil or herbs, spices, garlic or lemon rind beforehand. Foods rich in natural oil are ideal for smoking, while drier food will benefit from a spell in a marinade. An old metal basin or roasting dish full of water will create a steamy environment under the hood and will keep drier foods moist. The temperature of the barbecue should be low, although it can be slightly higher on a trolley barbecue if only part of the surface is covered for smoking.

Smoking is a surprisingly quick process. Tuna cut into 2 cm slices, marinated in a mix of oil and wine with some lemon peel, will take 10 minutes sitting on a rack over smoked sawdust with a few unpeeled slices of ginger root added. Lamb shanks, brushed with oil, garlic and rosemary, will take 15 minutes under the hood. Pork fillets can be first marinated in wine and oil and then cooked over a woody mix with a few crushed star anise and a cinnamon stick. They should take about 10 minutes.

The main thing to remember is that this process is *hot smoking*, designed for food to be eaten then and there. *Cold smoking* is an entirely different kettle of fish, when food is actually cured and consequently preserved.

Hitting the spot

After a barbecued lunch or before the evening meal is under way, a leisurely game of boules could hit the spot. With very few rules to argue over, boules or petanque is an easy game to play. The youngsters enjoy it and even the infirm or slightly addled can join in. Make up teams or have play-offs — it can be intensely competitive or just a bit of fun.

If you're really keen and have the space, it's not difficult to lay down a special petanque court. It'll save a lot of tedious future maintenance if the allotted area is dead flat and weed-free. Spray with Roundup or your chosen herbicide, burn it off with a blowtorch, or put down some weedmat as long as the area is completely clear. Outline the edges in raised wood or brick to contain the generous mattress of crushed shell or fine gravel you then spread over the entire area. That's about it. Alternatively, if you have a grassed area that is reasonably flat and hazard free, and where the occasional crater won't cause any strife, then that'll suffice for a good game. There are sets of cheap plastic water-weighted balls that are better on grass or sand. The handsome metal numbers are designed for gravel or shell surfaces.

The Recipes

FOCACCIA

Combine **1 tbsp dried yeast** with **50 ml lukewarm water** and rest this for 10 minutes or until the mixture becomes frothy.

In a food processor place **400 g flour, 1 tbsp olive oil, ½ tsp salt** and **175 ml cold water**. Add the yeast mixture and blend just until the dough forms a ball. Knead on a lightly floured board until the dough is smooth and elastic. Turn the dough into an oiled bowl, cover with plastic wrap and set aside in a warm, draught-free place (maybe the airing cupboard) for 1–1½ hours or until the dough has doubled in size. Punch down the dough and then press it into an oiled Swiss roll tin (25 x 35 cm). Cover and put back in the warm place for another 30 minutes until it has risen. Brush the top with more olive oil and sprinkle with **rock salt** and either **fresh thyme** or **rosemary leaves**. You can also add some **pitted olives**, pushing them into the surface of the dough. Bake in a hot oven (220°C) for 15–20 minutes until cooked.

TAMARILLOS

While tamarillos are delicious fresh, they also combine nicely in both sweet and savoury dishes. They give a good bite to jams and preserves and make an excellent chutney. My friend Johnny Heard makes the best chutney in the world and he kindly offered this recipe for this book.

Put in a large pot **2 kg peeled and quartered tamarillos, 1 kg peeled, cored and sliced apples, 1 kg peeled and chopped onions, 1 kg soft brown sugar, 1 kg white sugar, 1½ tsp each of salt and white pepper, 50 g pickling spices wrapped in gauze, 25 g all spice, 1.2 litres white wine vinegar**. Bring to the boil and then simmer for 2 hours until the mixture is thick. Cool then bottle in hot sterilised jars. For browner chutney substitute the white sugar with brown and use malt vinegar instead of white wine.

I have also added the fruit to a sauce to serve with vegetables. Its sharpness goes particularly well with green beans, broccoli and brussels sprouts in early winter. Whisk **3 egg yolks** and **1 tbsp of wine vinegar** in a bowl over simmering water until thick. Cool a little, then add **220 g melted butter** in a drizzle and **then 3 puréed tamarillos** and **salt** and **pepper** and for optional sharpness a **squeeze of lemon juice**.

And for the sweet-toothed, you can poach them whole with their stalks attached, in a syrup made of equal amounts of **sugar** and **water**. Simmer very gently in a covered pot with a **cinnamon stick** or crushed **star anise** for about 15 minutes. Remove the fruit and skin, but leave the stalks attached. Return to the pot, cover and cool slowly. Refrigerate until needed for a wonderful dessert.

TAPENADE

In a food processor put **2 cups black** or **green stoned olives, 1–2 tbsp well rinsed capers**, **3 anchovy fillets**, again well rinsed (some cooks soak the fillets in milk, then rinse and pat them dry), and **¼ cup olive oil**. Blend until the olives are to your desired consistency. (For some dishes, such as a sauce for pasta, the olives are best left chunky.) All kinds of ingredients can be added to this basic mixture. **1 or 2 tbsp canned tuna** gives more bite and goes well with grilled fish or veal. **Eggplant**, previously baked with **oil** and **garlic** until soft, can be scooped out and added to tapenade before it is blended. **Lemon juice** might be needed to enhance the flavour. This mixture will keep in a screwtop jar in the fridge for a couple of weeks.

SAGE ADVICE

The flavour of sage makes stirring music in pastas and risotto, and a burnt sage butter is delicious over veal or roasted pumpkin. Just cook some **sage leaves** with **butter** until they are crisp and the butter is brown. Sometimes I will add some **lemon juice** and freshly ground **pepper** and serve it over broccoli. Bunches of the small blade-like leaves can be fried to a crisp and crumpled over spaghetti, and a single fresh blade sits well on a poached breast of chicken and on diminutive risotto cakes to serve with drinks.

For an easy dessert, try this pear cream flavoured with the herb. **Combine 3 tbsp of warmed honey** with **2 tsp of finely chopped sage**. Peel and chop **3 very ripe, chilled pears** and blend in a processor with the honey mixture. Whip **¾ cup cream** until it forms stiff peaks and fold into the pear mixture. Alternatively, use **thick yoghurt**. Spoon into glasses and chill for at least 30 minutes before serving, topped with a whole sage leaf. This will serve 6.

PICCANTINA ALLA PAVOROTTI

With a rolling pin flatten slightly **800 g veal escalopes**. Dust these with **flour** and freshly ground **black pepper**. Heat **80 g butter** in a heavy-based frying-pan and fry the meat over a fairly high heat until it is browned on both sides and cooked. Keep veal warm on a serving dish. Drain the pan and add **20 g butter** and **60 g leg ham**, cut from the bone and then into fine strips. Cook over a low heat for 1 minute. Remove pan from the heat and add **1 tbsp of the best balsamic vinegar** you can get your hands on. Stir gently, then pour the sauce over the veal. Serve sprinkled with **2 tbsp chopped parsley**. Serves 4 but from what I've read of Pavorotti's appetite, maybe just one for a snack.

CHICKEN AND SILVERBEET TERRINE

You can use spinach instead of silverbeet for this dish, but the sturdy leaves of the latter hold their shape better while cooking. (Don't use the stems of either.) You will need **8–10 slices of bacon**. Wash and remove the stalks from **2 bunches silverbeet** (about 16 leaves). Flatten with a rolling pin **1 kg skinned and boned chicken breasts**. Lightly butter a 2-litre terrine, then line the base and sides with overlapping slices of the bacon. Sprinkle bottom of the terrine with **freshly grated parmesan cheese**, then start layering the main ingredients, commencing with silverbeet leaves, followed by chicken, then another sprinkling of parmesan. Make 3 or 4 layers, finishing off with chicken.

In a bowl beat together **3 eggs** and **300 ml cream**. Season with **salt** and **pepper**, keeping in mind that the bacon will be salty. Pour the egg mixture over the layers in the terrine. Cover the top of the terrine with a piece of buttered foil and place the dish in a bain-marie, that is, a roasting-dish filled with enough water to come half way up the sides of the terrine. Cook in a hot oven (200°C) for 1¼ hours. (You may need to top up the water half way through; use hot water so you don't interrupt the cooking.)

Remove the terrine from the bain-marie and put a brick or some full cans on top of the foil cover to weigh down the loaf. (Be prepared for some excess juices to overflow; a tray is useful here.) Refrigerate the weighted terrine overnight.

Next day, unmold your terrine and serve in slices. This should serve 10 people.

NOODLES WITH BUTTERNUT SAUCE

Peel and remove the seeds from **1 or 2 fresh butternuts**. Chop into reasonable sized pieces. In a little **olive oil** fry until fragrant **1 tsp red curry paste**. Stir in the **white part of a lemon grass stalk**, crushed and finely sliced, and **1 tsp each** of **ground coriander** and **ground cardamom**. Add the butternut pieces, a small **leek** and **1 celery stalk**, both finely sliced. Toss this all round the pan for a couple of minutes, then pour in **1 can coconut cream** and **1 litre of chicken stock**. Combine briefly and season to taste with **salt** and **pepper**. Bring the mixture to a slow simmer and cook for 25 minutes, or until the butternut is tender. Cook the required amount of **noodles** or **pasta** until it is al dente, drain and place in bowls. Spoon over the butternut sauce and top with some **coriander leaves** and, if you like, some **thin strips of fried chilli**.

RICOTTA CAKE

Grease a 20 cm springform tin with **1 tbsp butter** and coat bottom and sides with **2 tbsp breadcrumbs**, shaking away the excess. In a food processor put **1 cup loosely packed basil leaves, 1 cup loosely packed parsley leaves** and **½ cup loosely packed mint leaves**. Process these herbs until finely chopped. Add **500 g ricotta cheese** and **⅔ cup of cream** and blend until the mixture turns green. One at a time, processing between each addition, put in **2 eggs**. Transfer mixture to a bowl and fold in **1 cup freshly grated parmesan cheese**. Season to taste with **salt** and **pepper**. Pour the mixture into the prepared tin and, if desired, sprinkle the top with **1 cup pitted and sliced black olives**.

Bake cake in a moderately hot oven (190°C) for 30 minutes or until it is cooked and browned. This is best served straight away, but still tastes good cold.

PESTO

In a food processor put a **good handful of basil leaves**, at least **2 cloves of garlic** (preferably roasted), **1 cup freshly grated parmesan cheese**, **½ cup pinenuts**, lightly roasted, and a **pinch of salt**. Blend to a smooth paste. While the motor is still running, slowly add **½ cup of olive oil**. Pesto can be stored in a sealed container in the fridge for up to a week, or can be frozen for use in winter. The mixture freezes better without the cheese, which can be added if required on defrosting. Other herbs like **coriander** and **mint** can replace the basil, and **almonds** and, less often, **walnuts** can stand in for the pinenuts.

VEAL AND CHICKEN LIVER TERRINE

It was early on in my cooking that I learnt to appreciate the more tenacious qualities of thyme and bay which went in to slowly cooked casseroles and deliciously earthy farmhouse terrines that were coated with streaky bacon or even a chaud-froid sauce made with the jellied reductions of our own good stocks. Here's a veal and chicken liver terrine I still make and served with some bread and a green salad, it is perfect lunch or picnic fare.

Soak **250 g chicken livers**, cleaned and roughly chopped, **in 3 tbsp dry sherry or brandy** then blend with **125 g diced ham** and **2-3 cloves of crushed garlic**.

Soak **2 slices of bread** with the crusts removed in **4 tbsp milk**, add **250 g minced veal** and some finely chopped **parsley, and thyme** and season with **salt** and **pepper**.

Mix both lots together. Soften with a little **white wine** — the resulting mixture should be slushy. Line a terrine or loaf tin with **streaky bacon**, allowing for enough strands of the bacon to cover the top of the terrine once the filling is in the middle. Cover the tin with tin foil. Place in a bain-marie — a roasting tin filled with enough boiling water to come over half way up the sides of the terrine. Bake in a moderate oven (180°C) for 1-1½ hours. It will be ready when it begins to come away from the sides — mind you don't burn yourself when you look. The water in the bain-marie may need topping up during the cooking — do this with boiling water from the kettle so the cooking process isn't interrupted. The terrine will slice better if it is weighted after cooking. Place terrine or loaf tin inside a larger dish to collect the juices and put a brick or some heavy (unopened!) cans on top, and leave in the fridge overnight before turning out to slice.

BLACK BEANS AND TOMATO CORIANDER SALAD

Soak **2 cups of dried black beans** in at least twice their volume of **cold water** overnight. The next day, rinse them, put them in a pot, cover generously with water and bring to the boil. Boil for 10 minutes, lower the heat and then simmer for further ½ hour or until they are cooked. Drain the beans well. Allow beans to cool, then stir through **2–3 chopped tomatoes**, **2 capsicum**, seeded and chopped, **2–3 spring onions, chopped**, **½ cup chopped coriander leaves**, the **juice of 1 lemon**, **⅓ cup olive oil**, **1 tsp finely grated ginger root**, **½ tsp ground cumin**, **salt** and **pepper** to taste.

THAI PRAWN SALAD

Take a **3 cm lump of tamarind pulp** and soak it in **3 tbsp hot water**. Squeeze this with your hand to loosen it up, then strain. You should have **2 tbsp of tamarind juice**.

First make a dressing by bringing to the boil in a saucepan **2 tbsp of lime or lemon juice**, **2 tbsp fish sauce**, **3 tsp palm** or **brown sugar** and the already prepared tamarind juice. Remove pan from heat and allow the dressing to cool.

In a large bowl lightly mix together **1 kg cooked shelled prawns**, **8 finely chopped spring onions**, **4 stalks finely chopped lemon grass**, **2 large chillies**, seeded and finely sliced, **2 tbsp finely chopped ginger** (or **1 tbsp finely chopped galangal**), **2 tbsp finely chopped kaffir lime leaves** (or the zest of **1 lime**), and **1 good-sized bunch of coriander**, chopped, including the roots if they're fresh and soft. When the dressing is cold, pour it over the salad ingredients and allow the dish to stand for a couple of hours so that the marvellous flavours can develop.

THAI FISH CAKES

Thai fish cakes are tried and true cocktail fodder. I make them in baby muffin tins for bite-size treats, and their beauty is that they taste great at room temperature, which saves any fuss at serving time. Process **500 g of skinned and boned fish fillets** with a crushed **large clove of garlic, 2 finely chopped spring onions, 2 tsp of red curry paste or chilli sauce, ½ cup coconut cream**, a lightly beaten **egg**, the finely grated **zest of a small lemon and 2 tbsp each of fish sauce and finely chopped coriander roots and stems** — (those that don't like coriander will have to go without this time as the mixture benefits from its presence.)

Drop teaspoons of the mixture into oiled patty pans. Smooth the tops with a teaspoon dipped in water, forming a small hollow in each. Mix together **another ½ cup coconut cream** with **1 tbsp of rice flour or 2 tsp of cornflour** and a **pinch of salt** and spoon a little into each hollow. Top with a thin **strand of red chilli** and bake in a hot oven (200°C) for 10 minutes. They can be served with a small **basil** or **coriander leaf** on top of each little cake. This mixture will make over two dozen.

TABOULEH (LEBANESE BURGHUL SALAD)

Put **¾ cup fine burghul** in a bowl and cover with **cold water**. Leave this to soak for 30 minutes, then drain through a fine sieve, pressing with the back of a spoon to extract the moisture. Spread on a cloth to dry further, then put in a bowl and add **½ cup finely chopped spring onions**. Squeeze the mixture again so that the burghul absorbs the onion flavour. Add **2 cups chopped parsley** and **½ cup finely chopped mint**. Separately mix **¼ cup olive oil** with **2 tbs lemon juice, 1½ tsp salt** and **½ tsp pepper**. Add this dressing to the burghul and toss well. Peel and seed **2 firm ripe tomatoes** and cut into a dice, then gently mix through the salad. Cover and chill the tabouleh for at least an hour before serving. Serves 6.

The above mixture will keep for a few days in the fridge but is better stored for any length of time without the tomatoes, which can be added as you need them. Serve tabouleh in a bowl lined with **crisp lettuce leaves** and have a jug of **salted lemon juice** on the side for extra dressing. In place of the burghul you can substitute couscous made up according to the packet's instructions. Add the finely diced **rind of ¼ of a preserved lemon** with the other goodies.

SORREL SOUP

The lemony leaves of sorrel make a lovely soup and a sharp sauce for fish. The leaves actually turn an unattractive shade of grey when cooked, so I adapt by adding spinach, which remains green while still having the tangy lemon flavour of the sorrel. Take **2 or 3 good handfuls of both spinach and sorrel** — wash well and remove the central veins. Chop **2 medium-sized onions** and a well-washed **leek** into small pieces, cook gently in a **little oil or butter** till transparent, not burnt, then add all the drained leaves. Stir them around and add **enough vegetable or chicken stock** to barely cover. Simmer till barely cooked, still with a good colour. Put through a mouli sieve, blender or liquidiser. Add **salt** to taste. Thin with a little **milk**, or more **stock** if necessary. Or you can use **an egg** beaten into **thin cream or milk** and add when the soup is hot (but not boiling or it will curdle) — this gives a pleasant richness. The colour of the soup should be a bright emerald green. On a hot day it is good served chilled, with a **spoonful of yoghurt**.

Thai Fish Cakes

VICTORIA SANDWICH CAKE

The most versatile of cakes is the good old Victoria Sandwich. It is lovely just made in two rounds, sandwiched together with homemade raspberry jam and its top dusted with icing sugar. It can be coated in chocolate or whisky icing, and the same cake batter can be put into patty tins to make little individual cakes, iced and topped with a rosebud to complement its garden setting. It is one of those classic cakes that can be brought out time and time again.

Cream **185 g butter** and **1 teacup sugar** until light and fluffy. Add **3 eggs**, one at a time, allowing each to be incorporated into the mixture before adding the next. **Add ½ teaspoon vanilla essence** and then **1 breakfast cup sifted self-raising flour** and mix just until the flour has blended into the batter. Turn this batter into 2 greased and floured 20 cm sandwich cake tins and bake in a moderately hot oven (190°C) for 20–25 minutes or until a skewer comes out clean when you test them. Turn the cakes onto wire racks to cool before sandwiching them together with jam or icing. To make chocolate cakes, reduce the flour by 2 tbsp and add **2 dsp of cocoa**.

Simple Thai Chicken Curry

LEMON CHEESE TARTS

Little lemon cheese tarts are perfect afternoon tea fare. The notion may be old fashioned but these tarts make the most of the food processor, microwave and freezer to bring them into the modern age.

Put **2½ cups flour** and **3 tbsp icing sugar** into the processor and mix together. With the motor running drop in **250 g cold butter** (cut into cubes) cube by cube and continue to process until the mixture forms a ball. Wrap in plastic wrap and refrigerate for at least an hour. Roll pastry out, cut and line lightly buttered muffin tins. I use the little tins that everyone bought for bite size Christmas mince pies a few years back. Cook in a hot oven (190°C) for 8–10 minutes or until golden and cooked. This will make quite a number of baby pastry cases. They store well in a tin in the deep freeze and because of their size will thaw in a couple of minutes, so they really can be brought out at a moment's notice. As well as the following lemon cheese filling, they can be filled with a little stewed apple, fresh raspberries or strawberries and topped with cream. Fill once thawed.

Place the **2 eggs, 1 cup sugar, juice and zest of 2 large lemons** in a bowl or jug and cook for 6-8 minutes on the high setting of your microwave. Stop the cooking and stir every 2 minutes. Add **75 g cubed butter** at the end and beat it in well. Cool. This will make 2 small jars, which will keep for a couple of weeks in the fridge. A little can be spooned into the pastry cases and you can top with some lightly whipped **cream** if you like.

SIMPLE THAI CHICKEN CURRY

In a large pan heat some **oil** and sauté **1 chopped onion, 2 chopped cloves garlic** and **1 tbsp red curry paste**. Trim and skin any excess fat from **500 g chicken pieces**. Brown the pieces slightly in hot oil (optional), or add the chicken directly to the onion/garlic mixture. Pour in **1 can of coconut cream** and **1 cup chicken stock**.

Stir through **2 tbsp fish sauce** and **1 tsp sugar** or **honey**. Put on the lid and let the chicken simmer until cooked — about ½ an hour. I sprinkle over some chopped **spring onions** and either **parsley** or **coriander**, or both, to give the dish a bit of colour. Some bright yellow calendula petals also make a pretty garnish. Serve with fragrant jasmine rice.

LEEK RISOTTO

Before you start cooking this rice dish, have all the ingredients chopped and the required amount of stock simmering on the stock. You will need 5–6 cups of hot **chicken, beef or fish stock**, preferably homemade, to complete the risotto. Wash **2 mature leeks** (or 6–8 baby ones), discard the tough green tops and outer leaves, and chop finely. Finely chop **1 onion**, **2–3 cloves garlic** and add to the leeks along with **2 tbs finely chopped herbs**. In a large, heavy-based saucepan heat **3 tbsp olive oil** (or ½ butter, ½ oil if you prefer). In this, cook vegetables and herbs over a gentle heat until the onions are translucent. Add **2 cups arborio rice** and stir until each grain is coated with oil, then stir through the zest of a **small lemon**. Take 1 cup of hot stock and add it to the mixture, stirring constantly with a wooden spoon until the liquid is incorporated with the rice. Repeat these 1-cup additions, stirring all the time, until all the stock has been added, by which time the rice should be just about cooked. It should still be firm to the bite but will have lost its chalky taste. (If that taste still persists, I usually add **½–1 cup dry white wine** and continue stirring until that too has been absorbed into the rice.) When the rice is cooked, add **1 tbsp butter** and **1 cup of freshly grated parmesan cheese**, which produces a creamy texture. Season with **salt** and **pepper** and serve immediately with extra shavings of parmesan. Serves 6.

Leeks lend themselves to all manner of flavours and this risotto would make a fine meal served with poached chicken breasts or tossed with prawns and accompanied with a green salad.

VITELLO TONNATO

This dish calls for cold **veal slices**. The meat can be cooked in a variety of ways, depending on the cut; a fillet can be poached for about 10 minutes in **chicken stock** with a little **white wine** added; larger cuts roasted in a hot oven with appropriate seasonings. When cool, refrigerate the meat, preferably overnight, before slicing.

Prepare the mayonnaise by beating **4 egg yolks** in a food processor, then gradually adding **1½ cups olive oil** while the motor is still running.

When the mixture is thick and amalgamated, add **2–3 tbsp lemon juice**, **1 tbsp Dijon mustard**, **6 anchovy fillets** and the drained contents of a **200 g tin of tuna**. Process until smooth.

Slice the veal and arrange the meat on a large platter. Top with the tuna mayonnaise, sprinkle over a few **capers** or **caperberries**, cover with plastic wrap and refrigerate the dish until you are ready to serve. This will keep in the fridge for a few days — the flavours develop with time.

RENÉE'S LITTLE POTS OF CHOCOLATE

For this recipe, allow **30 g dark chocolate and 1 egg per person**. Separate the eggs, then beat egg yolks until they are pale and thick. Melt chocolate in a bowl over a pan of simmering water. Add a **knob of butter**. Let chocolate cool slightly, then add a spoonful of the egg-yolk mixture. Keep adding the chocolate, spoonful by spoonful, until it is all incorporated with the yolks. Beat the egg whites until they hold stiff peaks and quickly but lightly fold them into the chocolate mixture. Pour into bowls or coffee cups and refrigerate for at least an hour.

Vitello Tonnato

STRAWBERRY CREAM

Hull and then purée **500 g strawberries**. Beat together **4 egg yolks** and **1 cup of sugar** until the mixture is creamy and forms a ribbon when the beater is lifted. Separately whip **400 ml cream** until it forms stiff peaks. Add puréed fruit, then the egg and sugar mixture. Spoon fruit cream into a bowl or mold, and freeze. Serve decorated with fresh strawberries.

Raspberries could be used instead of strawberries, and yoghurt or créme fraîche can replace the cream to make a lighter dessert, which can be served frozen or softly chilled.

FLORENTINES

In a saucepan melt **125 g butter** with **½ cup sugar** and **2 tbsp honey**.

Remove from the heat and add **½ cup slivered almonds**, **⅓ cup chopped cherries** and **⅓ cup chopped peel**. Stir in **1 cup flour** and mix well. Drop small teaspoons of the mixture on to a tray lined with baking paper. Space them well apart as the biscuits spread considerably. Bake in a moderate oven (180°C) for about 8–10 minutes, keeping a good eye on them. Allow the biscuits to cool completely before removing them from the baking paper. Melt **125 g dark chocolate** in a bowl over a pan of simmering water. Spread a little of the melted chocolate on the flat side of each florentine. Mark with traditional zig-zag pattern, using a fork, then leave the biscuits on a rack to allow the chocolate to harden. These keep longer in a tin without their chocolate topping, although they will last a few days with it. Makes roughly 30 bite-sized biscuits or 10–15 larger ones.

PEACH SALSA

Combine **3 large peaches** which have been stoned, peeled and chunkily chopped, with **1 finely chopped Spanish onion**, **1 chopped red** or **yellow capsicum** and **2 tbsp chopped coriander** or **mint**. Stir through **2 tbsp olive oil** and **1 tbsp raspberry vinegar**. Set aside this salsa for at least an hour to allow the flavours to merge. Serve it with any grilled meats or poultry.

APPLE AND BOYSENBERRY RELISH

Core, peel and slice **2 Granny Smith, Braeburn or other cooking apples**. Put in a pan and add **4 tbsp red-wine vinegar**, **2 tbsp soft brown sugar**, zest and juice of **1 orange** and **1 tsp each of ground ginger**, **allspice** and **garam marsala**. Cook over a medium heat for 15 minutes until the apple is tender and most of the liquid evaporated. Add **200 g fresh boysenberries** and cook for a further couple of minutes. Set aside to cool. This is nice served with pork sausages or any other pork dish.

Strawberry Cream

Index

African fountain grass see *Pennisetum orientale*
Agave 28, 47, 56, 60, 71, 148; *A. americana* 60; 'Marginata' 60; 'Mediopicta' 60; *A. attenuata* 60
Ajuga repens 20; 'Alba' 23; 'Atropurpurea' 20; 'Braunherz' 20; 'Burgundy Lace' 20; 'Jungle Beauty' 23; 'Multicolour' 20; 'Variegata' 20
Alchemilla mollis 17, 18, 19, 39
Allium 42, 117, 119–20; *A. ampeloprasm* 119; *A. cernuum* 42; *A. christophii* 42; *A. giganteum* 42; *A. moly* 42; *A. sativum* 119
Alocasia macrorrhiza 59
Aloe 56, 59; *A. arborescens* 59; *A. bainesii* 59; *A. plicatilis* 59; *A. saponaria* 59
Alstroemeria 90
Alyssum 145
Amaranthus gangeticus 90, 124–25; 'Cascade' 125; 'Samson' 125
Angelica 106, 107, 110
Angel's trumpets see *Brugmansia*
Anigozanthos 43; *A. manglesii* 43; 'Bush Dawn' 43; 'Bush Gems' 43; 'Bush Glow' 43; 'Bush Noon' 43
Antipasto 31, 93, 103
Apple and Boysenberry Relish 156, 166
Artemisia 35–36, 37; *A. absinthium* 36; *A. arborescens* 36; 'Lambrook Silver' 36; 'Powis Castle' 36
Arthropodium cirratum 40
Artichokes see *Cynara scolymus*; *Helianthus*
Arugula 88, 125
Asian Mustard see *Brassica rapa*
Asplenium bulbiferum 67
Astelia 40, 47, 107; *A. chathamica* 'Silver Spear' 40
Aubergine see *Solanum melongena*
Aubergine Dip 102

Baby Squid 152, 155
Barberry see *Berberis thunbergii*
Basil see *Ocimum basilicum*
Bay 107, 118
Beans 88, 89, 103, 104, 112
Beef Salad 150–51
Beet 88
Berberis thunbergii 'Atropurpurea Nana' 24

Bergamot 90
Bergenia 90
Beta vulgaris 89
Betula pendula 148
Birch see *Betula*
Bird of paradise plant see *Strelitzia reginae*
Black Beans and Tomato Coriander Salad 162
Black-eyed Susan see *Thunbergia alata*
Bluebell 47
Borage 107, 126, 131
Bougainvillea 68
Boules 159
Box see *Buxus sempervirens*
Brachyglottis greyii 40
Brassica rapa 90
Broccoli 88, 91–92; 'Romanesco' 91
Bromeliads 56, 58, 67
Brugmansia 145, 146; *B. sanguinea* 145
Buddleja davidii 43; 'Black Knight' 43; 'Empire Blue' 43; 'Ile de France' 43; *B. fallowiana* 43; 'Lochinch' 43
Butia capitata 57
Butternut see Pumpkin
Buxus sempervirens 14, 24, 25–27; 'Elegantissima' 24; 'Suffruticosa' 25

Cabbage 23
Cabbage tree see *Cordyline*
Calendula officinalis 89, 115, 126, 133
Californian lilac see *Ceanothus*
Campanula persicifolia 16
Canna 62–63, 107; *C. x generalis* 63; 'America' 63; 'Fantasia' 63; 'North Star Coral Belle' 63
Capsicum 88, 89, 99–100, 113; 'Long Sweet Yellow' 100; 'Mandarin' 100; 'Marconi Red' 99; 'Marconi Yellow' 99
Carpinus betulus 22
Catmint see *Nepeta*
Cauliflower 88
Ceanothus 43; 'Blue Cushion' 43
Celeriac 93–95
Celery 31, 91
Centaurea cineraria 40; *C. macrocephala* 40
Cestrum 144; *C. nocturnum* 144; *C. parqui* 144
Cycad 56, 57–58
Chamaemelum nobile 10, 11; 'Treneague' 11
Chamaerops humilis 57

Chamomile see *Chamaemelum*
Château Vaux-le-Vicomte 157
Château Villandry 14
Chermoula 82
Cherry pie see *Heliotropium arborescens*
Chervil 107, 110, 111
Chervil Custards 108, 111
Chicken and Silverbeet Terrine 161
Chicory 124
Chives 42, 109, 110, 126
Chocolate leaves 149
Choisya ternata 24
Cilantro 116
Cistus 38; *C. landanifer* 38; *C. x purpureus* 'Brilliancy' 38; *C. salviifolius* 38; 'Silver Pink' 38
Citrus 78–82
Clematis 89, 137
Clivia miniata 64; 'Firelight' 64
Colocasia esculenta 59; 'Fontanesii' 59
Convolvulus cneorum 43
Coprosma 24; 'Beatson's Brown' 24; 'Beatson's Gold' 24; 'Coppershine' 24
Córdoba 47
Cordyline 66, 137; *C. australis* 66; *C. indivisa* 66; *C. pumilo* 66
Coriander 116; 'Iman' 116
Corokia 24; *C. x virgata* 'Cheesemanii' 24; 'Frosted Chocolate' 24; 'Geentys Green' 24; 'Yellow Wonder' 24
Cotton lavender see *Santolina chamaecyparissus*
Courgette see *Curcurbita pepo ovifera*
Country Terrine 115
Courtyard 142
Couscous 82
Cremolata 82, 110
Crocus 126
Crystallised petals 132
Cupressus sempervirens 44; 'Gracilis' 44; 'Stricta' 44; 'Swane's Golden' 44; 'Totem' 44
Curcurbit 103–104; 'Turk's Turban' 104
Curcurbita pepo ovifera 89, 102, 112, 113
Curry plant see *Helichrysum italicum*
Cynara scolymus 92–93, 105, 115; 'Camus de Bretagne' 92; 'Green Globe' 92; 'Purpurea

de Jesi' 92; 'Purpurea Romanesco' 92
Cyphomandra betacea 58, 160
Cypress see *Cupressus sempervirens*
Cyathea 67; *C. dealbata* 67; *C. medullaris* 67

Daffodil 47
Dahlia 14, 133
Daphne 143; *D. bholua* 143; *D. mezereum* 143; *D. odora* 143; 'Alba' 143; 'Leucanthe' 143; 'Rubra' 143
Date palm see *Phoenix canariensis*
Delphinium 145, 148
Dicksonia 67; *D. fibrosa* 67; *D. squarrosa* 67
Dictamnus albus 146
Dill 107, 126
Diospyros 74, 77–78; 'Fuyu' 78; 'Gailey' 78; 'Hirtanenashi' 78; 'Ichikikei Jiro' 78; 'Maekawa Jiro' 78; 'Matsumoto Wase Fuyu' 78; 'Omiyawase' 78; 'Tanenashi' 78

Echeveria elegans 51; *E. secunda* 51
Echinops ritro 43
Echium 41; *E. candicans* 41; *H. pininana* 40; *E. wildprettii* 41
Eggplant see *Solanum melongena*
Endive 122–124; 'Saint Laurent' 124; 'Toujours Blanche' 124
Eryngium alpinum 43; *E. bourgatii* 43; *E. giganteum* 36; *E. maritimum* 43
Eucalyptus 137, 148
Euphorbia characias subsp. *wulfenii* 18
Evening primrose see *Oenothera*

Fan palm see *Chamaerops humilis*; *Livistona australis*; *Washingtonia robusta*
Fennel see *Foeniculum vulgare*
Ferns 56
Ficus carica 74, 76–77; 'Black Ischia' 77; 'Brown Turkey' 77; 'Brunswick' 77; 'Sugar' 77; 'White Adriatic' 77; 'White Genoa' 77
Fig see *Ficus carica*
Fish 156
Flax see *Phormium*
Florentines 149, 151, 166
Focaccia 31, 160
Foeniculum vulgare 91, 107, 110; 'Purpurascens' 91; var. *azoricum* 'Albaro' 91

Forget-me-nots 14
Frosting flowers 126

Gardenia 147; *G. augusta* 'Professor Pucci' 147
Garlic 42, 89, 152; see also *Allium*
Gaura lindheimeri 145; 'Whirling Butterflies' 144, 145
Gazpacho 98, 114
Germander 23
Glaucium flavum 45
Grapefruit 78, 81
Grapes 83–85; 'Albany Surprise' 83; 'Concord' 83; 'Diamond' 83; 'Niagra' 83; see also Vine leaves
Gravel gardens 35–45

Haworthia 51; *H. attenuata* 51; *H. fasciata* 51
Hebe 24, 137; 'Lavender Lace' 24; *H. pimeleoides* 'Quicksilver' 43; *H. speciosa* 'Mauve Knight' 24
Hedera 15, 50, 144, 149; *H. helix* 'Goldheart' 144; 'Silver Queen' 144; *H. canariensis* 'Glacier' 144; 'Gloire de Marengo' 144; 'Ivy Lace' 50; 'My Love' 50
Helianthemum 38
Helianthus 93, 104
Helichrysum 39; *H. bellidioides* 39; *H. italicum* 23; *H. petiolare* 39; 'Limelight' 39, 144; 'Silver' 144
Heliotropium arborescens 143; 'Aurea' 144
Helleborus 136–39; *H. niger* 138; 'White Magic' 138; *H. lividus* 138; *H. orientalis* 138–39; *H. x sternii* 138
Hen and chickens fern see *Asplenium bulbiferum*
Herb Ricotta Cake 108, 110
Herbs 88, 106–125
Hesperis matrionalis 142
Hibiscus 61–63; *H. diversifolius* 63; *H. rosa-sinensis* 61; *H. syriacus* 63; *H. trionum* 63
Home-made Lemonade 81
Hornbeam see *Carpinus betulus*
Hosta 40, 47, 148
Hylocereus 144
Hyper-tufa pots 46
Hyssop 23–24, 152; 'Albus' 24; 'Roseus' 23

Ilnacullin 137
Ipomoea 145–46

Iris 42; *I. germanica* 'Florentina' 42
Ivy see *Hedera*

Japonica 126
Jasmine see *Trachelospermum jasminoides*
Jelly palm see *Butia capitata*

Kangaroo paw see *Anigozanthos*
Kniphofia 148
Kumquat 78

Lady's mantle see *Alchemilla mollis*
Lamb Kebabs 154
Lavandula 15, 23, 35, 36-37, 89, 107, 132; *L. angustifolia* 37; *L. dentata* 37; *L. stoechas* 37; 'Helmsdale' 37; 'Marshwood' 37
Lavatera 'Barnsley' 17; 'Bredon Springs' 17
Lavender see *Lavandula*; see also *Limonium latifolium*; *Santolina*
Leek 42, 105
Leek Risotto 149
Lemon 78, 80, 81, 82, 88, 105; Meyer 78, 82
Lemon balm 106, 107, 110
Lemon Cheese Tarts 164
Lemon grass 116-18
Lettuce 89, 90, 122; 'Black Seeded Simpson' 122; 'Diamond Gem' 122; 'Green Ice' 122; 'Little Gem' 122; 'Loma' 122; 'Lovina' 122; 'Merveille des Quatre Saisons' 122; 'Red and Green Salad Bowl' 122; 'Rosalita' 122; 'Rouge d'Hiver' 122; 'Royal Oak Leaf' 122; 'Sangia' 122
Lily 89
Lime 78
Limoncello 81
Limonium latifolium 43
Livistona australis 57
Lovage 110
Lychnis coronaria 39; 'Alba'; 'Oculata' 39
Lysimachia clethroides 145

Macleaya cordata 37; *M. microcarpa* 37
Mandarin 78, 81
Mandevilla 68
Manuka 137
Marigold see *Calendula officinalis*
Marlborough rock daisy see *Pachystegia insignis*
Matthiola longipetala 142
Meatballs 152, 154
Mentha 106, 109, 110, 118; *M. smithiana* 118
Meryta sinclairii 66-67, 71; 'Moonlight' 67
Metrosideros 66; *M. collina* 66; 'Tahiti' 66; *M. excelsa* 66; *M.*

kermadecensis 66; *M. robusta* 66; 'Mistral' 66; *M. umbellata* 66
Mexican orange blossom see *Choisya ternata*
Mibuna 122
Mint see *Mentha*
Mirabilis jalapa 146
Mizuna 122
Moonflower see *Ipomoea*

Nasturtium 90, 109, 115, 126, 152; 'Empress of India' 126
Nepeta 13, 15; *N. cataria* 15; *N. c. liminoides* 15; *N. faassenii* 15; *N. racemosa* 15; 'Six Hills Giant' 15
Nicotiana 142-43; *N. sylvestris* 143
Night-scented jessamine see *Cestrum nocturnum*
Night-scented stock see *Matthiola longipetala*
Niçoise Salad 149, 150-51
Nikau see *Rhopalostylis sapida*
Noodles with Buttercup Sauce 161

Ocimum basilicum 31, 90, 103, 109, 110, 112-3, 152; Genovese Giant' 113; 'Lettuce Leaf' 113; 'Purple Ruffles' 90; 'Red Rubin' 90
Oenothera 142; *O. biennis* 142; *O. odorata* 142; *O. speciosa* 142; 'Prima Donna' 142
Olea europaea subsp. *europaea* 31-35, 80; Barnea' 33; 'Manzanilla' 33; 'Mission' 33; Sevillano' 33; 'Verdale' 33
Olive see *Olea europaea*
Onion 105
Onion Marmalade 156
Ophiopogon japonicus 26
Orange 78, 81
Oreganum 107, 126

Pachystegia insignis 37
Palms 56, 57, 148
Pandorea 68
Pansy 126
Papaver pilosum 45; *P. somniferum* 43
Parsley 106, 107, 109, 110-11
Parterre 18-27, 157
Passiflora edulis 69-70; 'Crackerjack' 70; 'Robinson's Black' 70
Passionfruit see *Passiflora edulis*
Passionfruit Syllabub 70
Pavers 12
Peach Salsa 166
Pelargonium 47-50, 132; *P. peltatum* 47; *P. quercifolium* 49; *P. tomentosum* 49; *P. zonale* 47, 48-50; 'Attar of Roses' 49; 'Quantock' 49

Pennisetum orientale 36; *P. setaceum* 36
Penstemon 16-17; 'Firebird' 17; 'Garnet' 17; 'Purple Passion' 16; 'Sour Grapes' 17; 'Stapleford Gem' 17
Peony 28
Pepper see Capsicum
Perovskia 'Blue Spire' 43
Persimmon see *Diospyros*
Pesto 108, 162
Petanque see Boules
Petunia 14
Phoenix canariensis 57
Phoenix palm see *Phoenix canariensis*
Phormium 47, 67-68, 148; *P. cookianum* 67-68; *P. tenax* 68
Piccantina alla Pavorotti 161
Pineapple 58
Podocarpus totara 50; 'Aurea' 50
Pohutukawa see *Metrosideros*
Polyanthus 126
Pomegranate see *Punica granatum*
Poor Knights lily see *Xeronema callistemon*
Poppy 43, 80; see also *Glaucium flavum*; *Papaver*
Potager 87, 88-89
Pots 45-53
Pratia angulata 11
Primrose 126
Puka see *Meryta sinclairii*
Pumpkin 104-105
Punica granatum 74-76; 'Wonderful' 76

Queen palm see *Syagrus romanzoffiana*

Radicchio 90, 124; 'Guilio' 122; 'Red Verona' 124; 'Treviso Early' 124
Radish 31
Renée's Little Pots of Chocolate 149, 151, 165
Rhododendron see *Vireya rhododendron*
Rhopalostylis 65; *R. baueri* 65; *R. sapida* 65
Rheum 107; *R.* x *cultorum* 89
Rhubarb see *Rheum*
Ricotta Cake 164
Rocket see Arugula
Rose 16, 23, 89, 107, 126, 129-39, 145; 'Abraham Darby' 135; 'Ambrose Rose' 135; 'Aotearoa' 134; 'Bantry Bay' 134; 'Cécile Brünner' 131; 'Constance Spry' 135; 'Dublin Bay' 131, 134; 'Graham Thomas' 135; 'Iceberg' 135; 'Maggie Barry'; 'Olympiad' 134; 'Raspberry Ice' 131; 'Sexy Rexy' 134;

'Strawberry Ice' 131; 'Waikato' 131
Rose Vinegar 132
Rosehip Jelly 133
Rose-petal Punch 132
Rosemary see *Rosmarinus officinalis*
Rosmarinus officinalis 23, 31, 45, 107, 126, 153-54
Rudbeckia 90
Rue see *Ruta graveolens*
Ruta graveolens 'Jackman's Blue' 43

Sage see *Salvia*; *Perovskia*
Salad 120 2, 162 5
Salad burnet 125
Salad dressing 121
Salsa 154, 155, 166
Salvia 14, 39, 107, 126, 160; *S. argenta* 39; *S. madrensis* 39; *S. officinalis* 'Purpurascens' 39, 90; *S. tesquicola* 39
Santolina chamaecyparissus 39, 144; 'Bowles Lemon' 40
Sauces 24, 83; see also Salsa
Scleranthus biflorus 10, 12
Seafood 156-58
Sea holly see *Eryngium giganteum*
Sedum 51-53; *S. acre* 53; *S. kamtschaticum* 51; *S. pachyphyllum* 53; *S. rubrotinctum* 53; 'Variegatum' 51
Selenicereus grandiflorus 144
Sempervivum 51; 'Lavender and Old Lace' 51; 'Pacific Red Rose' 51
Senecio 40, 144; *S. cineraria* 40; *S. grandifolius* 59; *S. greyii* see *Brachyglottis greyii*; *S. serpens* 51
Silverbeet see *Beta vulgaris*
Silverbeet Terrine 90
Smoked food 158-59
Solandra 68
Solanum melongena 89, 100-102, 113; 'Bambino' 102; 'Violetta de Firenze' 102
Sorrel 106
Sorrel Soup 115, 163
Spinach see *Amaranthus gangeticus*
Spring onion 105
Stachys byzantina 'Silver Carpet' 43, 144
Strawberry Cream 151, 166
Strelitzia reginae 68, 69
Succulents 50-53
Sweet rocket see *Hesperis matrionalis*
Syagrus romanzoffiana 57

Tabacco plant see *Nicotiana*
Tabouleh 118, 163
Tamarillo see *Cyphomandra betacea*
Tapenade 31, 160

Taro see *Colocasia esculenta*; *Alocasia macrorrhiza*
Tarragon 107, 111-12
Tarragon Bread Sauce 111
Tecomanthe speciosa 68
Teucrium 38; *T. chamaedrys* 38; *T. fruticans* 38
Thai Chicken Curry 149, 164
Thai Fish Cakes 116, 163
Thai Prawn Salad 162
Thunbergia alata 50
Thyme see *Thymus*
Thymus 31; 107, 109, 110, 126; *T. coccineus* 11; *T. vulgaris* 114
Titoki 148
Tomato 89, 95-99, 113; Amish Paste' 96, 97; 'Principe Borghese' 98; 'Roma' 96; 'San Marzano' 96
Topiary 50; 157
Trachelospermum jasminoides 50
Trachycarpus fortunei 57
Tree ferns see *Cyathea*; *Dicksonia*
Tree tomato see *Cyphomandra betacea*
Tulips 14, 47

Veal and Chicken Liver Terrine 162
Verbascum 41, 142, 148; *V. bombyciferum* 41; *V. olympicum* 41; *V. phoeniceum* 41; 'Pink Domino' 41
Verjuice 83
Versailles 81, 157
Victoria Sandwich Cake 164
Villa Gamberaia 73, 80
Villandry 87, 88, 89
Vine leaves 84-85, 156
Viola 126, 132; *V. odorata* 127; *V. tricolor* 126
Violets see *Viola*
Vireya rhododendron 63-64; 'Java Light' 64; 'Kisses' 64; 'Littlest Angel' 64; 'St Valentine' 64; 'Simbu Sunset' 64; 'Tropic Glow' 64
Vitello Tonnato 149, 150-51, 165
Vitis coignetiae 84

Washingtonia robusta 57
Westringa fruticosa 24
Windmill palm see *Trachycarpus fortunei*
Winter savoury 109
Witloof 124

Xeronema callistemon 65

Yucca 61; *Y. elephantipes* 61; *Y. gloriosa* 61

Zinnia 133
Zucchini see *Curcurbita pepo ovifera*